MW01126995

Fisherman's Coast

An Angler's Guide to
Marine Warm-Water Gamefish
and Their Habitats

Aaron J. Adams, Ph.D.

STACKPOLE BOOKS

0 11557 03105 8

Copyright © 2003 by Aaron J. Adams

Published by
STACKPOLE BOOKS
5067 Ritter Road
Mechanicsburg, PA 17055
www.stackpolebooks.com

All rights reserved, including the right to reproduce this book or portions thereof in any form or by any means, electronic or mechanical, including photocopying, recording, or by any information storage and retrieval system, without permission in writing from the publisher. All inquiries should be addressed to Stackpole Books, 5067 Ritter Road, Mechanicsburg, Pennsylvania 17055.

Printed in the United States

First edition

10 9 8 7 6 5 4 3 2 1

Cover photograph by Aaron J. Adams. Professional guide Jim Locascio fishing on Sanibel Island, Florida
Cover design by Caroline Stover

Library of Congress Cataloging-in-Publication Data

Adams, Aaron J.
    The fisherman's coast : an angler's guide to marine warm-water gamefish and their habitats / Aaron J. Adams.—1st ed.
        p. cm.
    Includes bibliographical references (p.).
    ISBN 0-8117-3105-7 (alk. paper)
    1. Saltwater fly fishing—Atlantic Coast (U.S.) 2. Marine fishes—Atlantic Coast (U.S.) 3. Marine fishes—Habitat—Atlantic Coast (U.S.) 4. Saltwater fly fishing—Mexico, Gulf of. 5. Marine fishes—Mexico, Gulf of. 6. Marine fishes—Habitat—Mexico, Gulf of.
    I. Title.
    SH463 .A32 25004
    799.1'6614—dc21

                                                        2003011872

To my dad and to Uncle Frank.

They got me started, helped me on my way,
took me along on fishing trips, taught me all they know,
believed all my fishing stories, and never forgot
that it's just fishing.

And to my wife, Maria,
for sharing me with fly fishing.

Contents

Acknowledgments   ix
Preface   xi
Introduction   1

Chapter 1   **Life Cycles of Marine Gamefish and Their Prey**   **5**
                The Larval Stage   6
                The Juvenile Stage   7
                The Adult Stage   11
                ▨ APPLYING WHAT YOU'VE LEARNED:
                   Taking Advantage of Juvenile Prey   12
                Seasonality of Gamefish Prey   13
                ▨ APPLYING WHAT YOU'VE LEARNED:
                   Seasonality of Prey Species Life Cycles   14
                Spawning Gamefish   14
                Temperature   15
                Local Nuances   16

Chapter 2   **Seagrass**   **17**
                Species of Seagrass and Their Environmental
                   Requirements   20
                ▨ APPLYING WHAT YOU'VE LEARNED:
                   Reading Seagrass   24
                ▨ APPLYING WHAT YOU'VE LEARNED:
                   Spotted Seatrout   26
                Seagrass as Habitat   26
                Fishing in Patchy Seagrass   30
                ▨ APPLYING WHAT YOU'VE LEARNED:
                   Tailing Red Drum   34
                Gamefish Prey   35
                Time of Day   50
                ▨ APPLYING WHAT YOU'VE LEARNED:
                   Seasonal Strategies for Gamefish in Grass Beds   50
                Stewardship   52

Chapter 3	**Mangroves**	**53**
	Mangrove Species and Their Ecological Attributes	54
	Red Mangroves	55
	▪ APPLYING WHAT YOU'VE LEARNED:	
	Bonefish along the Mangroves	56
	Black Mangroves	59
	▪ APPLYING WHAT YOU'VE LEARNED:	
	Black Mangrove Shorelines	60
	Gamefish Prey in the Mangroves	61
	Location Matters	72
	Time of Day	74
	Seasons in the Mangroves	74
	▪ APPLYING WHAT YOU'VE LEARNED:	
	Gamefish in the Mangroves	77
	Stewardship	80
Chapter 4	**Oyster Bars**	**83**
	Ecological Requirements	85
	Types of Oyster Bars	86
	Currents	88
	Tidal Range	89
	Salinity	90
	▪ APPLYING WHAT YOU'VE LEARNED:	
	Exploring Oyster Bars	91
	▪ APPLYING WHAT YOU'VE LEARNED:	
	Basic Fishing Tactics	92
	Oyster Bar Habitats	96
	Seasonality	98
	Gamefish Prey	98
	▪ APPLYING WHAT YOU'VE LEARNED:	
	Fishing at Dawn and Dusk	103
	Resident Prey Fish	104
	Seasonal Prey Fish	107
	▪ APPLYING WHAT YOU'VE LEARNED:	
	Fly Selection	109
	▪ APPLYING WHAT YOU'VE LEARNED:	
	Be Ready for Baitfish	110
	Stewardship	112

Chapter 5   **Salt Marshes**   **113**
High and Low Marsh Zones   115
   ▓ APPLYING WHAT YOU'VE LEARNED:
   Finding Gamefish in Salt Marshes   119
   ▓ APPLYING WHAT YOU'VE LEARNED:
   Red Drum in the Salt Marsh   121
Tides   123
   ▓ APPLYING WHAT YOU'VE LEARNED:
   Fishing the Tides   125
Gulf versus Atlantic Coastal Salt Marshes   127
Salt Marsh Food Web   130
Gamefish Prey   131
   ▓ APPLYING WHAT YOU'VE LEARNED:
   Strategies for Murky Water   137
   ▓ APPLYING WHAT YOU'VE LEARNED:
   Seasonal Strategies   138
Stewardship   140

Chapter 6   **Beaches**   **143**
Waves   144
   ▓ APPLYING WHAT YOU'VE LEARNED:
   Basic Strategies for Fishing the Surf   146
Shifting Sands   149
   ▓ APPLYING WHAT YOU'VE LEARNED:
   Summer Beachside Snook   152
Gamefish Prey   153
   ▓ APPLYING WHAT YOU'VE LEARNED:
   Seasonality and the Fall Feeding Frenzy   158
Beaches of the Tropics   161
   ▓ APPLYING WHAT YOU'VE LEARNED:
   Tarpon Blitzes   162
   ▓ APPLYING WHAT YOU'VE LEARNED:
   Strategy for Fishing Protected Beaches   167
   ▓ APPLYING WHAT YOU'VE LEARNED:
   Tarpon at Dusk   168
Gamefish Prey   170
Tropical Beachrock Shorelines   171
Stewardship   173

Chapter 7   **Rubble Flats and Sand Flats of the Tropics**   **175**

Rubble Flats of the Backreef   175

Shoreline Rubble Flats   180

Sand Flats   183

Appendix A   **Table of Common Gamefish**   **189**

Appendix B   **Table of Major Prey Groups**   **191**

References and Further Reading   193

Index   207

Acknowledgments

My mom, Sandi Adams, and Bob Miller were very helpful with editing suggestions on drafts of this book. Bob Miller, Jerry Goldsmith, Joe Cronley, Paul Rudershausen, Anthony Martino, and Justin Bowles contributed by going fishing with me, talking about fishing, or suggesting good fishing locations that helped in writing this book. Dave Blewett of Florida Marine Research Institute was gracious enough to provide me with the results of his hard work examining stomach contents of snook in Charlotte Harbor, Florida. I give special thanks to Art Scheck, editor of *Saltwater Fly Fishing* magazine, for his willingness to take on "The Science of Saltwater Fly Fishing—Examining the Warmwater World," which formed the nucleus for this book.

Preface

Coastal environments provide a unique opportunity for fly fishing. They are at once intimate and infinite, secluded and expansive, seductive and unconquerable. Perhaps it is this mix of extremes that grabs anglers once they wet a fly line in salt water. Or perhaps it is the size and power of a fish that feeds in water so shallow its back is exposed, then eats a fly and flees at warp speed through water only inches deep. And surely the beauty of the coasts—where land meets sea and where salt water meets fresh—is a factor; there is a special excitement to catching a fish while surrounded by the unbridled colors and sounds of coastal environs. While scanning a flat for bonefish, I've often wondered how many hues of blue and green nature can pack into a single frame. On the better fishing days, this wonderment is broken by a tailing bonefish. On slower days, the wonderment continues uninterrupted.

Despite all these attractions, the aspect of saltwater fly fishing that most appeals to me is its diversity. In a single outing, I might encounter shallow grass flats, steep dropoffs swept by strong current, rocky outcrops, and sandy beaches. I might find the same species of fish around each turn or tangle with a handful of species in a single day. The diversity of prey available to these gamefish is just as impressive—shrimp, crabs, worms, clams, small fishes, urchins, brittle stars, and a seemingly endless number of baitfish species—many of which can be imitated with a fly. There is a certain satisfaction that comes from catching a fish with a fly you created to imitate a prey species you found while exploring gamefish habitats.

Some days a single fly might be all that is necessary: On a recent outing, I caught red drum, snook, spotted seatrout, crevalle jack, bluefish, and ladyfish all on a red and white Seaducer. Other days a single species of gamefish might change its preference of prey as the day progresses: Tailing red drum that eagerly ate a fly imitating a mud crab in the early morning may prefer small shrimp patterns as the sun floods the flat and the mud crabs head for cover. I once fished a pair of flats within sight of one another; the bonefish on one flat pounced on a Gotcha without hesitation, but bonefish on a seemingly identical flat just a mile away shunned the Gotcha in favor of a small crab fly. Helping the fly angler understand why these changes in fish behavior occur and how to use this information to find and catch fish is what this book is about.

I am doubly lucky. First, I've been a fisherman since the age of five. One of my first memories involves a fishing rod in my hand, rod bent double as a fish headed for the depths. That first big fish was a bullhead catfish—a five-pound fish, a whopper for a five-year-old. Hooking that fish didn't take any special knowledge, just a worm on a hook with a bobber. Just as vivid is the memory of my first experience with tides—a favorite bluegill hole on the tannin-stained edge of a tidal river was mysteriously full and then dry from one visit to the next. Realizing that fish change location and behavior due to water movement was my introduction to the importance of scientific literacy to fishing.

I fell naturally into a career in marine science. I'm not sure exactly when this career path started—probably back at that bluegill hole—but almost without planning, I've progressed through jobs and degrees in marine science to where I am today: a marine biologist who fishes and an angler studying marine science. For me, it is the perfect combination.

My goal in writing this book is to bring some of the science of coastal systems into the larger picture of saltwater fly fishing, presented in layman's terms. There are plenty of books that describe in great detail what flies and fishing tactics work for different gamefish. Some of these books even tell you where to go, what time of day to fish, what fly to use, and how to fish the fly—all in order to catch your favorite gamefish. This approach provides useful information, but there is little explanation of the "whys," and I think many of us find that unfulfilling. What's more, if the conditions vary from what is described in those books, you are out of luck.

That said, this book is by no means exhaustive. With each read through my drafts of the text, I noted new items I could include. Local nuances were the most common new items for inclusion—the differences between northern and southern Indian River Lagoon, for example. But I quickly realized that the local nuances were endless, and I could probably spend the rest of my life revising and updating each chapter and still never include everything. I reached a point where it was time to put down the pen and go fishing.

You can take as much or as little out of this book as you wish. Enough information is provided to allow you to adjust your strategy to your levels of skill and interest. Rather than write a book that is old news after a single read, it is my intention that this book will serve as a reference, providing new insights as your experience level increases and as you venture on to new locations. When you reach the point where you want to find additional information, you can use this book as a base for more detailed personal research.

I hope you find as great a reward in reading this book as I have found in writing it.

AARON ADAMS
Pineland, Florida
March 22, 2003

Introduction

Whether you've waded the waters of warm-water coasts for the first or the fifth or the fiftieth time, you've discovered how perfect they are for fly fishing. Not only have you found these picturesque, diverse, and dynamic coastal habitats relatively shallow and accessible from shore by wading or from small boats, you've also realized that they are home to many species of gamefish willing to take a fly. We anglers can feel fortunate to be fishing at a time when modern equipment makes success possible for anyone with the desire and motivation to venture into coastal habitats.

But do you know that the life cycles of many gamefish depend on coastal waters such as beaches, estuaries, and wetlands? And that this dependence is what makes these fish accessible to fly anglers? In some species, the younger fish inhabit these inshore areas and are caught by fly anglers, while the largest fish reside mainly in deeper waters. Red drum follow this pattern, the majority of red drum in estuaries being immature or young adults. In other species, such as bonefish, both young and adult fish inhabit shallow coastal waters for all or part of the year, and fly anglers will encounter a variety of sizes of those fish.

Now that our sport has the tools that make saltwater fly fishing as accessible to the fly angler as freshwater fly fishing, it seems essential that anglers learn about the environments they are fishing. *Fisherman's Coast* draws from scientific research and literature, as well as from my scientific and angling experience, to provide relevant information in anglers terms.

This book contains what I think has been lacking in the world of saltwater fly fishing: information on the types of habitats where gamefish can be found, the kinds of prey they prefer, the ways they behave in and use their environment, and how they pursue different prey—in a sense, the coastal environment from a fish's-eye view. Given this information, my hope is that an angler will be able to figure out what tactics and flies might work best in a particular situation. This is a book for the thinking angler.

The newness of scientific information in the world of saltwater fly fishing is certainly not the fault of the pioneers of saltwater fly fishing. The pursuit of saltwater gamefish with a fly rod is relatively new and is just now maturing to the point where this type of book, like those that have preceded it, is appropriate. The entomology books so common now in freshwater fly fishing were also a step behind the earliest freshwater fly anglers.

Much as freshwater entomology and ecology books did for trout anglers years ago, my aim with this book is to teach saltwater fly fishers about the ecosystems where they fish, so that they are better able to figure out a fishing system on their own. And in the process of learning how coastal environments work, it is my hope that these fellow anglers become better stewards of these unique warm-water treasures.

What attracts many of us to fly fishing—the enjoyment of the cast and bringing a fish to hand, and a connection with and growing appreciation for gamefish environments—is enhanced by the different approach of this book. Presented here is information on gamefish habitats, the different prey available in those habitats, and the ways gamefish use these environments under different conditions. Once connected to this ecology of gamefish, you can formulate your own strategies for many species, in many habitats, and under many scenarios.

This book includes a lot of marine science. When many people hear the word *science*, their eyes glaze over and their minds wander. Fear not; this is not that kind of book. There are no complicated formulas or confusing graphics. The science I refer to is the research that has been done on the ecology of coastal marine communities, especially gamefish. This includes what gamefish species eat what prey and when; how gamefish diets vary among regions, habitats, and seasons; how the age of a gamefish might influence its diet; and how different habitats provide different opportunities and challenges for both gamefish and anglers. I have sifted through volumes of scientific research and present here only the points useful to anglers. However, ecological science is complex and has few absolutes. In that sense, many of the ecological characteristics in this book are generalities—they are all valid, but the complexity of ecology means there will always be exceptions. Combining this information with my fishing experience, I provide examples throughout the book to mesh the science with the angling. I have also incorporated the knowledge I have gained from fishing with and talking to some great anglers—knowledge that has been ingrained into my fishing. This is, in every sense, a book about fishing.

Beginning saltwater fly fishers may at times feel overwhelmed by sections of this book. But as they spend more time on the water and gain experience, the information contained here will make more sense and will become part of the learning experience. My hope is that in time their experience combined with this book will make them better anglers.

Because the book is about how gamefish use their habitats, the more you know about gamefish, the more you will learn from this book. For the most experienced anglers, much of the information may be old hat, but even a seasoned angler should gain something, perhaps a better understanding of why a fish behaves a certain way in a certain situation. Reading this book may help those anglers fill some gaps in their fishing knowledge.

The book examines coastal habitats through the eyes of gamefish, or at least as close as scientific research can get us. To a certain extent, the information provided herein should be applicable for your pursuits of any gamefish that use these habitats. The examples and fishing strategies presented focus on the most common gamefish in coastal habitats. Combining your knowledge about what a habitat has to offer and what types of prey a gamefish prefers will allow you to formulate a strategy for the gamefish of your choice.

Chapter 1 outlines the life history of gamefish and their prey and focuses on the basic concepts and information you will find referenced throughout the book. It serves as an introduction to ways gamefish and their prey use coastal habitats.

Because each habitat has unique characteristics that make it attractive to gamefish, and each has a different mix of prey, the five major coastal habitats are addressed in separate chapters. Each chapter begins by outlining the ecology of the habitat, the basis for the rest of the chapter. I then dive into specifics on where, when, and why gamefish use the habitat and which prey they are most likely to find. The imaginative reader or experienced angler will be able to formulate fishing strategies that go beyond the examples I provide.

Although the basics of each habitat type are similar across geographic zones, there are also important differences. We'll examine the warm-water coasts in three geographic zones as defined by average and low temperatures, plant and animal distributions, geological history, and many other well-established scientific criteria. The zones are as follows:

Tropical—includes the Caribbean, the Florida Keys, and the Bahamas
Subtropical—southern Florida and southern Texas
Warm-temperate—the Gulf of Mexico from central Florida through Texas, and the southeastern Atlantic coast from central Florida to Cape Hatteras

A word of caution: Don't give in to the temptation to skip straight to the chapter that covers your favorite habitat. I suggest you read the chapters in order. General ecological themes are similar in all habitats, and they are often described in early chapters and only referred to in later chapters. By skipping ahead, you may miss important points to consider when fishing in your favorite coastal habitat. In addition, you may find some strategies and examples for one habitat equally applicable in another habitat.

Since common names for fish change from region to region and can be confusing, I use the standard common name for each gamefish species as it appears in fisheries science texts, such as red drum instead of redfish, channel bass, or spot-tail bass. The scientific names are also provided for certain identification and to make it easier for you to do additional research. An Internet search for *Cynoscion nebulosus* will result in more useful information on diet, habitat, and growth than a search for spotted seatrout. In addition, a search through scientific literature will necessitate use of the scientific nomenclature.

The appendixes list the common gamefish and prey covered in this book to provide a quick point of reference for connecting the habitats, gamefish, and prey. Although not an exhaustive list, the references section at the end of the book provides the interested reader a jump start on additional resources. After all, no single book can cover every single aspect of a habitat, every possible prey item, or every fishing scenario, but this book should provide a good foundation.

Consider this book another tool in your tackle box. Your appreciation for the importance of coastal habitats will grow beyond what brought you to fly fishing on the coast in the first place. And your knowledge of the life cycle of the species you're casting for will increase your enjoyment of the sport and translate into a richer angling experience.

Chapter One

Life Cycles of Marine Gamefish and Their Prey

Coastal habitats are essential to the survival of many gamefish and the species they depend on for food. The food, shelter, temperature, salinity, and overall water quality of these habitats are some of the characteristics that make these areas so important to so many gamefish, which in turn make so many gamefish accessible to fly anglers.

How and when gamefish use different habitats depends, in many ways, on their life cycle patterns. To understand how, when, and why both gamefish and prey species use coastal habitats is to take a giant step toward approaching fishing from the fish's perspective of coastal habitats. You will also learn why habitats you might never fish—such as tiny marsh creeks—are essential to the survival of your favorite gamefish.

Challenges confronting fish in coastal habitats are complex and vary depending on a fish's size and age. Among the challenges are competition with other fish for food and shelter; finding appropriate food while avoiding becoming a meal for a larger fish; and finding an area with the right type of habitat, salinity, and temperature. These challenges change as the fish grows. The type of food required by a juvenile fish is usually different from that for an adult, and the way a fish uses a habitat changes as well. A juvenile gamefish in a seagrass bed can search for food and can hide from a predator among the grass blades. An adult in a seagrass bed will search for larger prey than a juvenile of the same species and won't be able to feed on the small items among the grass blades as efficiently as a juvenile. And while the adult gamefish might use camouflage coloration to blend in with the seagrass to avoid being eaten, there is no place for such a large fish to hide in a seagrass bed, so adults may be more wary in these shallow habitats than their juvenile counterparts.

Most saltwater fish species pass through three distinct life stages in their relatively short lives: larval, juvenile, and adult. The species that follow this strategy, which include all of the gamefish discussed in this book and most of their prey, reproduce through a behavior known as broadcast spawning, rather than laying eggs in a nest like largemouth bass or trout. Adult females and males, either as pairs or in groups, release their eggs and sperm into the water column, the water between the bottom and the surface, where fertilization takes place. While this may seem to be a risky approach to reproduction, females of many species can produce hundreds of thousands to millions of eggs for a single spawning period, so even though there is no parental care, sheer numbers virtually ensure that some larvae make it to the juvenile life stage.

THE LARVAL STAGE
The fertilized eggs hatch within hours to days, depending on the species and water temperature. The time it takes an egg to hatch is different for each species; within the range of temperatures that a species can tolerate, the warmer the water, the shorter the time needed to hatch. Once they hatch, the larvae live as plankton—small, free-floating individuals in the open waters of the ocean or estuary.

Although larvae are able to swim, their swimming abilities are minimal, so they are unable to fight most currents and can be transported wherever the currents take them. Larvae of many species are able to migrate vertically in the water column to take advantage of different currents at the surface and below, and in this way they maintain some control over where they travel. Larvae of some species remain in coastal waters; others may be transported out into the open ocean. Where and when the larval stage occurs depend on both the species' requirements— where and when the adults spawn, what type of environment the larvae need to survive, and the best season for growth and survival of larvae and juveniles, among other factors—and luck.

Snook, which are associated with estuaries for most of their lives, spawn in passes and channels at the mouths of estuaries near the end of an outgoing tide during a full or new moon in summer, May through September. Adult snook spawn mostly at the mouths of estuaries because the eggs and sperm require salt water to be viable, and farther into the estuary the salinity might be too low. Once the eggs hatch, incoming tides carry the larvae far into the estuary. The tides around the new and full moons, known as spring tides, are the strongest, so these tidal currents will carry the larvae farthest. Summer is best for several reasons: Adult snook are most active in warm months, the warm water temperatures result in faster growth rates of larvae than would occur in winter, and with juvenile snook using the low-salinity headwaters of difficult-to-reach backwater creeks, the wet season is when the creeks experience the highest freshwater flows of the year.

The larvae live as zooplankton (animal plankton), eating small phytoplankton (plant plankton) and other zooplankton for periods of days to months, depending on the species. Depending on currents and how long they spent as plankton, surviving larvae may end up close to their place of origin or far away, even drifting from one island to another in the Caribbean, for example.

Most larvae are small, less than an inch, and look nothing like their parents. Many are transparent, or nearly so, which is great camouflage in clear ocean water. Some have spines and other protrusions for protection, and many aren't even shaped like adult fish. Most are voracious predators and adopt predatory behavior early in life. Despite their camouflage and long spines, more than 90 percent of larvae are eaten or die. That may seem like a lot, but remember that 10 percent, or even just 1 percent, of millions of original eggs and larvae is a substantial number. Such a strategy has worked well for many species for a long time.

THE JUVENILE STAGE
At the end of the larval life stage, surviving larvae undergo a rapid and drastic transformation, changing from mostly clear, often spiny larvae to a form recognizable as a miniature fish, thus starting the juvenile life stage. While the larvae are getting ready to transform into juveniles, they are searching for the right type of bottom habitat. So if they were lucky enough to have survived the treacherous open water, the larvae must be lucky yet again: They must have ridden the currents so that they are near the right kind of bottom habitat at the time they are ready to start their juvenile life stage.

In some species, like tarpon, these new juveniles are miniature versions of the adults and can be easily identified. In other species, like amberjack, the juveniles have a different coloration than the adults and change color, becoming more like adults, as they grow. The juveniles of many species of jacks are difficult to distinguish from one another.

Since many of the larvae riding the same or similar currents toward their nursery habitats were spawned at the same time, many will reach the larvae-to-juvenile transformation stage at the same time. And because larvae often arrive at juvenile habitats on spring tides, the juveniles often appear in distinct pulses over short time periods.

This is true of other marine species as well. You can often detect distinct size groups of juveniles that reflect these pulses of larvae entering

Juvenile snook *(shown here)*, tarpon, red drum, and other gamefish and their prey use mangrove creeks or salt marshes as nurseries, and adults return to these rich habitats to feed.

the juvenile habitats. While these size groups may not seem important to an angler, understanding that these pulses occur, and that larvae of different species arrive at different times and in different habitats, will aid in the selection of flies for different times and locations.

The seasonality of pinfish *(Lagodon rhomboides)*, an important prey species for fish in the subtropical and warm-temperate environments, is a good example. Pinfish spawn in coastal waters from late fall through winter. Small juveniles of one to two inches become abundant in estuaries in winter and early spring. Small, yellow and white, high-bodied flies are good pinfish imitations for this early-season fishing. As the summer progresses, these same pinfish grow to greater than three inches in length and are joined in the estuaries by adult fish of six inches or longer from previous years that have migrated back for the summer. So by late summer, your one-inch flies from spring will likely be too small and should be replaced by pinfish imitations three inches long or larger.

Knowledge of the occurrence of pulses of prey might also help explain those instances when you see fish actively feeding but your normally successful fly patterns don't even get a first look. It might be that the fish are feeding on a brief but intense occurrence of a particular prey species. With some effort, you might be able to figure out the time of day, season, type of habitat, tide, temperature, and other conditions when such an event occurs and be ready for it the next time it happens. The famous crab and worm "hatches" of tarpon lore are good examples.

Juvenile Nursery Habitats

For many saltwater fish, especially the gamefish species covered in this book, coastal areas provide many of the habitats essential for the survival of juveniles. These are known as nurseries. Without these habitats, few juveniles would survive to become adults.

Shallow coastal habitats such as seagrass beds, mangroves, marshes, oyster reefs, and shorelines are heavily used by juvenile fish because they provide the best food and shelter necessary for this life stage. In the most general sense, there are two types of nursery habitats: those with plants and those without. Although plants, such as seagrasses, mangroves, and marsh plants, are not necessary for an area to support juvenile fish, plant-based habitats do provide several advantages.

Shallow coastal areas furnish two commodities important for supporting plant growth: appropriate nutrient levels and sunlight. In turn, plants provide three important habitat functions to juvenile gamefish. First, plants are able to harness sunlight and nutrients into a form many prey species can use. Prey species feed on plant material or on the smaller organisms associated with the plants, which are in turn fed upon by juvenile gamefish. Second, by holding sediments together, plants keep the bottom, shoreline, and associated habitats intact, which protects the integrity of the habitats. Stable habitats are good habitats for juvenile gamefish. The rooted plants then trap organic matter, which is food for crabs, shrimp, small fish, and other prey items for juvenile and adult gamefish. Third, plants create habitat structure that provides shelter from predators for the juvenile fish. Many of the same features that attract juvenile gamefish to these habitats also support species that are prey for juvenile, adolescent, and even adult gamefish.

This combination of food and shelter creates great habitat for many species, resulting in a diverse community. Juvenile gamefish are able to take advantage of this dual bounty of shelter from predators and abundant food to grow quickly. And as juveniles face their greatest risk of being eaten during the early days in their nursery habitat, and larger fish are less likely to get eaten by predators than smaller fish, the faster the juvenile gamefish can grow, the better.

A number of gamefish use plant-dominated habitats as juvenile nurseries. Adolescent and adult fish of some of these species also inhabit these areas, at least occasionally.

Juvenile permit are most often found near shallow seagrass beds that lie next to low-energy, sandy beaches, where they feed mostly on small crustaceans. As they grow, these permit can be found along sandy beaches with moderate wave energy.

Juvenile tarpon and snook are most abundant at the headwaters of tidal creeks and in backwater mangrove lagoons, usually in low-salinity water, and often use shallow mangrove lagoons. As these juveniles grow, they gradually move down the creeks toward open estuaries, which is one reason mangrove creeks are good places to find baby tarpon and small snook throughout much of the year.

Juvenile bonefish can also be found in mangrove lagoon habitats, but they also use shallow seagrass areas as nurseries and can be found in the same beach habitats used by juvenile permit.

Juvenile barracuda are abundant among and near mangroves when very small, one to two inches. When they are this small, they look and behave like small twigs suspended near the water surface. As they grow to catchable size, some barracuda remain near the mangroves, while others find good feeding areas along shallow beaches.

Juvenile red drum can be found in seagrass, marsh cordgrass, and tidal creek habitats, depending on the location and the types of habitats available. As they grow, they widen their use of habitats and can be found in just about any type with appropriate food.

Juveniles of many species of snapper and grouper use shallow seagrass habitats before moving to deeper habitats as adults.

A host of other organisms, fish and otherwise, also use these areas as nurseries. Juvenile blue crabs are dependent on estuarine seagrass areas, and juveniles of numerous coral reef fish, such as grunts, use seagrass and algae in lagoons. The list of organisms that use coastal habitats as nurseries is large indeed, and in many cases, it is these organisms that we attempt to imitate with our flies.

Coastal habitats without plants also support juvenile gamefish, though generally not as many as areas with plants. These often are areas that have appropriate levels of nutrients but can't support plant growth because they are too deep or too murky for sunlight to penetrate, have too much variation in salinity to support seagrass, or have too much current. A variety of organisms that don't need sunlight are able to take advantage of these areas and can provide habitat for juvenile fish. Reefs of oysters, mussels, or worm tubes are examples of this type of living coastal juvenile fish habitat. In the tropics, rocky shorelines and tidepools provide habitat for juveniles of numerous species of gamefish. Like plants, these structures provide shelter from predators and support communities of organisms that are food for juvenile fish.

You are likely to find juvenile members of the jack family (family Carangidae) along beachrock shorelines in the Caribbean. Juvenile horse-eye jacks *(Caranx latus)*, barjacks *(Caranx ruber)*, blue runner *(Caranx crysos)*, and jack crevalle *(Caranx hippos)* are the most common. Some of these juvenile jacks along beachrock shorelines will be large enough to catch with a small Clouser Minnow. Casting a size 2, chartreuse and white Clouser with bead-chain eyes with a 6-weight rod is one of my favorite ways to fish a beachrock shoreline.

Coastal habitats such as sand or mudflats, with neither plants nor other habitat like oyster reefs, support fewer juvenile gamefish. Although some organisms, such as worms and clams, may inhabit these areas, there is little shelter for small fish. In general, survival of juvenile fish is higher in areas with complex shelter than in areas of open bottom, like sand or mud. Fish species that use shallow, open-bottom areas as juvenile habitat include flounder and, in some locations, red drum.

Don't large, predatory fish know about these nutrient-rich, diverse communities in coastal areas? Of course, and that's one reason large gamefish are often accessible from shore or by wading. These shallow, rich habitats and the communities they support attract large fish within range of shorebound fly anglers.

THE ADULT STAGE

After surviving the gauntlet of the open ocean and then escaping predators in their nursery habitats, most remaining juveniles grow to adulthood. The transformation from juvenile to adult is not as rapid or drastic as from larva to juvenile, and there tends to be some overlap in habitat and diet between juveniles and adults. For some species, the juvenile-to-adult transition occurs within the same general area as the nursery, so juveniles and adults can be found together. Spotted seatrout *(Cynoscion nebulosus)* use estuarine seagrass habitats as juveniles, young adults, and adults. However, juveniles are usually found in dense seagrass, while adults venture into patchy areas. In other species, individuals gradually move from nursery areas to adult habitats. Juvenile and young adult tarpon often use mangrove lagoons, while larger adults generally use more open areas and often undergo lengthy seasonal migrations.

A fish's diet and behavior usually changes as it grows, allowing the fish to take advantage of a wider array of habitats and prey. Knowing this can help you choose your flies to target what is available in a given situation. Spotted seatrout are a great example. Juveniles and young adults tend to form large schools, while larger, older fish, often called "gators," adopt a more solitary existence or a looser affiliation with other large spotted seatrout. As spotted seatrout grow, they move from a small juvenile's diet of small mysid shrimps to increasingly larger shrimp species as young adults, and eventually to a more varied diet consisting of shrimp, fish, and crabs as older adults.

Red drum show a similar change in diet with age, subsisting on small shrimp and crabs as juveniles before moving to a more varied adult diet of shrimp, larger crabs, and fish. A similarity among the life stages is that red drum often school as both juveniles and adults. Casting a size 1/0 Deceiver at a juvenile red drum may get the interest of the young drum, but it is just as likely to send the fish swimming in the other direction. That same fly cast to a larger adult red drum has a decent chance of being eaten, because fish such as mullet become an important part of the adult diet.

You've probably noticed seasonal changes in the abundance of your favorite gamefish in coastal waters, and maybe even in their diet. While the reasons for this seasonality are many, food availability and temperature are major factors. Juveniles of many organisms that use coastal habitats as nurseries are most abundant in spring and summer. This is true even in the Caribbean, where the abundance of juvenile fish is highest in summer months. Gamefish and other predators may shift their diet and feeding locations to take advantage of this seasonal abundance of prey.

APPLYING WHAT YOU'VE LEARNED:

Taking Advantage of Juvenile Prey

My experience on a summer research expedition to the Caribbean provides a vivid example of gamefish use of seasonal prey. I had just finished a session of intensive fieldwork. Using scuba gear, I had been counting juvenile fish on coral reefs. After being in the water for more than six hours a day for three weeks, I had seen all the juvenile fish I cared to. I was taking a couple days of R&R before heading home, and on this particular day I was wading across a large sand flat in search of bonefish. Out in the middle of the flat, I came across a broken-down piece of old, dead mangrove that must have been washed onto the middle of the knee-deep flat in a storm. The closest live mangroves were more than a half mile away along the shoreline.

I slowly walked over to the old mangrove to see if it might hold some juvenile snapper, because mangroves provide important habitat for them. Small snapper would be perfect for my 6-weight rod and small Clouser Minnow. As I reached the old mangrove, I saw two torpedoes speed off—bonefish! This really piqued my curiosity, because I had never before seen bonefish so closely associated with structure in this fashion, especially on a shallow sand flat where I expected to see them cruising and feeding, always on the move.

Once I was close enough to the mangrove, I saw why the bonefish were so attracted. There were hundreds of one-inch-long juvenile grunts (family Pomadasyidae, similar in appearance to snapper, family Lutjanidae) huddled among the mangrove branches and roots. From their size, I figured the juvenile grunts had made the transformation from larval to juvenile stage about a month earlier. The bonefish had found the jackpot and were happily feeding to their hearts' content until tide, or an angler, forced them away. An event like this would happen only in summer, when juvenile grunts are at their greatest numbers. Had I anticipated this, I might have fooled the bonefish with a small yellow and white Clouser Minnow.

SEASONALITY OF GAMEFISH PREY

Spotted seatrout also undergo seasonal shifts in diet that are important for an angler to know about. In Indian River, Florida, adult spotted seatrout feed mostly on shrimp in summer and early winter but switch to a diet dominated by small fish in late winter and early spring. There are always exceptions to general rules, but choosing a fly based on these general seasonal trends is a good start. In the Virginia portion of Chesapeake Bay, spotted seatrout venture into shallow grass beds in the spring (May and into June) in search of juvenile and shedding adult blue crabs.

In contrast, the closely related red drum (both the spotted seatrout and red drum are in the drum family, Sciaenidae) has a diet similar to spotted seatrout, eating fish, shrimp, and crabs, but it may have different diet preferences depending on location. On Florida's Gulf coast, red drum in coastal habitats prefer small fish such as menhaden and anchovies in winter and spring and crabs and shrimp in summer and fall. Along the coast of Mississippi, many red drum prefer shrimp in winter, crabs in spring and summer, and small fish in the fall.

This type of information comes from studies of populations of red drum in certain locations and reflects the overall amounts of different prey items in the stomachs of fish captured for the study. In other words, for the studied population of gamefish, certain prey items appeared in stomachs more often and in greater numbers than other prey items. This information should help you decide what types of prey items to imitate with your flies, but it shouldn't be interpreted as being a complete list of prey. Although gamefish have diet preferences, they are also opportunistic and might take advantage of what they perceive as an easy meal and take a fly that is not high on the list of common prey items. There are also local variations. Although studies showed that red drum on Florida's Gulf coast preferred baitfish in winter, I found that red drum feeding in estuarine seagrass beds in winter eat crabs and shrimp.

Seasonality of Prey Species Life Cycles

While living on St. Croix in the Virgin Islands, I discovered another example of seasonality of prey in the Caribbean. A small baitfish, known locally as fry, forms into dense spawning aggregations along the shores of protected coves in early April. These large schools of fry attract a host of predatory fish, including tarpon, bar jacks, and barracuda. But most exciting is that bonefish feed aggressively on these schools of fry and are suckers for a white Crazy Charlie. At other times of year, these same bonefish feed mostly on shrimp and crabs, so a tan Gotcha is the most productive fly. In areas of the island where large schools of baitfish are not present, the bonefish feed almost exclusively on bottom organisms such as clams, crustaceans, and worms.

How did I figure out those bonefish were feeding on fry? It became obvious when a pair of bonefish rushed through a tightly packed school of fry, acting more like marauding jacks than the typical bonefish. I already knew about the seasonality of the schools of fry, so it was easy to put the two together.

SPAWNING GAMEFISH

Another reason to learn about the life cycles of fish is the influence of spawning on their location and behavior. Knowing where and when adult snook spawn narrows where to look for adult snook in summer months. Between spawning events—that is, between the full and new moons— snook feed along ocean beaches and in grass beds that are near the passes, often in very shallow water. As they get ready to spawn, large groups of fish can be found staging—gathering in groups—near passes and channels.

I've found the best snook fishing along the beaches to be in the early-through late-morning hours, when they can be found as close to shore as the water depth will allow. One of my favorite spots for summertime fishing for snook along an outer beach is about a half to one mile from a pass where snook spawn. I like to stand high enough on the beach that I can see approaching snook and cast to fish as they cruise by on their way to the pass. The fish often travel in small groups of three or four, with some occasional large, solitary females. How do I know the big fish are females? Snook are protandrous hermaphrodites, which means that most snook first mature as males and then undergo a sex reversal to become females once they reach a larger size. So most snook less than twenty-four inches are males, and almost all the monster snook of legends are females.

In contrast, bonefish spawn in deeper water outside reefs, so they aren't accessible to shoreline anglers. They rely on offshore currents to carry their larvae to the appropriate juvenile habitat. Unlike snook, bonefish spawn during winter, so the juveniles occupy the nursery habitats in early spring and have the whole summer growing season ahead of them.

Although the impact of catch-and-release of spawning fish is unclear, the conservative approach is to to avoid targeting fish that are actively spawning. Spawning consumes a lot of the fish's energy and may also make them more susceptible to large predators such as dolphin and sharks. Many fish are ravenous prior to spawning as they build up an energy stockpile, and they can be just as hungry after spawning as they replenish their lost reserves. I think these pre- and postspawn fish are generally in good health and can handle catch-and-release fishing.

TEMPERATURE
Fish are cold-blooded, and their physiology is adapted to operate most efficiently within a limited temperature range for which each species is best adapted. Some species migrate long distances to take advantage of the largest area they can within their preferred temperature range. Tarpon migrate southward from the Carolinas and Gulf of Mexico in the fall and return northward in late spring. Other species stay in the same region throughout the year but alter their behavior and habitat use patterns to remain within acceptable temperatures. Red drum are present in North Carolina throughout the year but can be hard to find during the cold fronts of winter.

Regardless of the method gamefish use to stay in an appropriate water temperature, the result is seasonal changes in their availability. These temperature-related changes in gamefish abundance and behavior are most notable in warm-temperate and subtropical areas and occur to a lesser extent in the tropics.

In general, the number of gamefish species in subtropical and warm-temperate regions is greatest during the warmer months. Species that spent the cold winter months offshore where water doesn't get as cold as along the coast, or that migrated south when fall arrived, return to subtropical and warm-temperate coastal habitats as the water warms in spring. In addition, many of the species that remained throughout the winter become more active with the warming waters of spring. So summer brings the widest variety of gamefish to shallow coastal habitats.

In contrast, other species seem best adapted to the cooler temperatures in summer—spotted seatrout in the subtropics and some warm-temperate areas, for example—and the dog days of summer can send these species into deeper water. Red drum may become scarce in shallow habitats during summer and either feed in the shallows at dawn or dusk or move to cooler ocean waters outside their normal estuarine haunts. Spring and fall, or even winter, can be the best times of year for these species, even though they are present and can be caught throughout the year.

Fall is a special time in warm-temperate and subtropical regions because so many species aggregate for migrations. Not only are the seasonal gamefish ready to move out, but so are the species they depend upon for food. These coinciding migrations can result in some amazing action as gamefish gorge on tightly packed schools of panicked baitfish. Most exciting for fly anglers is that these large concentrations of bait often occur along shallow beaches or even in shallow protected bays, so they are within easy reach.

LOCAL NUANCES

Every location has its own nuances, so there is no single recipe for a successful strategy. You have to investigate your home waters to figure things out. More experienced anglers probably already have experiences from their home waters similar to my Caribbean bonefish stories. The obvious patterns are easy to figure out, but many more subtle activities occur that require more study. If you are traveling, your knowledge of these general patterns will help you be in the right spot at the right time casting the right fly. If you're in doubt, a local shop may be able to give you tips, and you can match those tips with information you'll gain from this book for a successful outing.

Chapter 2

Seagrass

Seagrass beds are my favorite coastal and estuarine habitats to fish. These beds are where many juvenile gamefish get their start. They are full of species that gamefish use as prey and are used as feeding areas by many adult gamefish. Seagrass beds come in different forms: They can be thick, dense stands of continuous grass; thick grass pockmarked by deep, sandy potholes; a patchwork of grass and open bottom; or sparse blades scattered over an otherwise open sand or mud bottom. Numerous species of seagrass can make up a grass bed, each with unique characteristics that make a difference to gamefish and their prey. The combination of how a grass bed is arranged, the different types of seagrass, and the bed's location poses different opportunities and challenges for both gamefish and anglers.

At first glance, seagrass beds may seem like lush underwater lawns with a limited number of organisms living among the blades of grass. But closer inspection reveals a habitat teeming with life. Since these beds are shallow and very productive areas that provide food for many species, they are attractive areas for numerous small organisms, many of which are cryptic (well camouflaged to match their surroundings) and very adept at using the seagrass blades for shelter. Many of these organisms are prey for gamefish.

Although seagrass habitat provides shelter for small organisms, such as shrimp, crabs, and small fish, there is inadequate shelter for large fish. This is one reason why large fish often forage in shallow seagrass beds but retreat to deeper water when they feel threatened. Figuring out the strategies gamefish use to capture prey while avoiding predators in these shallow habitats is a giant step toward finding and catching more gamefish in seagrass beds.

The more you know about the gamefish's home, the more you know about the gamefish and the more fish you are likely to catch. And the more you know about what these habitats need to exist, the better equipped you'll be to make sure these habitats remain healthy so you can continue to catch fish there in the future.

Seagrass beds are widely distributed in shallow, protected coastal waters throughout the tropics and subtropics and, to a lesser extent, in warm-temperate environments. In the Gulf of Mexico, seagrass beds are common as far north as the Florida panhandle. Seagrass beds along the northern Gulf coast, from the western Florida panhandle through eastern Texas, are scattered and sparse compared with those along the Gulf coast of Florida and in the tropics. These beds become more prevalent again from southwestern Texas south into Mexico and Central America. Along the Atlantic coast, they are present as far north as Indian River Lagoon, Florida, and then are largely absent until you reach North Carolina's Outer Banks and associated sounds.

Seagrass beds of the tropics, subtropics, and warm-temperate regions may contain as many as nine species of seagrass, but you are mostly likely to encounter only four species: turtle grass (*Thalassia testudinum*), shoal grass (*Halodule wrightii*), widgeon grass (*Ruppia maritima*), and manatee grass (*Syringodium filiforme*). In the tropics, you will mostly encounter turtle grass and manatee grass, whereas in the subtropics, you may regularly encounter all four species. Beds in warm-temperate North Carolina contain mostly eelgrass (*Zostera marina*), with some shoal grass in the southern Outer Banks of North Carolina and some widgeon grass in backwater areas.

All seagrass species are similar to a great extent. All are green plants that are attached to the bottom, and they all share some basic environmental requirements, such as the need for sunlight and for low-energy areas, which have moderate to low wave action and currents. Knowing these common requirements of seagrass will help you find the most likely locations for seagrass beds as you explore new areas and may give you some clues as to why an old seagrass bed disappeared or a new one formed, or why beds in some locations seem more lush.

All seagrass species require sunlight for photosynthesis and thus are limited to shallow coastal waters. The depths at which you may find seagrass depend on water clarity—the clearer the water, the deeper you will find seagrass. In clear tropical waters, you can find it at depths of thirty feet or more, though you won't likely be fishing this deep, but it is uncommon to find seagrass in greater than eight-foot depths in Florida estuaries, and even shallower in the northern Gulf of Mexico.

Seagrass serves an important ecological function by acting as a baffle, reducing the velocity of currents that flow over grass beds so that sediment particles suspended in the water by these currents settle to the bottom. This acts as a filter, preventing sediments from reaching reefs and keeping the water clear. Too much sediment, however, can smother seagrass; in addition to blocking sunlight from penetrating the water, high amounts of water-borne sediment can overwhelm seagrass that is already established. Areas with high amounts of sediment suspended in the water support seagrass in only the shallowest locations.

In some locations where there is not much sediment in the water, the water is stained the color of coffee from high loads of tannins from mangroves and other wetland and shoreline plants, and this too decreases the depth that sunlight can penetrate, as well as the depth at which seagrass can grow. Still other areas have soft bottom sediments that are easily stirred up by waves and currents, and the water is too murky for sunlight to penetrate so frequently that seagrass can't survive.

Seagrass also requires low-energy conditions. If you've ever been caught by a wave in the surf, you will know water can exert extreme force. In high-energy environments such as beaches with strong wave action or areas with strong currents, grass blades can be broken and entire plants ripped out of the bottom, so these types of areas aren't suitable for grass beds. Waves and currents also move sediment, and the shifting bottom makes it difficult for seagrass to become established and grow. This is why seagrass is most abundant on the protected, downwind, lee sides of barrier islands, like the Chandeleur Islands and the back sides of the barrier islands on the Outer Banks; in estuaries and lagoons, like Indian River Lagoon; on flats, like the backreef flats at Turneffe Island; and along coastal areas, like Apalachee Bay, Florida—all areas that receive little in the way of wave energy.

Seagrasses are able to tolerate a wide range of salinities. This refers to the salt content of water, measured in parts per thousand, with typical ocean salinity around thirty-five parts per thousand. Too much variation in salinity, however, may prevent seagrass from becoming established or may eradicate existing beds. Each species has a preferred range of salinities but can tolerate brief periods, usually up to a couple weeks, of very high or very low salinity. Long periods of high salinity followed by long periods of low salinity are usually too stressful for a species of seagrass to become established. In the tropics and subtropics, where there are distinct wet and dry seasons, the area where a river runs into an estuary may be full ocean salinity during the dry season and almost full fresh water during a strong wet season. In such an area, the bottom near the river mouth, where salinity varies most, will likely have no seagrass.

The shape and number of seagrass blades can be influenced by salinity. In areas where salinity is high and doesn't vary much, such as the lower portion of an estuary or a lagoon protected by reefs in the tropics, turtle grass blades tend to be wider, longer, and brighter green in color, and the grass occurs in dense stands. In the upper portion of an estuary, where salinity is lower and more variable because of river flow, turtle grass blades tend to be thinner, shorter, dark green, and less dense.

Putting the basic requirements of light, low energy, and salinity together gives you a good idea of where you are most likely to find healthy seagrass beds. The first locations to eliminate in a search for seagrass are the mouths of rivers that carry heavy sediment loads. Beaches that are exposed to strong waves and areas exposed to strong currents are also off the list. You can eliminate the deep spots, although the actual depth depends on where you are fishing. The clearer the water, the deeper and more widespread you will find seagrass. Locations that seem to have muddy water a lot of the time also are not likely to harbor seagrass beds, because not enough light gets to the grass blades or the grass blades get smothered as the sediment settles out of the water column. In regions with notable wet and dry seasons, seagrass is often absent from the lower portions of rivers and where rivers meet estuaries or ocean because of changes in salinity—even if the river flows are not full of sediment. And within an estuary, the thick, dense grass beds tend to be closer to the mouth, where there is the least variation in salinity. In Pamlico and Albemarle Sounds in North Carolina, for example, the most extensive grass beds are on the inland sides of the barrier islands, with only smaller pockets of seagrass farther into the sounds and in the rivers.

SPECIES OF SEAGRASS AND
THEIR ENVIRONMENTAL REQUIREMENTS

Each species of seagrass has advantages over the others under different environmental conditions, and each species grows best and is most common where it has the advantage. Many beds have mixed species of seagrass, but others are composed mostly of one species, or different species may grow in different parts of the bed.

The type of seagrass present in a location reflects the long-term conditions there—tides, current, salinity, depth, and wave energy. Gamefish know the typical conditions for a grass bed and behave accordingly. Knowing the environmental requirements of each seagrass species will help you decipher patterns from one location to another and devise an effective strategy for fishing those locations.

Turtle grass is the most common seagrass in shallow coastal and estuarine areas of the tropics and subtropics. This is the seagrass you most often see in the beautiful panoramic pictures of clear, tropical flats. Of the four most common species in the tropics and subtropics, turtle grass blades are the widest and act best as current baffles, sometimes creating areas of soft bottom.

Although turtle grass can tolerate salinities as low as 3.5 parts per thousand (ppt) and as high as 60 ppt, it grows best in salinities between 24 and 35 ppt. Its tolerance for salinities below 15 ppt is limited by the time of exposure. After more than a couple weeks, turtle grass becomes stressed and dies. This means that turtle grass won't grow in portions of estuaries that receive significant amounts of fresh water for an extended period of time.

In the tropics, turtle grass grows throughout the year, but in the subtropics and the areas of the warm-temperate northern Gulf of Mexico where it exists, turtle grass can become dormant during winter. In these more seasonal areas, there may be a thinning of the grass beds during winter as the blades that die or break off are not so readily replaced as during summer, or they may remain short for extended periods. In summer, these same grass beds will have more densely packed and longer blades.

Although turtle grass can grow as deep as one hundred feet, it is usually found much shallower due to light requirements for photosynthesis. In clear tropical water, beds of turtle grass may be as deep as thirty feet, whereas in less clear waters of estuaries, turtle grass is usually found in waters less than ten feet in depth. As fly anglers, we are most interested in the shallow grass beds six feet or less in depth.

Turtle grass can tolerate occasional exposure to air during low tides, but it won't grow in spots that are dry too frequently or too long. During periods of extra low spring tides, turtle grass in shallow areas may have blades that are burned brown from exposure to the sun and air. These blades are soon replaced by new growth once tides become less extreme. In the Caribbean, turtle grass is the dominant species on the flats—if there is seagrass, it is probably turtle grass—so it is not uncommon to find shallow areas with burned blades, though shoal grass does grow in some shallow areas. In contrast, in the subtropics and northern Gulf of Mexico, the shallowest-growing seagrass is often shoal grass.

Like turtle grass, shoal grass has a pretty wide range of salinity tolerance—from 12 ppt to much greater than 35 ppt—and although shoal grass is also unable to tolerate extended exposure to fresh water, it is more tolerant than turtle grass. Shoal grass can be found growing among the blades of turtle grass and is often overlooked because its blades are so much thinner. Shoal grass is often overlooked even in areas where it sometimes dominates, because during winter in subtropical and warm-temperate

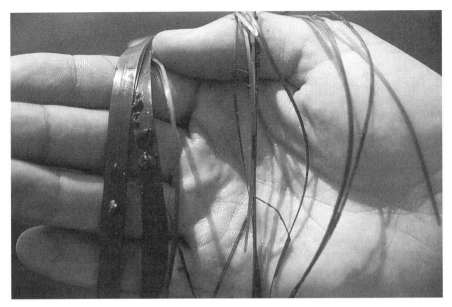

Shoal grass *(right)* is flat-bladed, like turtle grass *(left)*, but much narrower. Shoal grass is common in shallow areas in the subtropics and, to a lesser extent, in the tropics.

regions, plants can become dormant and blades can break off entirely, leaving a bare sand bottom. When water warms in spring, the buried root system sends new growth into the water column. These newly emerging, springtime grass beds quickly attract small organisms such as shrimp, crabs, and small fish, which are readily eaten by gamefish.

In general, shoal grass is better able to tolerate recurrent exposure to air and wave energy than turtle grass. Because of this advantage over other seagrass species, shoal grass is often most abundant in the shallowest areas, thus its name. This doesn't mean that other grass species won't also grow in areas that are exposed at the lowest of low tides, but it does mean that, in general, shoal grass is your best indicator of where the shallowest areas are on a grass flat.

During winter in the subtropics, even though seagrass blades, especially those of turtle grass and shoal grass, are not being quickly replaced as they die or break off, many beds still provide good shelter. In most locations, the loss of blades isn't so great that the grass beds disappear. At the same time that seagrass growth slows or stops in late fall and winter, drift algae becomes more abundant, reaching its peak in late winter into early spring.

Drift algae is like the tumbleweed of the sea, sometimes attached to grass blades, but often carried by tidal and wind-driven currents and deposited in areas where the current slows. As the drift algae grows through the winter and is moved around by currents, it often collects in depressions and along windward shorelines. Sometimes there is so much drift algae that it carpets the bottom and can be more than two feet deep. Overall, I've found that areas with such thick accumulations of drift algae don't hold as many prey and don't offer the best fishing.

Eelgrass is found from the Outer Banks of North Carolina north to Canada and is limited in its southern range by warmer temperatures. Eelgrass blades are similar in shape to turtle grass, and their width is between that of turtle grass and shoal grass blades. This means that eelgrass provides good habitat for small organisms and juvenile gamefish. Eelgrass has a wide range of salinity tolerance (7 to 35 ppt), though it prefers the upper end of the range, so it grows well in the estuarine waters of the Outer Banks and locations farther north. Strong currents, waves, and areas exposed to frequent strong winds that muddy the water limit the growth of eelgrass. The most extensive eelgrass beds can be found on the leeward sides of the barrier islands of the Outer Banks and in shallow, clear areas protected by marsh islands. Only isolated beds grow close to the rivers.

Widgeon grass has many blades branching from each stalk and thus provides good hiding places for small organisms. This grass grows in shallow water in depths similar to turtle grass and shoal grass. Its greatest advantages are its wide range of salinity tolerance, 2 to 70 ppt, and its ability to tolerate high and low salinities for extended periods. You will likely find the greatest concentration of widgeon grass in areas of low salinity that might experience large changes in salinity that last for weeks at a time. Shallow mangrove or marsh creeks that drain large wetland areas experience low salinities during the wet season and high salinities in the dry season. In such areas, widgeon grass may occur seasonally, with highest growth in the wet season. Similar shallow coastal areas, such as in the Louisiana backcountry where water is clear enough, are also good places to find widgeon grass.

Of all the seagrasses mentioned here, you will probably have least direct contact with the round-bladed manatee grass. Manatee grass is usually the deepest-growing of the four species, is found in low-energy conditions, and has little tolerance for exposure to air. It has the least tolerance for fresh water, with a narrow preferred salinity range of 24 to 35 ppt. Manatee grass often grows among turtle grass blades. It grows in patches or sparsely arranged blades in deeper water as well. A deep-growing bed of manatee grass probably indicates an area that sees relatively mild currents and clear water—an area where gamefish may pass through but are not likely to hold and wait for baitfish to be swept through on currents. These areas are best fished with a sinking fly line.

The most notable exception to these general rules is the Laguna Madre of south Texas. Because the southern Laguna Madre is mostly enclosed and isolated from the Gulf of Mexico and receives almost no fresh water, salinities are extremely high—greater than 50 ppt in many places. Nonetheless, seagrass grows in the shallow waters of the Laguna Madre. Before the lower Laguna Madre was connected via dredging, the dominant grass was shoal grass, but now that the salinities are lower, turtle grass and manatee grass dominate.

APPLYING WHAT YOU'VE LEARNED:

Reading Seagrass

Now that you're aware of the environmental requirements of each species of seagrass, let's apply this information to a fishing situation. Having learned the general environmental conditions required for seagrass beds, you now know where to look for seagrass when exploring new areas, and you also know that different species of seagrass grow best in different conditions. You will find that even if you encounter a grass flat that is unfishable at high tide, you can get an idea of how the flat might look, and where fish will most likely be, at a better fishing time near low tide. Here is a likely scenario.

Picture yourself fishing in a subtropical estuary. At high tide, you encounter a grass flat with a mixture of grasses. Some areas on the flat have mostly turtle grass, while others have mostly shoal grass. You think the flat will be good for sight-fishing for tailing red drum near low tide, but it is expansive—if you are in the wrong spot, you might never see the red drum you are certain will be there. Your increased understanding of environmental factors influencing seagrass distribution will help you figure out where the shallow spots and deeper troughs are most likely located. You can place yourself in the spot where you have the best chance of seeing fish expose their positions as they travel through and feed in the shallowest water, and then watch the avenues they are most apt to use to retreat during low water.

Why use the type of seagrass to determine depth if you can look at the bottom to see which area is deeper? Though this is true, it only works on a rough scale—say, the difference between one and two feet. Whether you find tailing fish, however, might be measured in inches of difference in water depth. A red drum might move along a trough of turtle grass that is only a few inches deeper than a ridge of shoal grass, and where it can feed without showing a tail. If you have enough sunlight to sight-fish, you can position yourself along the higher ground and search for fish feeding in that trough. If you are unable to see fish because of low-light conditions or murky water, but you still want to cast to sighted fish, find the shallower ridges and wait for tailing fish to move onto these areas to feed as the tide rises.

The presence of shoal grass might also indicate exposure to waves—that is, the outer side of a bar. If environmental conditions are consistent enough to cause a change from turtle grass on the protected side of the bar and shoal grass on the outer side of the bar, these conditions are also likely to influence fish distribution. Unless the weather has been particularly calm for a number of days, your best bet to search for tailing fish is on the inside of the shallow bar. During an extended calm period, you might find that fish take advantage of the conditions and feed on the outer edge of the bar in the shoal grass.

When fishing on the inside of the bar in turtle grass, your best strategy is to use an unweighted, weedless fly. On the outer side, where the shoal grass is likely more sparse and doesn't pose as much of a fly-snagging challenge, a lightly weighted fly that gets to the bottom quickly might be a better choice.

Here is an example from the tropics of the importance of reading seagrass. In the eastern Caribbean, the difference in water depth between typical high and low tides is less than ten inches, frequently even less. Despite the slight change in water depth, permit enter shallow backreef flats to feed on the latter half of incoming tides and are usually absent after the first hour or so of dropping tides. The difference in water depth is almost imperceptible to an angler, but it sure makes a huge difference to the permit. Knowing the requirements of turtle grass, you can figure out locations of feeding and travel lanes that permit are most likely to use on a flat. Sparse, short grass blades, maybe with some of the blades burned brown from a recent extralow tide, indicate a shallow spot. A trough of thicker, longer blades probably indicates a slightly deeper area. As the tide rises, you might find permit using the deeper trough as a traveling lane to access shallow feeding locations.

Spotted Seatrout

Spotted seatrout like to hang out in deep spots at low tide and ride the rising tide into shallow grass beds to feed. During winter, rising tides heated by the midday sun seem to bring the most spotted sea-trout into shallow grass beds, whereas the rising tides of dusk are best in the heat of summer. In either case, if you find deep water next to shallow grass beds, there is a good chance you will find spotted sea-trout on a rising tide. One of my favorite places to fish for seatrout is a large bed of turtle grass separated from deep water by a series of sandbars and troughs, with shoal grass growing on the bars and in the troughs. At low tide, I like to pole along the bar and cast into the thicker patches of shoal grass in deeper spots in the troughs. On the good days, a handful of spotted seatrout rest in many of the small holes, waiting to ride the flooding tide into the shallow bed of turtle grass. The holes that hold fish are usually close to a trough that cuts through a sandbar, which provides a travel avenue from the deeper holes into the turtle grass.

Another good location for spotted seatrout is deep beds of turtle grass that grow on a bottom that slopes into shallow water. These grass beds allow spotted seatrout to find the most comfortable water temperatures by moving between deep and shallow water, without ever having to leave the food-rich seagrass bed. In the heat of sum-mer, you'll find spotted seatrout using the deeper areas during the day to remain cool and moving into the shallows in the evening. An extreme case of spotted seatrout using deep seagrass are the offshore seagrass shoals in the Big Bend region of Florida. In winter, spotted seatrout spend most of their time in the deep grass to avoid the cold water of the shallows; on warm sunny days, they move into the shal-lows to warm up in the midday sun.

SEAGRASS AS HABITAT

One of the most important functions of seagrasses is their ability to har-ness sunlight, along with nutrients in the water and sediment, to produce food and provide shelter for other organisms. Many organisms, such as snails and numerous fish species, graze directly on the blades and are in turn eaten by larger predators. A diverse array of algae and invertebrates don't graze on the seagrass, but they do live on the blades. The algae are called epiphytes, the invertebrates are known as epifauna, and both groups combined are referred to as epibionts.

Seagrass also holds sediments in place, just as plants on land help prevent erosion. A stable bottom habitat attracts and supports a wide array of species that are prey for gamefish.

The ability of seagrass to act as a current baffle is another important function. Even in areas where you find current strong enough to bend over grass blades, the water near the bottom of the blades is nearly still. The slowing of currents as water passes over a grass bed causes many particles that are suspended in the moving water, such as sediment and broken blades of grass, to fall toward the bottom. Microorganisms often coat the floating material, and as the sediment and decaying plant material falls to the bottom, they provide food for numerous organisms that feed on the microorganisms. This collection of sediments and plant and animal matter is called detritus.

The productivity of seagrass beds supports a rich food web that brings larger fish into these shallow waters. The food chain in these habitats can be given in simplified form as follows: Sunlight and nutrients support seagrass and algae, which creates sediment and detritus, which feed epibiont invertebrates, which feed larger invertebrates and small fish, which are prey for larger fish.

The shelter provided by seagrass beds also sustains high numbers of small organisms that are potential prey for gamefish. The large amount of prey attracts gamefish to these shallow habitats. The behavior of the prey influences when gamefish are most likely to find a particular prey, in what types of seagrass beds the prey may be found, and the different strategies gamefish use to pursue different prey. If you understand the habitat, the feeding behavior of a gamefish can often tell you which prey it is pursuing.

Seagrass beds support an incredibly high diversity of species that are potential prey for gamefish: small fish, crabs, shrimp, small crustaeceans called isopods, miniature shrimplike creatures known as amphipods, various worms, algae, echinoderms such as sea urchins and starfish, and a host of other organisms. Though many of these organisms aren't appropriate for imitating with a fly (most amphipods would require a size 30 hook), they all are important prey items for juvenile or adult gamefish. Only a few of the fish species found in seagrass beds are targeted by recreational anglers, but many of the smaller fish provide food for these gamefish. It's a complex food web that suffers if any part is missing.

Not all seagrass beds have exactly the same prey species. The abundance and types of species found in a seagrass bed may change depending on location. So although the general list of prey items available to gamefish may be similar, the actual prey items eaten by gamefish often vary among locations. This explains, in part, why some flies are pounced upon by fish on one seagrass flat but are completely ignored in other locations. If you have a general list of prey species a gamefish will feed on, however, you can move quickly through a short list of flies to find an appropriate imitation for just about any situation.

One reason the prey species differ among grass beds is that each seagrass species provides different advantages and disadvantages to gamefish and their prey. Turtle grass has the widest blades and seems to provide the most shelter to small organisms. A grass shrimp will move around a grass blade, keeping the blade between itself and the gamefish, in order to hide. While this is an effective strategy with turtle grass, the strategy is probably not as successful with the thin-bladed shoal grass. The grass shrimp is wider than the blades of shoal grass and thus is more likely to be spotted by a gamefish. If you examine stomachs of spotted seatrout, you might find that trout that have been feeding on grass shrimp will have some grass blades in their stomachs as well. A mouthful of shrimp and seagrass is better than no shrimp at all.

Another factor is how the grass beds are arranged. If you compare the numbers and types of small fish, crabs, shrimp, and other potential prey species found living on an open sand bottom with those in a nearby grass bed, the difference is immediately apparent. Far more species in far greater numbers are found in the seagrass, which provides both food and shelter from predators. Here, small fish can feed on epibionts living on the grass blades and flee into thick stands of grass to escape pursuing predators.

If there were no larger predators, small fish might be found in equal numbers in areas of open bottom and beds of dense seagrass. The small fish are predators, too, eating even smaller organisms that also use the seagrass as shelter. From the perspective of the small fish as predator, the less shelter its prey has to hide in, the more efficiently it can find and eat prey. Although there are things in the seagrass bed for the small fish to eat, there are also things to eat on open bottom—and they are easier to get to.

As gamefish do exist, however, the small fish not only have to be concerned with finding something to eat, but they must also find shelter to keep from being eaten. With a predator around, you are unlikely to find any small fish in open-bottom habitat; they will be in the seagrass. The small fish can't feed as efficiently as if they were on the open sand bottom, but they have less chance of being eaten by gamefish. This tradeoff—between eating and being eaten—is an important factor that helps determine which seagrass beds hold more prey and more gamefish.

Between the two extremes of open bottom and dense seagrass is a range of seagrass habitats: thick, dense stands of continuous grass; thick grass with scattered patches of open bottom; a patchwork of seagrass and open bottom; or sparse blades scattered over an otherwise open bottom. The density of the seagrass and the landscape—how the mixture of grass and open bottom is arranged—factor heavily into the dynamics of eating and being eaten. This helps explain why some seagrass beds consistently hold more gamefish than others.

Beds of dense seagrass hold a lot of prey, but it can be difficult for gamefish to capture prey in such areas. If the seagrass is too thick for a gamefish to swim through, it is forced to swim above the blades. It is also easier for small fish to swim above the grass blades, but they can usually see a gamefish approaching and quickly dive into the cover of the dense grass until it has passed. In these situations, a good strategy for the angler is to use an unweighted streamer fly and either strip it slowly, so that it hovers above the grass blades, or use quick, short strips. The slow, hovering fly is a good imitation of a small fish that has not seen an approaching predator and might trigger an ambush attack by a gamefish. The quickly stripped fly imitates a small fish that has seen a gamefish and has elected to flee over the grass rather than dive among the grass blades.

In the subtropics, spotted seatrout often rove through dense seagrass beds looking for unwary prey and can be fooled by streamers fished just above the grass blades. In the tropics, barjacks cruise above the dense grass blades at high speed, hoping to surprise an unsuspecting small fish. Jacks are suckers for chartreuse and white Clousers with bead-chain eyes that are not so heavy that they sink into the grass, but whose jigging action imitates small fish searching for the cover of seagrass.

In dense grass, you are likely to find gamefish searching for organisms they can root for in the bottom rather than chasing fish among the blades. Red drum, permit, and bonefish often root for shrimp, crabs, and worms in the bottom of dense beds. The challenge for the fly angler in these situations is twofold: first, to see the fish in the midst of the dense grass, and second, to get a fly into the fish's strike zone. Meeting the first challenge comes with practice. A flicker of the tip of a tail above the water may be all that gives a fish away, or you may pick out the well-camouflaged body of a bonefish sliding through the grass blades. Spotting these brief signatures of a feeding gamefish becomes second nature over time. Once you've spotted a fish feeding in dense grass, you have to make an accurate cast—close enough that the fish sees the fly among the blades, yet gentle enough to avoid spooking the fish. Weedless flies are a must in these situations.

Areas of sparse seagrass usually don't have as many prey species as you will find in dense seagrass. These areas are easier to fish, however, because it is easier to spot a fish, there is less seagrass to snag a fly, and a gamefish is more likely to see your fly.

I've found beds of sparse seagrass to be hit-or-miss fishing spots. They can be good places for gamefish such as jacks, ladyfish, and even cobia that are moving in search of baitfish or other tasty prey, but you have to be there at the right time to intercept these fish. Sparse seagrass beds can be good places to find red drum or bonefish tailing on a rising tide as they root for worms, shrimp, and crabs that burrow into the bottom. Snook visit sparse beds that are exposed to current or are pockmarked by potholes.

Jacks—crevalle jacks, barjacks, horse-eye jacks, and others—can provide great fun on flats of sparse seagrass. Jacks cruise through these areas, often at high speed, hoping to surprise baitfish. You can often spot cruising jacks by the bow wake they push as they move through shallow water. When casting to a fish in this situation, lead the fish by at least five feet, as it is at least a couple feet ahead of its wake. At times, you might actually see the fish. Don't be fooled; these fish are probably moving faster than it appears. Force yourself to lead the fish with your cast more than you think is necessary, especially if the jacks are in deeper water. Without actually seeing the fish, I have been able to track jacks as they cruise across a flat by following the trail of small eruptions of baitfish. I connect the dots of baitfish activity to guesstimate the path of the jacks, and then cast into the area where I think they will be next. This strategy has worked well enough to catch fish I otherwise would not have sighted. Small streamers such as Clouser Minnows or Deceivers work well for these fish. You will get some refusals, but more often than not a well-placed cast will result in a strike because the jacks are cruising the shallows in search of a meal.

In regions where there is little or no seagrass, the lack of seagrass is not really an issue. Coastal Louisiana has a lot of marsh mud bottom yet little seagrass in most areas, and it still has plenty of red drum. Although there are areas with seagrass, the ecosystem in this region is centered around marshes, mud bottom, and oyster bars, and the types of prey are different than in grass beds. Red drum are able to use the marsh and mud bottom areas with great success, even though seagrass is not common.

FISHING IN PATCHY SEAGRASS

Beds of dense seagrass hold a lot of prey but can be tough to fish, whereas bottoms with sparse seagrass don't hold as many prey or gamefish but are easier places to see and cast to fish. What's a fly angler to do? Find the best of both worlds: areas of mixed open bottom and hearty seagrass. A mixture of seagrass and open bottom supplies both good habitat for shelter and areas for easy feeding.

Overall, there are probably more species and more total numbers of prey items in the areas of thick grass, but the feeding efficiency of gamefish is higher in more open areas. This is one reason why anglers often find snook lying in wait in open patches in the seagrass to ambush small fish, and why spotted seatrout often hide among the grass blades near the edge of a seagrass bed and dart out into the open to grab a fly as it passes by. These open areas are also easier for fly anglers to fish because the fly is more visible to the gamefish and there are fewer snags.

Areas of open bottom in seagrass beds are often slightly deeper than the surrounding bottom in the bed and thus are known as potholes. Most gamefish species that are found in seagrass beds use potholes or edges of the beds as places to ambush prey. Some species use the ambush strategy extensively. Barracuda, snook, tarpon, seatrout, and snapper often rest near the edge or bottom of a pothole waiting for small fish, shrimp, or other prey to venture out of the protection of the grass and into the pothole. Other species rest in potholes between feeding forays into the seagrass or while waiting out low tide but will take advantage of an easy meal. Red drum and bonefish often use potholes as rest stops but always seem to have an eye open for a potential meal. Snappers often reside in

This snapper was caught with a Clouser Minnow cast into a pothole in a bed of thick turtle grass.

Barracuda are common catches from sandy potholes in seagrass beds. They use their ability to change color to blend into the background as they wait to ambush prey. Many species of gamefish and prey are able to change their colors or patterns of bars and spots to more closely match their surroundings.

larger potholes during the day and venture into the grass bed at night to feed, but like red drum and bonefish, they are opportunistic feeders if prey ventures into the pothole. Jacks cruise from pothole to pothole if the water is deep enough in the surrounding grass bed.

Another advantage to fishing in open-bottom areas in grass beds is that while the structure of the seagrass habitat makes it almost impossible to fish flies that imitate many of the prey species eaten by gamefish, areas of open bottom, or sparse seagrass are more amenable to using flies that imitate some of these prey species. Most worms and urchins move slowly, or not at all, along the bottom of the grass beds and thus are difficult to imitate with a fly in areas of thick seagrass. Casting a fly that imitates an urchin or worm into a dense stand of seagrass and letting it sit is rarely productive. But casting the same fly so that it lands in an open area in the path of a bonefish, permit, or red drum is a worthwhile endeavor.

Drift algae tends to be more common in areas of mixed open bottom and seagrass, and many of the small animals that reside in seagrass also take refuge in drift algae. Grass shrimp, pink or brown shrimp, pipefish, mud crabs, juvenile blue crabs, gobies, blennies, and brittle stars are present throughout the year and use both seagrass and drift algae. Juvenile fish also use drift algae during the winter, when the algae is most abundant, because its complex shape provides good shelter. All of these species are eaten by one gamefish or another.

I've seen red drum rooting in clumps of drift algae with such intensity that they did not hear my approaching skiff. In a couple instances I was able to drift over the feeding fish before they spooked from the shadow of the boat passing over. I've examined the stomach contents of red drum feeding in such areas and found, from most to least abundant, mud crabs (often the common mud crab, *Panopeus herbstii*), snapping shrimp (genus *Alpheus*), and small gobies and blennies. The mud crab can be imitated with many of the common crab fly patterns in olive green, size 4. The snapping shrimp is also olive green and about one to two inches long. Gobies and blennies are easily imitated by small brown streamers such as Muddler Minnows.

The following story shows why it's important to know where you are most likely to find seagrass and why; how the types of seagrass provide clues on currents, tides, and waves to tell you where and when to fish an area; and how the density and landscape of seagrass will affect prey and feeding strategies of gamefish.

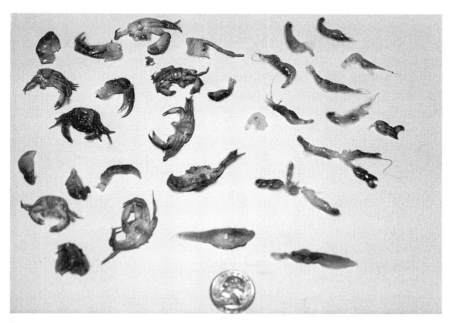

Typical stomach contents of a red drum feeding in a seagrass bed. The owner of these stomach contents was caught tailing in patch seagrass. *Left:* mud crabs; *upper right:* grass shrimp and pink shrimp; *middle right:* snapping shrimp; *lower right:* gobies or blennies.

Tailing Red Drum

The tide was so low I had to get out of my small skiff and push it over the sandbar. The sandbar had only a sprinkling of shoal grass, indicating that it was probably exposed frequently at low tide. As the boat slid off the sandbar into slightly deeper water, the shoal grass became more dense, with scattered clumps of turtle grass mixed in.

I jumped back on the skiff and slowly poled across the mirrorlike water surface. As the water got just a little deeper, the grass changed to mostly turtle grass, with the tips of the blades poking into the air in scattered bunches. The tide had just turned and was starting to flood. I hoped to find red drum feeding in the grass bed in the slightly deeper water between the sandbar and the mangrove shoreline some two hundred yards away.

With the morning sun at my back, I could make out the patchwork of seagrass and open bottom. Some areas were covered by large sections of dense turtle grass, and I could picture the flurry of activity among the blades as grass shrimp, snapping shrimp, gobies, brittle stars, mud crabs, and many other species moved about in search of food. Although a variety of animals also inhabit the sections of open bottom, many live within the sediment, so it appears less active aboveground than in the seagrass. And imitating any of the belowground creatures with a fly is a difficult proposition at best.

With a quick sideways push of the pole, I turned the boat and headed into my favorite section of the grass bed—a mixture of turtle grass interspersed with open bottom. The thick seagrass provided shelter and food for some of the red drum's favorite prey items. In the patches of open bottom and sparse seagrass, the feeding drum could more easily capture prey that ventured from the shelter of the denser grass to feed. They also gave me perfect opportunities to cast my flies to feeding or cruising fish. In these open or sparsely vegetated patches, red drum were more likely to see the fly, and the fly was less likely to get snagged on the grass. I targeted these open areas so I could use crab and shrimp flies that sank quickly to the bottom and could be moved ever so slightly, if at all, with a short, quick strip—just like the real prey. A quick-sinking pattern would get lost among dense grass blades before a red drum could see the fly and would easily snag in the grass.

As soon as I'd turned the boat, I saw the reflection of the morning sun on the square copper tail of a red drum as it broke the water surface about fifty yards away. I gave a good shove to the push pole to send the boat moving toward the tailing fish and immediately saw another tail waving, this one much closer. I quickly stowed the pole, grabbed my fly rod, threw a quick backcast, and shot the fly toward the tailing fish. The olive-colored crab fly plopped down in front of the fish just as it stopped tailing and was readying to move forward. This was a lucky break for me, because the fish saw the fly as it dropped the ten inches to the bottom. The line jumped as the fish surged forward and took the fly, and with a strip strike, the fight was on.

Other grass beds where I've found and fished for tailing red drum are full of thick, dense turtle grass. These present a real challenge. In such situations, I use an unweighted, weedless shrimp fly, casting it just about on top of a tailing red drum's head. If I'm lucky, the tailing fish hears the plop as the fly hits the water and investigates the source of the noise. If I'm unlucky, the splashdown of the fly scares the scales off the fish, and it speeds off. If the fish doesn't hear the fly hit the water and doesn't spook, I let the fly slowly drop toward the bottom, giving it slight twitches and hoping the red drum sees the fly among the grass blades. When the drum does see it, there is no mistake as the fish rushes the fly, pushing a bow wake in the process. This is real excitement that will test your patience; don't strike too soon and pull the fly from the fish's mouth.

The reason I like to cast the fly on top of the fish's head is that if the fly is more than a few inches away, the fish will not see the fly because of the thick seagrass. I liken casting to these fish in thick grass to casting to a moving teacup, the teacup being the red drum's circle of vision as it moves and feeds in the thick grass. I think this is one reason why red drum can appear picky—despite your apparent perfect cast, the fish just never saw the fly. This situation serves to illustrate why so many prey species prefer the shelter provided by dense seagrass habitats.

Black drum also inhabit grass flats in some locations. Florida's Mosquito Lagoon hosts perhaps the largest schools of shallow-water black drum. Schools of black drum also appear elsewhere in shallow water in large numbers in the fall through early winter, and although they don't provide the feeding frenzy action of other species, they are great shallow-water gamefish. The same strategies for red drum are good for fishing to black drum, with a slight difference: Slower is better when giving action to the fly.

GAMEFISH PREY

Although the number and types of prey species may vary among locations, most seagrass beds have members of particular families of organisms living among the blades. You can use this information to narrow the list of probable prey items you might find in a particular seagrass bed and to choose the minimum number of fly patterns with the greatest potential for catching fish there.

In *Fly Fishing for Bonefish,* Dick Brown provides a good example of differences in prey among locations and how these differences influence what gamefish eat. Brown summarizes the findings of a number of scientific studies that examined the availability of prey, food preference, and overall diets of bonefish found in shallow-water habitats, including seagrass, in Puerto Rico, Florida, and the Bahamas. In each of these locations, the types and abundance of prey species varied, as did bonefish prey preferences and diets. Most of the Florida bonefish had crustaceans in their stomachs, whereas clams were most frequent in the stomachs of bonefish from Puerto Rico.

I found similar differences in prey preferences for permit in the Virgin Islands. On St. Croix, in the U.S. Virgin Islands, where permit come into shallow seagrass beds mixed with coral rubble to feed, analysis of stomach contents revealed a preference for small clams and small sea urchins. At locations in the nearby British Virgin Islands, where permit are most often found in shallow seagrass beds intermixed with sand flats, crabs and shrimp are high on the menu. These differences in diets of bonefish and permit among locations are most likely due to differences in the abundance of prey items.

I'd be hard-pressed to come up with a workable fly pattern that imitates a clam, so in the areas where bonefish and permit eat a lot of clams, it's best to focus on the next most common items in their diets. The list of bonefish and permit prey usually includes crustaceans—shrimp and crabs. Some species of shrimp and crabs are widespread, but numerous other species have smaller ranges, so the species of crustaceans eaten by gamefish can vary from place to place. There can also be variations in coloration of the prey to match the surroundings—green in one location and mottled tan and green in another. All this variation in species and color might make your head spin with the countless fly pattern possibilities—you'd need a caddy to carry all of your fly boxes—but there is a common theme throughout that will allow you to use a few fly patterns to cover most possibilities.

Crabs and Shrimp

Although the species and color pattern of crabs and shrimp may vary among locations, the general colorations and behaviors within each group can be strikingly similar. Swimming crabs (family Portunidae) and walking crabs (numerous families) are the most common small crabs in seagrass beds. Crabs from both families are well camouflaged in their surroundings, whether green in areas of thick turtle grass or mixed tan and green in areas where coral rubble, shells, or rocks are mixed with the seagrass. Most of these crabs scurry for cover rather than try to outrun a pursuing fish.

Species of swimming crabs are present in all three regions covered in this book, are similar in shape (think of blue crabs), and are probably the most active crabs in grass beds. They can be voracious predators and scavengers and are always on the move. Their color varies, from the olive green of blue crabs to tan with eyespots for small tropical species. Swimming crabs can be found along the bottom of grass beds, clinging onto grass blades, swimming near the surface, or digging small holes in patches of open bottom as they excavate a clam dinner. When chased, swimming crabs may make a quick dash to escape, either by scurrying along the bottom or swimming quickly through the water, before burrowing into the bottom or hiding under shells, rubble, or rocks. When fleeing a gamefish, swimming crabs usually swim sideways. When cornered and unable to bury themselves, swimming crabs attempt to ward off a gamefish by waving and slashing with their claws, regardless of the relative sizes of crab and gamefish.

The first consideration in choosing a fly pattern is color. Mottled green and tan is one of my favorite color combinations for crab flies because it

Juvenile blue crabs and other swimming crabs are common in shallow coastal habitats and are eaten by most species of coastal gamefish.

includes the colors present in a grass bed. All green and all tan crab flies are also in my arsenal in the event the gamefish are keyed in on a particular color, so I am prepared for whatever species of crab might be on a flat. A second consideration is orientation and shape of the fly. You need a fly that, when stripped, appears to swim sideways, so the fly should be longer along the axis of the hook shank. Finally, the fly must be weighted so it sinks to the bottom, where natural crabs seek shelter when chased by gamefish.

When fishing your fly, the action you give it has to convince a gamefish that it's an easy meal. A nice thing about fishing flies that imitate swimming crabs is that you can give the flies substantial motion to get the gamefish's attention, since a natural crab will first attempt to get out of the neighborhood without being seen. Once it realizes it's been spotted, a crab will then attempt to hide. You can mimic the same behavior with your fly. First strip your line so the fly swims through the water or scurries over the bottom until seen by the gamefish. Then let the fly sink to the bottom as if to hide. Often the gamefish will take the fly as it drops to the bottom.

I have found blue crabs measuring up to four inches across in the stomachs of eighteen-inch speckled trout. While a four-inch crab is a bit too large to imitate with a fly, this gives you a good indication of how much spotted seatrout and other gamefish like to prey on blue crabs. Cobia also venture onto grass flats in search of blue crabs and can be taken on crab flies. Permit are well known for their crab-laden diet; live blue crabs are a favorite bait for permit anglers using spinning gear. Like spotted seatrout, cobia and permit eat blue crabs whole.

Bonefish also like blue crabs but sometimes do not eat them whole, instead picking at them to dismember them, then eating the mortally wounded crabs. This can be frustrating for anglers casting a blue crab imitation to bonefish. When bonefish try to feed on a crab fly in this manner, you have to patiently wait for the bonefish to turn with the fly in its mouth before setting the hook. In case the fly is not fully in the bonefish's mouth, strip strike to ensure that the fly remains within reach of the bonefish. Juvenile blue crabs of the size preferred by gamefish are most abundant in summer in warm-temperate latitudes but can be present throughout the year in the subtropics and tropics.

Numerous species of walking crabs can be found in seagrass beds, with the species varying by region. In the tropics, reef crabs (members of the spider crab family Majidae), usually green in areas with seagrass and algae and tan in areas with a lot of coral rubble, are the most common. In subtropical and warm-temperate areas, mud crabs (family Xanthidae) can be found throughout the year in seagrass beds with soft bottoms. Mud crab color varies but is typically a dark shade of green with or without brown and black spotting.

Walking crabs always maintain a close association with the bottom. In the tropics, reef crabs are often found feeding among rubble and shells that lie among grass blades; they scurry for the undersides of these shelters when chased. In the subtropics, mud crabs can be especially abundant in clumps of drift algae in winter, when it is most common. Mud crabs are most at home feeding along the bottom; they hide at the base of grass blades or burrow into the soft bottom when chased. They usually make more of an effort to hide rather than defend themselves with a showy slashing of claws.

While conducting research in grass beds in southern Florida one winter, I found numerous large (one inch across) female mud crabs with eggs hiding in drift algae. Perhaps this is one reason I found red drum feeding so intently in patches of drift algae during that same season. The red drum's intense feeding behavior is yet another reason why I try to cast the fly so it just about hits tailing red drum on the head to be certain that they see the fly.

Although seagrass beds in the tropical, subtropical, and warm-temperate regions have different species of walking crabs, they have some similar characteristics that you can apply to your fly-fishing strategy. First, your choice of color can be simplified to green and tan. Second, the action you give to the fly should be minimal—all species of walking crabs remain close to shelter, whether under a rock, among seagrass blades or algae, or burrowing into the bottom, and don't scurry over long stretches of open bottom. You may want to give the fly a couple twitches to get the gamefish's attention, and then let the fly sit still. If you give too much action to the fly, the fish will know something is amiss and move on.

As with crabs, the species of shrimp found in seagrass habitats vary depending on location, but most species are similar enough to be imitated with a couple good patterns. Shrimp often take on the coloration of their surroundings, so it's worth carrying multiple color variations of your favorite shrimp fly patterns. Some species of grass shrimp are mostly clear, so they blend in with any background color. Larger shrimp are too large to be translucent and usually take on a coloration that blends in with their surroundings. In an area with a mixture of seagrass and open bottom, you're more likely to find shrimp that are almost clear or have a sand tint. In beds of dense grass, you're likely to find shrimp with a greenish cast.

The most familiar species of shrimp found in seagrass beds are members of four families. Common shrimp (family Peneidae), which are the

Pink shrimp and other members of the family Penaeidae (common shrimp) use seagrass, mangrove, salt marsh, and oyster bar habitats as juveniles.

familiar commercially caught species, are found in all three regions. The shrimp eaten in restaurants belong to this family. These shrimp often use seagrass beds as juveniles and migrate to deeper water as adults, although you can find some large individuals in seagrass as well. Common shrimp are usually found in grass beds with soft sediments and are typically a shade of tan or green, depending on the type of bottom where they are living. In areas of mixed seagrass and open bottom, tan is the more common coloration.

Mantis shrimp (family Squillidae) live in holes among coral rubble or shells and in burrows in sand-bottomed seagrass beds. They are also present in all three regions. Mantis shrimp are similar in appearance to the praying mantis insect, thus the name. These shrimp are usually tan when living among sparse seagrass with coral rubble or open sand bottom or green when living in dense seagrass. The claws of the mantis shrimp are incredibly powerful and come in two basic types: a club and a slicer. Mantis shrimp knock their prey, including small fish, unconscious with a blow from the very powerful club claw. With the slicing claw, they can quickly and mortally wound prey. Mantis shrimp range from an inch or so in length to well over six inches. Because of their powerful claws, only the smaller mantis shrimp are eaten by gamefish.

Mantis shrimp usually don't venture far from their burrows and scurry back into their burrows if approached. Species of mantis shrimp that do venture from their burrows in search of prey are most active at night. When snorkeling, you can sometimes see the eyestalks of mantis shrimp peering out from these burrows. Permit and bonefish readily catch and eat small mantis shrimp that have ventured too far from their burrows or are unaware of the approaching fish. When chased, mantis shrimp can swim rapidly backward with a flip of the tail or walk quickly along the bottom. Their defense posture is to turn and face their adversary while retreating backward.

Depending on the species, snapping shrimp (family Alpheidae) found in grass beds are associated with rubble or shells or live in burrows in areas of mixed seagrass and open bottom. These shrimp are high on the menus of bonefish, red drum, permit, and spotted seatrout. Snapping shrimp found in grass beds are usually green to brown in color and range in length from less than an inch to two inches. They move slowly along the bottom, if at all, and retreat into shelter when they see a predator approaching.

Although the snapping shrimp has an enlarged claw, gamefish don't seem to notice whether snapping shrimp fly patterns have claws, attested to by the success of the impressionistic Fernandez Snapping Shrimp. Adding a rattle to a snapping shrimp imitation can attract a gamefish that doesn't see the fly. I've had some success with this approach while fishing for red drum in grass beds. Once the fish has located the rattle fly, I stop stripping the fly and allow it to rest on the bottom.

Often the most abundant shrimp in seagrass habitats, grass shrimp (family Palaemonidae) are frequently overlooked because of their small size, at less than an inch. Grass shrimp live on and among the grass blades. To escape predators, these shrimp, depending on the species and habitat, burrow into the sediments, hide among the bases of the blades, or grab onto blades and try to appear as part of the seagrass.

Grass shrimp are a major prey item for spotted seatrout, and other gamefish feed on them as well. These shrimp are present in grass beds throughout the year, yet their abundance changes seasonally; they are most abundant in summer and least abundant in winter. Many of the females have eggs attached to their undersides in late winter to early spring, so you might want to tie a few fly patterns to reflect the presence of eggs on grass shrimp at this time of year. There are times when spotted seatrout and red drum won't take larger shrimp flies but will take smaller flies imitating grass shrimp. Shrimp patterns in size 4 or 6 are worth trying in these situations.

Most gamefish will take the opportunity to feed on shrimp or crabs if given the chance. Crustaceans arguably pack the greatest reward for the effort for gamefish because they are very high in caloric content for their

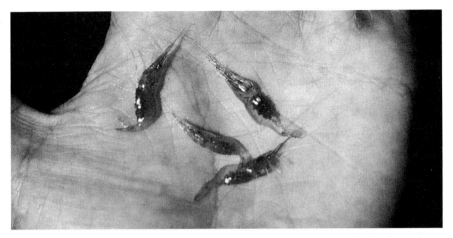

Grass shrimp are small but abundant enough to be on the menu of most gamefish in salt marsh, seagrass, oyster bar, and mangrove habitats.

size. For this reason, even in areas where crustaceans might not be the most common food item, such as on St. Croix, where clams are a favorite for permit, flies imitating crabs and shrimp should be high on your list.

Flies imitating crustaceans can be effective either weighted or unweighted to match a given situation. When fishing for red drum, permit, or bonefish in areas of dense seagrass, an unweighted, weedless shrimp pattern is probably the best choice. When fishing with a floating line, you can allow the fly to sink slowly toward the bottom, using occasional strips to pull it back toward the surface. This method allows you to keep the fly in a very small area for a long time and gives the fish a better chance of finding it. In areas of sparse seagrass, open patches, or deeper water, a weighted pattern is best for getting the fly down to the bottom in a hurry. Once the fly is on the bottom, you might make a couple short, quick strips to get the fish's attention, and then let the fly rest on the bottom. You don't have to worry so much about snagging the fly on grass, and you will be able to quickly put the fly in the fish's area of vision on the bottom and keep it there. This is especially crucial when casting to fish on the move.

Resident Prey Fish

Any particular seagrass bed can be home to dozens of species of fish. One recent survey of a seagrass bed in the Caribbean recorded ninety-one species. Some are present year-round and are therefore considered resident species. This group includes gobies (family Gobiidae), blennies (family Blenniidae), and some species of wrasse (family Labridae) and parrotfish (family Scaridae). Most resident fish are relatively small, generally less than four inches, and thus are potential prey for gamefish.

In warm-temperate areas, small fish are most abundant in warmer months, and the total number of species is generally lower than in the subtropics and tropics. In winter in subtropical and warm-temperate regions, when many of the seasonally abundant prey species, such as pinfish, croaker *(Micropogonias undulatus),* and mojarras (family Gerreidae), are absent or scarce, the resident prey species become even more important in the diets of gamefish.

Gobies and blennies live on the bottom, are present in all three regions, and seldom venture to the tops of the grass blades. They are common in most grass beds but are unseen to all except the most observant angler. They live among the grass blades, in drift algae, and in shells. Gobies and blennies dart about with short, rapid movements to feed or to chase competitors from their territories. They rest on the bottom when they aren't feeding. Although the pattern and tone of coloration varies for each species and among locations, green and brown dominate.

All gamefish species found in seagrass habitats will eat gobies and blennies if given a chance. If a blenny or goby seems oblivious to a gamefish's presence, the larger fish will likely take advantage. Gobies are shaped somewhat like a pencil, with a larger head tapering to a more slender tail, and are usually only an inch or two long. Blennies tend to be larger and more heavy-bodied, both taller and wider. One of my favorite flies for imitating these prey fish is a Muddler Minnow–style fly with a brown deer-hair head, gold body, and brown tail. I use a weighted or unweighted version, depending on the conditions, and fish it with short, quick strips to give the fly a darting-and-resting motion.

Killifish (family Cyprinodontidae) can be found year-round in the subtropics in shallow areas of dense seagrass close to shore. Their abundance in grass beds may increase during the wet season and decrease during the dry season, probably because they are changing location in relation to changes in salinity. Killifish are small, about one inch, and a dark brassy olive color. They fall prey to snook, red drum, spotted seatrout, and jacks as the gamefish venture onto the shallow grass flats on a rising tide.

Wrasses and parrotfish are limited to the tropics and swim among and just above the grass blades. When threatened, they may flee across the tips of the blades in a zigzag pattern or dive into the grass for shelter. The most common wrasses in Caribbean seagrass beds are the slippery dick *(Halichoeres bivittatus),* tan to tan-green in color with a thin black line along the midbody from head to tail, and the blackear wrasse *(Halichoeres poeyi),* a medium to bright green in color. Both species are generally cigar-shaped and a few inches in length. To imitate a wrasse, I like to cast a tan and white or chartreuse and white Clouser Minnow over grass beds that are a few feet deep, and then strip the fly so it swims erratically over the grass. Barjacks, yellow jacks, blue runners, and barracuda cruise over grass beds looking for an opportunity to eat a wrasse that doesn't see them coming in time and are likely candidates to grab your fly. You might also hook up with a bonefish or snapper.

Only a few species of parrotfish are habitually found in seagrass beds in the Caribbean. The most common, the bucktooth parrotfish *(Sparisoma radians)*, often swims in small schools along the tops of the grass blades. These fish feed on blades of turtle grass, leaving crescent-shaped cutouts. Usually grass green in color, these small parrotfish are a few inches long and shaped like a stereotypical fish, a size and shape best imitated by a Deceiver or bendback pattern. Since the bucktooth is generally in grass beds of a couple feet or deeper, weighted flies and sinking or intermediate lines are best. Larger jacks, barracuda, and occasional tarpon and snook are your most likely catches with this approach.

Seasonal Prey Fish
Juvenile fishes are seasonal residents of grass beds and are also potential prey for gamefish. These may be juvenile gamefish, such as snapper, grouper, or spotted seatrout, or juveniles of nongame species. Often these species are found in grass beds only as juveniles, with the adults living in other habitats. The seasonality of the presence of juvenile fish is due to the life cycles of these species. Although the seasonality of these species in seagrass beds is similar in all three regions, generally with more juveniles of more species in summer, the species vary from the tropics to subtropics to warm-temperate zones.

During summer months in the tropics, juvenile fish can be important food items for gamefish that feed in grass beds. Most species of coral reef fish spawn in spring and summer, so the larvae and juveniles are most abundant from May through October. Juveniles of some coral reef fish species use seagrass habitats before moving to coral reefs as young adults. Grunts (family Pomadasyidae) are perhaps the most common juvenile coral reef fish in seagrass habitats in summer. When small, most grunts are similar in appearance and have a basic yellow and white or silver coloration with various striping patterns. Yellow and white Clouser Minnows or small yellow and white Deceivers are my standby patterns.

Juvenile snapper (family Lutjanidae) are also seasonal residents of shallow grass beds in the tropics. Most common are juvenile yellowtail snapper *(Ocyurus chrysurus)* of two to three inches. A yellow and white fly of three inches or so, fished just above the grass blades, is a good way to imitate these juvenile fish. Juvenile mangrove, lane, and mahogany snappers also use grass beds, mostly in summer.

In subtropical and warm-temperate areas, a somewhat different variety of juveniles invade seagrass beds. The majority appear in spring and summer. Juvenile croaker and mojarra first appear in shallow areas, including grass beds and areas of mixed seagrass and open bottom, in spring. Juveniles of both species are almost all silver and can be imitated with one- to three-inch white Deceivers or similar patterns. Both species feed on organisms in the bottom and thus are most often found in areas of sparse seagrass or open areas within grass beds. Larger croaker are usually found in deeper areas of open bottom. Depending on the species, larger mojarra, three to four inches or more, can be found throughout the summer on open bottoms intermixed with seagrass or along mangrove shorelines.

Juvenile spotted seatrout also make an appearance in seagrass habitats in spring and summer. The juveniles look like miniature versions of the adults and are most common in areas of dense and continuous seagrass. As they feed on small shrimp and fish found among the blades, they can fall prey to larger fish—including adult spotted seatrout. Juvenile spotted seatrout are generally longer than they are high or wide, so white and silver flies with long profiles are good imitations.

One of the most interesting and important prey species in subtropical and warm-temperate seagrass beds is the pinfish. This is an extremely important prey item for gamefish, especially snook. David Blewett, a biologist with the Florida Marine Research Institute who has conducted extensive research on the snook diet, has found that pinfish constitute a major part.

Pinfish show distinct seasonality in size, abundance, and habitat use. Pinfish larvae enter estuaries and other shallow areas with seagrass in the winter months, generally November through March. These larvae then transform into juveniles that are less than an inch long and look like miniature versions of the adults. When given a choice, these small juvenile pinfish prefer grass beds that contain drift algae, probably because the algae provides the necessary food and shelter.

Pinfish grow very quickly. A fish that was less than an inch in March will be a few inches long by summer. As pinfish grow, they change their diet and behavior, lose their association with drift algae, and forage throughout the seagrass beds. Thus there are changes over the year in the average size of pinfish in grass beds: a lot of small fish in winter; a mixture of small to medium fish in late winter; medium to larger fish in late spring to summer; and the largest fish in early fall before the adults migrate to deeper water for winter. This seasonal change in size parallels

Pinfish larvae enter the estuaries in late winter and early spring, grow quickly during the summer, and migrate to deeper water in the fall. They are among the most abundant prey fish in grass beds.

a change in habitat use—from drift algae in seagrass beds by the smallest pinfish to seagrass beds and even deeper habitats by larger pinfish.

Blewett's research shows that snook seem to select a particular size of pinfish. Although he found pinfish from one-half to five inches in the snook stomachs he examined, most were between one-and-a-half and three inches long. Even more interesting is that the size of pinfish Blewett caught while sampling with seines was dominated by smaller pinfish between one-half and two inches. In other words, snook selected a certain size pinfish from what they had available. Given what we know about seasonality and pinfish size, you'd expect the size of pinfish preferred by snook to be available mostly during summer. And Blewett's data reflect this. Although the total number of pinfish caught during sampling with a seine was highest in spring, these pinfish were small. In contrast, although there were fewer total pinfish in summer, they were in the preferred size range for snook. So although snook ate pinfish in all but the winter months, summer is when snook ate the most pinfish.

Your fly selection should include a range of different sizes of flies to imitate pinfish through the seasons. I like yellow and white Deceivers of one to two inches for winter, one to three inches for spring, and three to five inches for summer and fall. Ken Bay of Ormond Beach, Florida, has come up with a fantastic pinfish imitation made entirely with artificial materials. Ken has spent time developing this pattern, and the extra effort has paid off because the fly is a dead ringer for a juvenile pinfish. The fly is tied on a hook from 1 to 1/0 with the hook point well hidden in the belly of the fly. The fly has a belly of white fibers with light blue and some yellow fibers mixed in from the mid-body upward. The back is a golden-green. Ken ties in a few strands of blue and yellow Krystal Flash along the upper third of the fly and uses a black permanent marker to make vertical bars, just like the real pinfish. Ken ties the fly sparsely, so the light can shine through the materials, giving the fly a more lifelike appearance. Ken must've really done his research because the size of his fly pattern is just the size snook seem to prefer during summer. When imitating juvenile pinfish, I like to strip the fly so it swims just above the drift algae and sea-grass, using short, quick strips to give the fly a darting motion. For larger pinfish, I like to cast over seagrass and along the edges of grass beds and use longer strips of the fly line.

Imitating Prey Fish Behavior
An important component of using a fly to imitate small fish in grass beds is the fish's behavior. It is well worth the time and effort to snorkel in the grass beds to get a fish's-eye view of how the prey species use the habitat. Snorkeling lets you observe how pinfish and mojarra zigzag through the grass blades. If you snorkel over a seagrass bed, you may see fishes swimming just above the tips of the blades. As you approach these fish, they will either dive into the blades for cover or speed quickly away, skimming the tips of the blades as they flee in a zigzag pattern. The latter behavior is one that is most amenable to imitation in the design and fishing of flies in these areas.

Snorkeling in grass beds will also give you insight into how crabs and shrimp move among the blades and on the open bottom. Your observations will undoubtedly give you ideas for new fly patterns and strategies for how to fish these new flies. One of the toughest aspects of sight-fishing with shrimp and crab patterns is that an angler's first instinct is to strip the fly when the fish approaches. However, as you will see when you snorkel a grass bed, the first response of shrimp and crabs to being chased by a predator is to hide among the grass blades or burrow into the bottom. If that fails, a shrimp or swimming crab might try to make a run for it, but probably not. This means that when you cast a shrimp or crab fly to a tailing red drum, bonefish, or permit, once the fish sees the fly, it's best to leave it motionless on the bottom.

Midwater Baitfish
Another group of small fish in seagrass beds remain in the mid and upper levels of the water column. Most often, these species are found just below the water surface, especially when being harassed by gamefish. The numerous species of herrings (family Clupeidae, which includes herring, sardine, menhaden, and shad), anchovies (family Engraulidae), and silver-

sides (family Atherinidae) are what most people picture when they think of baitfish. In the tropics and subtropics, seagrass lagoons are attractive to these species because these areas are relatively shallow, sheltered, and calm and are not as heavily populated by predators as nearby reefs or coastlines. These baitfish species tend to school during the day and disperse at night to feed. In lagoons with mangrove shorelines, schools of these baitfish can often be found along the mangroves, seeking shelter among the roots. In warm-temperate areas, large schools of baitfish seek association with open bottom as much as with seagrass habitats. They probably appear in these areas because the shallow water provides some protection from predators, rather than for an affinity for seagrass habitat. Since seagrass grows in shallow waters, however, there is always the chance of finding baitfish in these areas.

The abundance of baitfish varies seasonally. In the subtropical and warm-temperate regions, baitfish are in lowest abundance in winter. This is especially true for the species in the herring family, which migrate to offshore waters during late fall and winter. Warming waters of spring prompt the return of many of these baitfish, but in the spring and summer, juvenile baitfish also appear. The larvae enter the shallows in spring and early summer and grow throughout the summer. By fall, you will find the greatest numbers of baitfish in grass beds. Fall is the season when you are most likely to experience a feeding blitz in the shallows, when schools of marauding gamefish corral schools of baitfish and thrash the water to a froth with their feeding.

Although members of the herring family of baitfish are mostly silver, they can take on a range of colors on the dorsal surface, most notably a green hue when in grass beds. The list of herring species you might encounter over grass beds is lengthy, but the shape and coloration of the different species are similar. In estuaries with tannins, the baitfish may have a brassy sheen. In clear tropical waters, even minor splashes of color, such as yellow ventral fins, become more prominent. Your selection of flies should incorporate the local color variations.

My favorite fly pattern for herring species is a Deceiver with color variations. I begin with a base body of white and vary the color of the back, using dark green, black, or green and brown for stained or darker waters and chartreuse or blue for clear tropical waters. I carry a range of sizes to match the baitfish that are most common at a particular place or time: two-inch patterns early in the spring and summer, when the juveniles first make their appearance, and three- to five-inch patterns or larger in late summer and fall.

Silversides and anchovies are year-round residents of grass beds, but show a seasonality in abundance similar to the herrings. They are most abundant in summer and least abundant in winter. Small juvenile silversides are too small to adequately imitate with a fly and are mostly eaten by small species we generally don't target, such as needlefish, or by very small juvenile gamefish. For this reason, I only use flies that imitate adult silversides. Numerous species of silversides inhabit grass beds, but they are all similar enough in appearance that a single pattern is adequate.

Most anchovies and silversides range from three to four inches, but some, like the tidewater silverside *(Menidia peninsulae),* can reach six inches. Members of both families have long, slender bodies with silver stripes on the sides. They are bland in color, and some are almost colorless. The silver-lined gut and relatively large eyes are prominent features. Most fly pattern books are full of silverside and anchovy imitations.

Mullet are present in shallow waters of tropical and subtropical areas throughout the year, but they show distinct seasonal changes in size and abundance as well. Adult striped mullet in the subtropics gather in channels, cuts, and mouths of creeks in winter to spawn: not long after, you can find small juvenile mullet in shallow areas, including grass beds. In late winter to early spring, these juvenile mullet are small—an inch or two long—but by midspring into summer, when tarpon and snook can be found on the flats, the juveniles are in the medium-size class, at four to eight inches long, so a medium-size mullet fly is a good choice in late spring. In addition to snook and tarpon, red drum, crevalle jacks, spotted seatrout, and cobia feed on these juvenile mullet.

Some lucky anglers have witnessed large gamefish feeding on mullet in shallow grass beds. It's a spectacular sight: Schools of mullet erupt from the water en masse and splash back into the water like a giant hailstorm; tarpon, snook, or red drum crash through the tightly packed schools of mullet, their large backs and tails spraying water and sending wakes rolling across the surface. These feeding frenzies are easy to see and easy to fish. Often all it takes is a well-placed cast with an approximate imitation to hook a large fish. In other instances, there can be so many mullet or other baitfish that your fly gets lost in the crowd. When this happens, I often switch to a fly that will stand out from the crowd—one with more flash, a brighter color, or even a popper.

Try to overcome the temptation to cast into the middle of the school of mullet or other baitfish. A better strategy is to cast to the sides of the school of bait and move your fly along the edge of the school and away. When the grass bed is shallow, the gamefish work the bait from the edges of the school. In this scenario, a fly cast along the edge of a school of bait is more likely to be found by a gamefish.

TIME OF DAY

There are notable day-night changes in the activities of many species found in seagrass beds. This is especially true for crustaceans, many of which are far more active at night. One reason dusk and dawn can be great times to target large fish feeding in shallow water is that these are the changeover times for the day and night groups of species, so fish feeding during these times have access to prey both coming out to feed and returning to shelter.

Another reason gamefish feed at dusk and dawn is that they have a stalking advantage. It is easier for the gamefish to find and see prey than it is for the prey to see the gamefish, and gamefish take advantage of this. The eyesight of many species of gamefish is adapted to see well at dawn and dusk, whereas that of many of the species they prey upon is better adapted to either day or night. Gamefish are also able to take advantage of their lateral lines to feel the vibrations of prey as it moves through the water.

So although many recreational species can be found feeding throughout the day, their most active feeding times might be when light is lowest. On Caribbean islands, large snapper often forage in shallow seagrass beds at night and can be targeted with a fly rod at both dawn and dusk. Bonefish and permit can be found searching for small swimming crabs along shallow seagrass shorelines at dawn and dusk. Snook are notorious dusk feeders, and once you hear the *slurPOP* of a snook slurping a baitfish from the surface, you will find yourself fishing in grass beds at dusk more often. Red drum can also be found feeding at dawn and dusk because many of the species they eat, such as shrimp and crabs, are nocturnal and thus are active in low-light conditions.

APPLYING WHAT YOU'VE LEARNED:

Seasonal Strategies for Gamefish in Grass Beds

Just like their prey, gamefish undergo seasonal changes in their use of seagrass habitat, even in the tropics. Tarpon are most abundant in subtropical seagrass habitats from spring through fall, often with a brief early-summer hiatus, when many adults briefly disappear for spawning.

Bonefish have a limited temperature range and can be difficult to find if the water is either too warm, as during August in Florida or the Bahamas, or too cold, such as after a cold front passes through south Florida. When the water is too warm, bonefish may switch to a dawn and dusk feeding pattern. During cold spells, they often retreat to deeper water, returning to the shallows once the water has warmed. In general, the changes in water temperature in the Caribbean are more moderate, getting neither as cold nor as warm as in Florida. Accordingly, I've never tracked water temperature while fishing for bonefish in the Caribbean.

In the subtropics, snook may be found through the warmer months in patches of open bottom in grass beds—either in potholes or in smaller openings in the seagrass. During winter, they often migrate into freshwater creeks or find deep holes in estuaries in which to seek refuge from cold temperatures. Seagrass flats adjacent to mangrove-lined creeks that empty onto the flats can be good places to fish during warm spells in winter, because snook will venture out of the creeks during warmer weather and sun themselves on the dark, shallow bottom of the seagrass bed. These flats are also good places to fish in the spring, when snook first start to migrate out of the creeks onto flats and toward their summer habitats. Snook move along habitat corridors that extend from creeks onto grass beds, so the grass beds are good places to intercept these hungry early-season snook.

When I fish grass flats adjacent to creeks, I prefer to anchor the boat and wade. I start by fishing the deep hole that usually occurs at the end of the creek and the inner edge of the flat. I then fish my way along the shallow shoreline to either side of the creek or pole the boat along a track parallel to the mangroves looking for snook sunning themselves in open patches in the seagrass.

In the subtropics and northern Gulf of Mexico, although red drum can be caught in seagrass throughout the year, the sight of redfish tailing in grass beds is most common during midday in winter or early and late on summer days. In winter, low tides occur during midday, and red drum enter the shallows to feed as the tide turns and floods. They also seem more energetic as the sun warms the water. In summer, the lowest tides occur mostly at dusk or dawn, and the warm water is coolest during these times.

Spotted seatrout are present in grass beds throughout the year, but they may change locations and depth depending on temperature, tide, availability of prey, and summer spawning. You'll want to fish deeper edges of grass beds at low tide and the middle and shallow portions of grass beds at high tide.

The warming temperatures of spring bring a host of other gamefish onto grass beds in search of a meal. In the subtropics and northern Gulf of Mexico, crevalle jacks, tarpon, and cobia cruise the grass beds in search of prey. Tarpon are likely to stay in deeper grass beds or along deeper edges of shallow grass beds but occasionally venture into the shallows. I have seen large cobia feeding on blue crabs on a seagrass flat that was so shallow that the cobia's back was out of the water.

Seasonal changes in warm-temperate grass beds are more extreme, with most species migrating to warmer water either offshore or to the south during winter. When these gamefish return to the grass beds in the spring, they are hungry after a long winter and want to replenish their lost fat reserves. In the fall, these same gamefish take advantage of the abundance of prey to fatten up for the long winter.

STEWARDSHIP

It's impossible to overstate how much the communities found in seagrass beds depend on the food and shelter that only a healthy environment can provide. But seagrass beds are under threat from a number of sources. Sedimentation from coastal development can smother seagrass. Too many nutrients from sewage, fertilizer runoff, and other sources can cause algae blooms, which decrease the clarity of the water and cause the seagrass to die due to lack of light. Too many nutrients can also cause so many epiphytes (algae) to grow on the grass blades that the blades are smothered and die. Water management practices that remove all fresh water from an estuary, or alternately hold and then release all fresh water, create conditions that are unsuitable for the growth of seagrass. These threats to seagrass are associated with various nonfishing human activities, but they endanger the seagrass that gamefish depend on and should be of concern to anglers.

Perhaps one of the greatest threats to seagrass that can be directly addressed by anglers is its destruction by boat propellers, called propscarring. Prop-scarring is caused by running a boat in water that is too shallow, so that the propeller digs a trough through the seagrass. This has become a major problem to the overall health of seagrass in the subtropics, especially south Florida. It is a problem that can be solved to a great extent by boating anglers.

Regardless of the cause, seagrass beds that are damaged lose some of their ecological integrity and are unable to support the full and diverse communities that help to support gamefish. Maintaining the health of these ecosystems is paramount to ensure a productive recreational fishery, so fish these areas responsibly.

Chapter 3

Mangroves

Mangroves are tropical trees that grow along marine and estuarine shorelines in the tropics, subtropics, and some locations in warm-temperate portions of the Gulf of Mexico. Like seagrass, they play several important ecological roles in the coastal environments where they occur. They filter sediments from land that would otherwise smother seagrass and corals, stabilize shorelines against erosion, and are an important component in the nutrient cycle that forms the base of the food web of the coastal environment. In short, mangroves are an essential part of a healthy coastal ecosystem.

Mangroves provide seasonal habitat for juvenile fish and some invertebrates, such as the spiny lobster, and there is a resident community of fish and invertebrates that spend almost their entire life cycle within the mangrove ecosystem. The year-round residents and the juveniles that live in mangroves seasonally are important prey for gamefish that live or feed in these habitats.

These trees are better able to tolerate large fluctuations in salinity than are most seagrasses, but they require a marine or estuarine environment to survive. In salty environments, mangroves have an advantage over other plants because they are able to process and excrete the salt from the water, which would kill most other land and intertidal plants.

Mangrove habitats present different challenges to gamefish than do seagrass habitats. They exist on the edge of the marine environment and provide a habitat that transitions from the marine to terrestrial. The habitat that is directly important to gamefish and their prey comes from the mangrove roots, not the branches that tower above the water. Mangrove roots are solid structures immovable by gamefish, in contrast to the completely submerged, flexible habitat provided by seagrass. A snook pursuing a shrimp in a seagrass bed can grab the shrimp in a mouthful of grass, but it must capture the shrimp cleanly among the mangrove roots.

The trees that tower above the mangrove root habitat are indirectly important to fish because they create a shaded haven from the hot mid-day sun of the tropics and subtropics. The shade also gives gamefish an advantage in pursuing prey: Gamefish resting in the shadow of man-groves are less likely to be detected by baitfish swimming by in sunny areas, so an ambush-style predator like the snook is able to get closer to its prey before striking. This ambush advantage is analogous to a person standing in the darkness outside a house at night and being able to see into a lighted room, while a person inside the lighted room is unable to see outside into the darkness.

For all the advantages, in areas where mangroves are growing in intertidal zones, the shelter they provide can be fleeting. At high tide, the mangrove roots are partially or completely submerged, so they provide ample shelter for gamefish and their prey. But at low tide, the mangrove roots along shallow shorelines may be high and dry, leaving gamefish and prey no place to hide. So while mangroves may provide a more solid shelter, seagrass may provide a more consistent shelter. This is why my favorite time to fish for snook, small tarpon, red drum, and other game-fish along mangrove edges is at low tide, when they are forced from the shelter of the overhanging branches and can often be found resting along the outer edge of the roots. This is when they are most accessible to fly anglers.

Learning how to read these and other nuances of mangrove habitats is important to successfully fish these areas with a fly rod. While the general ecology of mangrove habitats is similar wherever mangroves are found, the species of gamefish and prey that fill each ecological role often differ among regions.

MANGROVE SPECIES AND THEIR ECOLOGICAL ATTRIBUTES

Sixty-five mangrove species exist worldwide, but only two species in our coverage area are considered fish habitat: red mangrove (*Rhizophora mangle*) and black mangrove (*Avicennia germinans*). Both species are unique in their ability to tolerate seawater due to a variety of special physiological and physical adaptations. Throughout their range, mangroves are found in similar conditions: along low-energy shorelines. Shorelines that are consis-tently buffeted by high energy from waves and strong currents are not suitable for these plants. In the tropics, this means you will find mangroves on lee sides of islands, in lagoons, on flats where the large expanse of shal-lows protects the mangroves from wave energy, along shorelines that are protected from waves by coral reefs, and in estuaries. In the subtropics of south Florida and from southwestern Texas into northern Mexico, mangroves are most common in estuaries and lagoons, on the landward sides of barrier islands, and in expansive, low wave-energy, shallow areas like Florida Bay. The red mangrove's northern limit is central Florida and southernmost Texas. Black mangroves are found as far north as some portions of the warm-temperate northern Gulf of Mexico.

RED MANGROVES
When fishing, you will most often encounter red mangroves. One of their most important adaptations is the support structures, called prop roots, that elevate the plants above the water. Because the prop roots support most of the plant above the water, red mangroves are able to take advantage of submerged areas that other land-based plants can't. And since many of these areas are exposed at low tides, they aren't suitable areas for seagrass to grow, so mangroves are the only source of shelter and food for gamefish. From an angler's point of view, the most important feature of red mangroves is that prop roots create a complex labyrinth of habitat for a large, nearshore community of gamefish and their prey that is accessible to fly anglers.

Red mangroves are an important part of the food web in coastal environments. The combination of sediments trapped by the mangrove prop roots, the continual dropping of leaves from the trees, and by-products of organisms within the mangroves forms the detritus that is the center of the food web in mangrove habitats. Bacteria, fungi, and even some fish, such as mojarra, feed on the detritus. An extensive community of algae, sponges, barnacles, oysters, clams, mussels, and other organisms—often referred to as the fouling community—grows directly on the prop roots. Small organisms, such as shrimp, crabs, worms, and small fish, feed on the detritus and on organisms in the fouling community, and are then preyed upon by larger organisms. The often turbid water, the structure of the mangrove prop roots, and the abundant food combine to make these great habitats for small fish and invertebrates, which in turn attract gamefish.

Prop Root Fouling Communities in the Tropics
There are numerous differences between mangrove prop root communities in the tropics and subtropics. One of the primary differences is in the fouling communities. In the tropics, a large variety of organisms, including numerous species of barnacles, mangrove oysters, algae, mussels, sponges, and anemones, compete for space on the mangrove prop roots.

The species of a fouling community tend to grow at different locations on the prop roots, resulting in a transition in species from the top to the bottom of the mangrove prop root. You can use knowledge of how this competition influences the community to your advantage. The top of the fouling community is dominated by barnacles, because they can tolerate exposure to air on every tidal cycle. The barnacles at the top of the prop roots are dry at just about every low tide. A smaller barnacle species is usually at the top, with a larger species just below. Mangrove oysters are usually next; they can tolerate some time out of the water, but not as frequently or for as long a time as barnacles, so they grow in the midtide range that is exposed for only brief periods at low tide. The fouling community on the portions of the prop roots covered by water in all but the lowest tides is dominated by mussels and algae. Sponges and anemones can tolerate only occasional exposure to air, if at all, so they are lowest on the prop roots.

Even if you have a tide chart, the direction, strength, and duration of the wind and changes in barometric pressure can have significant effects on water level, resulting in higher or lower water than predicted by the tide charts. While these differences may seem minor to us, they can influence gamefish behavior. Numerous days of strong onshore winds can make high tides higher than predicted and prevent low tides from dropping as low as predicted. Offshore winds have the opposite effect: Both high and low tides are lower than predicted. If you are very familiar with an area, you will know what the "normal" tide levels should be and can adjust your fishing strategy according to wind effects. However, if you are new to or visiting an area, if you are fishing in an area without reliable tide charts, if you left the tide charts on the kitchen table back home, or if you aren't quite sure of the effect of wind on the local tides, you can examine the prop root fouling community to determine what the normal water levels should be, and then adjust your strategy if necessary.

Knowing the types of areas that provide the best conditions for red mangroves—low-energy shorelines or flats—and interpreting clues to determine how water level may be affecting the gamefish can improve your fishing.

APPLYING WHAT YOU'VE LEARNED:

Bonefish along the Mangroves

While living in the Caribbean, I had a favorite bonefish fishing location—a mangrove shoreline on a small island that wasn't really much more than a big sandbar. It was a great spot to find tailing bonefish on an evening high tide. It wasn't an easy place to get to, so it was important to make the trip only when there was a good chance of finding feeding bonefish. Knowing the tides was the best way to choose the best times for the long trip, because bonefish fed along the mangroves on the late rising tide. Even for such a remote location, with practice I was able to predict the tides. Unfortunately, I couldn't predict the winds.

An hour before dusk, I was wading the mangrove shoreline in search of tailing bonefish. It was late in the incoming tide, and I expected to find bonefish riding the flooding tide into the mangrove prop roots to feed on crabs. Although I was fishing on the lee side of the island, I could hear a decent breeze whistling over the tops of the mangrove trees and could see whitecaps dancing over the deeper water in the distance. These strong winds were not predicted by the most recent weather forecast.

I'd been wading the shoreline for thirty minutes and had not seen a tail, mud, or a wake, and I hadn't heard the telltale swashing of a bonefish tailing within the flooded prop roots. In a forehead-slapping moment, I noticed that the water barely covered the mangrove oysters growing on the prop roots, even though it was nearly high tide. The strong wind had kept the water off the flat, which had caused a lower-than-expected high tide. The bonefish I was searching for had this figured out long before I did. In what was left of the daylight, I waded out onto the flat to try to save the evening's trip and was able to find a few cruising fish.

What I experienced wasn't a huge difference in water depth, and it would have been difficult to predict even with tide charts and an accurate weather forecast. But it was enough of a difference to keep the bonefish in deeper water and away from what I expected to be an evening casting to fish feeding along the shoreline. Seeing the barnacles high and dry was the information I needed to change my strategy for the evening.

Prop Root Fouling Communities in the Subtropics

In the subtropics, you're likely to find several species of oysters growing on prop roots in many locations, the eastern oyster being the most common, and these oysters dominate the fouling community. Here it is the oysters that create complexity in the prop root community that provides habitat for numerous small invertebrate species. Because oysters can cover the entire submerged portion of a prop root, they give fewer clues to the water level, as there is no transition in species like you'll find in the tropics. However, there are some clues. The upper end of the oyster clusters growing on prop roots will be at the upper portion of the intertidal range.

The leaf line of these red mangroves shows you the limits of the typical spring high tide, and the exposed oysters tell you that this is a rather low tide. Snook and red drum that were well hidden in the prop roots during high tide often remain in the shallow, open bottom right next to the prop roots at low tide, providing great sight-fishing opportunities.

Oysters can tolerate exposure to air, closing their shells and waiting for water to cover them again before opening, but they need to be in water for the majority of the tidal cycle, so they will grow only as high on the prop roots as most midlevel tides will cover. The upper limits of oyster growth indicate the height of the typical midtide. In contrast, mangrove leaves can't tolerate being submerged in salt water on a regular basis, so the water will reach the lowest mangrove branches only on strong high tides.

The differences in requirements of oysters and mangrove leaves result in a gap between the uppermost oysters and the lowest mangrove branches. When water fills the gap between the oysters and mangrove branches, or if it is as high as the mangrove branches, you know you are experiencing an especially high tide. A typical high tide covers the uppermost oysters. A typical low tide exposes the upper two-thirds of an oyster-encrusted prop root. You can use the water depth in relation to the oyster growth on prop roots and the height of mangrove branches as a rough guide to water level in relation to what is typical for that area.

BLACK MANGROVES

Black mangroves are also ecologically important in coastal environments but are limited to areas closer to the high-tide line than red mangroves. Instead of prop roots, black mangroves have pencil-size aerial roots called pneumatophores, which stick up vertically from the mud bottom. You can recognize black mangroves because they have tens or hundreds of these sticklike pneumatophores surrounding the area around the base of the tree. This strategy allows the black mangrove roots to exchanges gases with the air while living in sediment that is naturally hypoxic, or low in oxygen, and full of sulfur, which gives marsh mud its rotten egg smell.

Although pneumatophores are very successful adaptations that allow black mangroves to thrive in tough environments, they can't tolerate long periods underwater as well as the prop roots of red mangroves. Black mangroves are generally on the inland side of red mangroves where they occur together, or in backwaters with a relatively minor tide range, so that the pneumatophores can be exposed to air for at least some of the tidal cycle.

In the Caribbean, where the tidal range is small, black mangroves are found in shallow, usually soft-bottom backwaters that are not as frequently encountered by fly anglers in pursuit of bonefish, permit, and the like. These are often areas that tend to be too shallow for larger gamefish most of the time. In the subtropics, where the tidal range is often greater, black mangroves are most often found in two types of locations: inland of red mangroves in shallower water closer to the high-tide line, and along shallow, often muddy shorelines, such as the protected, murky backwaters and creeks of an estuary or lagoon. Both of these locations are frequented by gamefish such as red drum.

Because black mangroves don't have large prop roots like red mangroves, they provide a different type of habitat that is smaller in scale and less complex than that of prop roots. There is no fouling community on black mangrove roots. Instead, the marine community associated with black mangroves revolves around the bottom. Fiddler crabs, marsh crabs, mud crabs, and small fish that feed on the bottom detritus are most common.

In addition, since the pneumatophores are near the high-tide line and often are submerged for only part of the tidal cycle, they provide only limited shelter to the small fish found along these shorelines. The areas adjacent to black mangroves are usually open bottom—either muddy or sandy sediment—which also doesn't provide much shelter for prey. Gamefish know all about the habitat limitations of black mangroves and take advantage of the limited shelter this habitat provides to their prey. A section of deeper water adjacent to a black mangrove shoreline is a good place to look for gamefish feeding on small baitfish huddled along the muddy shoreline at low tide.

Black Mangrove Shorelines

During the high water associated with spring high tides, red drum and other gamefish ride the higher water well into the black mangrove root habitat to feed on fiddler and other crabs. Fiddler crab burrows are usually near the high tide within the intertidal zone. Although fiddler crabs are usually most active at low tide, when they can be found feeding on detritus and debris left by the previous high tide, red drum and other gamefish still take advantage of high tides to search for fiddler crabs that might venture outside the safety of their burrows during high water. The following experience is a testament to this behavior.

I paddled my canoe along a mangrove shoreline at high tide, hoping to find snook cruising the outer edge of the red mangrove prop roots. I heard a soft splash way up in the mangrove forest—not the *slurpPOP* of a feeding snook, but a much softer sound. I heard the sound again and was able to determine a direction, so I poked the bow of the canoe into the mangroves to take a look. As my eyes adjusted to the dim light in the mangrove forest, I turned my head as I heard the soft splashing again just in time to see a red drum tail waving among the pneumatophores of black mangroves.

It's impossible to get a fly to these fish, but it's worth exploring these areas to find small openings in the mangroves that are close to areas with flooded black mangroves or to a spot where you can see or hear a red drum feeding. If you're lucky, you might be able to intercept the fish as it moves along the shoreline. Or if you find areas where red drum are feeding in the flooded black mangroves at high tide, casting into the shadows of the red mangroves near low tide may fool a red drum that is resting in the shade.

Many flats along edges of red mangroves are covered by relatively clear water. But other red mangrove shorelines and most black mangrove shorelines are in areas with murky water. Along murky mangrove shorelines, getting your fly noticed is more important

Fiddler crabs, which are abundant in marshes and among black mangrove roots near the high-tide line, are high on the menu of red drum.

than using an exact imitation. Flies with a lot of flash (like Crystal Crabs), bright colors (orange, white, and yellow Seaducers), undulating motion (marabou shrimp), and noise (crab patterns with a rattle) are all appropriate for these conditions. How you fish a fly is also important. Sometimes a fly that splats onto the water will attract the attention of a foraging fish that otherwise would never notice your fly.

GAMEFISH PREY IN THE MANGROVES
The communities of fish and invertebrates that inhabit mangroves are generally made up of both resident and seasonal species. Resident species are present throughout the year and are usually the most common; seasonal species are present for only a portion of the year and are fewer in number. However, the seasonal species can dominate mangrove communities for short periods, such as during the summer pulse of juveniles, and are targeted by gamefish during these times.

Crabs and Shrimp
There are many different species of invertebrates living in mangrove habitats that are eaten by gamefish and can be imitated with a fly. The most common groups amenable to imitation with a fly are crabs and shrimp.

Crabs are very important prey items for gamefish feeding in man-grove habitats. Fortunately for anglers faced with choosing a crab fly pattern, although there are at least three families, and perhaps a dozen species, of crabs that live in mangrove habitats and are preyed on by gamefish, most of these crabs are similar in color, and they come in only three general body shapes.

Swimming crabs (family Portunidae), which include the blue crabs *(Callinectes sapidus)* and related species (the genus *Portunus* is well repre-sented), are more important prey for gamefish in seagrass beds, as these beds are where the juveniles are most often found. Depending on the location, however, small swimming crabs may be found among prop roots and surrounding bottom habitats and along the edges of black mangrove habitats, so they are always a potential prey item. Swimming crabs are usually olive to tan, depending on bottom coloration. They are able to swim sideways using their rearmost legs. These crabs are wider from side to side than they are from front to back and have pointed ends on their shells. When cornered by a gamefish, swimming crabs use one or more of three escape strategies. A first strategy is to swim rapidly sideways through the water out of the gamefish's field of view. If pursued, a swim-ming crab will often dive to the bottom, and quickly bury into the sedi-ment. As a last resort, the crab may spread its claws in a defensive posture and snap at anything that comes close. Such behaviors explain why the best strategy for fishing a fly that imitates a swimming crab is to move the fly until the fish sees it, then let the fly rest still on the bottom. Only crabs in the family Portunidae are able to swim. None of the crabs in the two families listed below are able to move by swimming; they rely entirely on walking.

Bonefish, permit, red drum, and even snook and tarpon will feed on mangrove crabs and marsh crabs (family Grapsidae). Mangrove crabs live on prop roots and branches of red mangroves and feed on mangrove leaves. Marsh crabs live in burrows in mud around mangrove branches. Crabs in this family have square bodies and are relatively small, most being one-half to one or two inches across. They are dark colored—dark purple, olive, brown, or reddish brown—and often mottled. These crabs are not able to swim; they scurry among mangrove prop roots and branches or on the shoreline above the low-tide line. When threatened, they flee into the water, either running from shore or dropping from man-grove branches, and a gamefish that finds itself in the right place at the right time will take advantage of such an opportunity.

Fiddler crabs (family Ocypodidae) live in burrows in the sediment between the high- and low-tide lines of mangrove shorelines. Because

Mangrove-dwelling crabs in the family Grapsidae make their living on the mangrove prop roots and branches, but if they fall into the water, they are quickly slurped up by any gamefish lucky enough to be nearby.

they require intertidal areas to dig their burrows, they are most common among black mangrove pneumatophores or at the most landward portion of a red mangrove stand. Fiddler crabs usually retreat into their burrows during high tide and come out to feed during low tide. But the burrows may be shallow enough to attract red drum and bonefish, or some fiddler crabs may remain active at high tide. Although the enlarged claw is the most notable characteristic of fiddler crabs, it is not a necessary component of a fiddler crab fly. Only the males have this appendage, which is associated with territorial and courtship displays. Females do not have an oversize claw, so when tying flies to imitate fiddler crabs, I suggest you concentrate more on matching the general color, size, and shape of fiddler crabs than imitating the oversize claw.

In the mangroves in the tropics and subtropics, you may encounter five or more species of fiddler crabs, all in the genus *Uca*. Burger's fiddler crab *(Uca burgesi)* and the Caribbean fiddler crab *(Uca rapax)* are the most common species on sheltered mudflats near mangroves in the Caribbean. Ive's fiddler crab *(Uca speciosa)* is perhaps the most common in the upper intertidal zone from south Florida to Mississippi and from eastern Mexico to Cuba in the Gulf of Mexico. The lavender fiddler crab *(Uca vocator)* is common in mud bottoms partially shaded by mangroves and is a common fiddler along the Texas-Mexico coast. Each species prefers a different type of sediment and salinity, so you will encounter different species depending on where you are fishing.

Fiddler crabs are similar enough in appearance that you don't have to be able to distinguish among the species or even know the types of sediments they prefer. As fiddler crabs live in the intertidal zone, you know what types of areas to look for and what locations are likely best for using fiddler crab flies. Explore an area at low tide to determine whether fiddler crabs are abundant. If they are, you will see their burrows scattered throughout the intertidal zone and may even see some crabs scurrying across the ground. Fiddler crabs have squarish bodies and are dark in color. Typical colors include olive, brown, mottled brown, tan, and orange-brown, usually with a white-tipped claw. These crabs range from one-half to almost one inch in body size.

A few species of mud crabs (family Xanthidae) live in mangrove swamps and are on the menu of bonefish, permit, and red drum. The mud crabs you will find in mangrove areas are also dark in color—reddish, grayish, brownish green, or black—often with white-tipped claws. They are from one-quarter to one-and-one-quarter inches across.

Although gamefish feeding in mangrove habitats have many species of crabs to choose from, the similarities of these crabs will allow you to get away with a just a few fly patterns. Most of your crab flies should be less than one inch across and dark-colored, perhaps with white tips on the claws. The greatest difference will be in the way you fish the flies: You can give more action to a fly that imitates a swimming crab, whereas a fly that imitates one of the walking crabs should be given minimal motion, and then only enough to imitate a crab moving slightly on the bottom.

Among the shrimp, the common shrimp (family Penaeidae, which includes the shrimp we eat) can be abundant as juveniles in mangrove habitats. These shrimp all have a similar appearance, tending to be somewhat translucent, with shades of brown and green to match the surroundings. When searching among red mangrove prop roots, I've found these types of shrimp to be most abundant in areas where seagrass is nearby.

Snapping shrimp (family Alpheidae) can also be abundant in mangrove habitats and are either the same species as those in seagrass beds or similar ones. *Alpheus armillatus, Alpheus heterochaelis,* and *Alpheus viridis* are the most likely species. Size two or one, long-shank shrimp flies in olive green to brown with one enlarged claw, and perhaps a small rattle, are suitable imitations of snapping shrimp in mangroves. These flies should be fished with minimal movement on the bottom, because snapping shrimp are not fast walkers or swimmers.

Insects
Surprisingly enough, insects, which are an important component of the above-water mangrove community, can also be an important part of the diet of juvenile tarpon. The presence of insects in the stomachs of juvenile tarpon living in mangrove-lined estuaries may help explain why small poppers often work so well for these small tarpon in the backcountry.

Resident Prey Fish
The core group of residents are important prey items for gamefish throughout the year, so you should be familiar with these prey species. Important families of fish in this group include herring (family Clupeidae), silversides (family Atherinidae), anchovies (family Engraulidae), mojarra (family Gerreidae), mullet (family Mugilidae), killifish (family Cyprinodontidae), gobies (family Gobiidae), and blennies (family Blenniidae).

Gobies and blennies are found living on the bottom among the mangrove roots. The species of gobies and blennies will vary, but they all have a similar appearance and behavior. Just like their relatives in grass beds, these fish are generally small, brown to dark green, and alternate between resting on the bottom and darting about to grab food or chase off intruders.

Gobies are common residents of most low-energy coastal habitats.

Gobies and blennies never make the top five prey items found in the stomachs of gamefish because they remain hidden in or near the bottom, are often well camouflaged to hide in their surroundings, and are not highly abundant like silversides. Given the chance, however, most gamefish will take advantage of an opportunity to make a meal out of these small fish. I have counted numerous gobies in the stomachs of red drum that were feeding along mangrove shorelines.

Numerous species of small fish are common along quiet mangrove shorelines in backwaters and creeks. Species in the family Cyprinodontidae, including the sheepshead minnow *(Cyprinodon variegatus)* and rainwater killifish *(Lucania parva)*, are among the most common, as well as the sailfin molly *(Poecilia latipinna)* and mosquitofish *(Gambusia holbrooki)*, which are in the family Poeciliidae. These species are especially abundant in brackish areas, but they are less abundant in the Caribbean and much of the tropics and thus are most important in the subtropical and warm-temperate backwaters. All of these species are similar in color—brassy to dark brown-olive, some with bars, stripes, or other markings. They are generally blunt-nosed and somewhat cigar-shaped. Earthy-colored streamers of two to three inches with gold flash are good for imitating these species.

Mojarra (family Gerreidae) are important prey for many gamefish. They are very common along mangrove shorelines and over mud and seagrass areas next to mangroves. They feed on the small invertebrates or detritus on the bottom. The many species of mojarra are silver to silvery over tan in color, have a large eye, and are generally high-bodied. Among the more common species are the silver jenny *(Eucinostomus gula)*, slender mojarra *(Eucinostomus jonesi)*, spotfin mojarra *(Eucinostomus argenteus)*, and yellowfin mojarra *(Gerres cinereus)*. Some of the species have faint vertical bars, striping, or mottling on their sides. To a certain extent, the color and patterns vary depending on the area where the mojarra is living. A mojarra in backwaters stained by tannins from mangroves will have a more tannish hue, whereas one in clear water will be mostly silver. The mojarra you encounter in or near mangrove habitats will range from three to almost sixteen inches, depending on the species.

Seasonal Prey Fish

The second part of the community of fish and invertebrates found in mangroves is made up of the species that use these habitats on a seasonal basis. These species are most often represented by juveniles that use the mangrove habitat as a nursery area and then migrate to different habitats as they grow larger. They are usually in highest abundance during the summer and fall and are either absent or in low abundance at other times of the year.

These small juveniles are a good seasonal source of food for gamefish. The fact that most fish don't make it past the juvenile stage because predation is so high indicates that gamefish and other predators feed heavily on these small fish. Including flies in your selection that imitate small fish in this vulnerable life stage is a good strategy.

Many of the species that use seagrass habitats as nursery areas are also found in mangroves in the same seasons, which should help keep your fly selection a reasonable size. There are, however, some species whose juveniles are more abundant in mangroves. Fortunately, many juveniles are similar enough in appearance that they can be imitated with the same flies.

Grunts (family Pomadasyidae) are most abundant in the tropics, with french grunts *(Haemulon flavolineatum)*, white grunts *(Haemulon plumieri)*, bluestriped grunts *(Haemulon sciurus)*, and sailor's choice *(Haemulon parrai)* often the most common, depending on location. Juvenile grunts all have a yellow and white background coloration, with minor dark lines or markings that differ for each species. A yellow-over-white Clouser (size 1 or 2) or yellow and white Deceiver (size 1) cast along the mangrove edge makes for a decent imitation of juvenile grunts. Since the majority of grunt larvae enter the mangrove habitat during summer, it is best to use smaller flies during summer and larger flies in fall. Often the juvenile grunts will migrate away from mangrove habitats to adult habitats on reefs by winter, but this is not always the case. Sometimes larger grunts of more than four inches can be found along the mangroves throughout the year.

Snapper (family Lutjanidae) can also be abundant among mangrove prop roots. Like grunts, juvenile snapper are most abundant during summer and migrate to adult habitats in fall or winter. However, in areas where mangroves are along a steep shoreline or next to a channel, you might find some large snapper year-round. Species that are represented by a lot of juveniles during summer in the tropics are schoolmaster snapper *(Lutjanus apodus)*, yellowtail snapper *(Ocyurus chrysurus)*, and gray or mangrove snapper *(Lutjanus griseus)*. In the subtropics, gray snapper is probably the most abundant species. In the tropics, you may find larger schoolmaster and gray snappers among mangrove prop roots in deeper water, while adult yellowtail snapper are found in deeper reef areas.

Juvenile parrotfish (family Scaridae) can also be found among mangrove prop roots, mostly during summer. Juveniles of most species found among mangrove prop roots are light in color, have a typical fish shape, and often have longitudinal alternating dark and light stripes.

Juvenile jacks (family Carangidae) occupy mangrove prop roots in loosely associated schools before moving to other habitats as they grow larger. Many juvenile jacks have vertical barring over silvery sides, are similar in shape to adults, and can be imitated with a three-inch all-white Deceiver. The vertical bars on juvenile jacks and the mottled patterns on some mojarra may explain the success of the Glades Deceiver along mangrove shorelines.

Different locations may have different collections of juveniles, so it may take a little investigation on your part to determine which flies are most appropriate. The extra investigation is likely to pay off.

Seasonal Prey: Juvenile Lobsters, Shrimp, and Crabs
The list of invertebrates that use mangroves as juveniles on a seasonal basis and can be imitated with a fly is much shorter. At the top of the list in the tropics is the juvenile spiny lobster *(Panulirus argus)*. Although they are not plentiful, with a little searching you can often find small spiny lobsters among mangrove prop roots. These small lobsters are like candy for mutton snapper and permit that cruise the edge of the mangrove roots. In fact, a large mutton snapper will engulf an adult lobster given the chance, so juveniles are easy targets. Juvenile spiny lobsters remain hidden among the prop roots during the day and venture out to feed on the bottom adjacent to mangroves at night. Lobster-imitating flies tied on long-shank hooks in sizes 1 and 1/0 are appropriate for sight-casting to mutton snapper and permit that cruise mangrove shorelines. The larval stage of spiny lobsters can range from six to twelve months long, and this is reflected in the variation in times of year when juveniles are most abundant. Although juvenile lobsters might be present in mangrove habitats at any time of year, it seems that late spring and summer are peak times of juvenile lobster abundance. You will also find juvenile shrimp among the mangrove prop roots, which can be imitated with the same patterns you use in seagrass.

The proximity of mangroves and seagrass provides a great situation for juvenile blue crabs. These crabs require the shelter of thick seagrass as juveniles but can forage among the mangroves once they are larger. Juvenile blue crabs are most abundant in late spring and summer. In contrast, mangroves with mud adjacent are unlikely to harbor juvenile blue crabs, although adults may be present. It is important to notice such connections between habitats, because juvenile blue crabs are on the menus of numerous gamefish found in the subtropics, including snook and my favorite, red drum. Given an opportunity to sight-fish for red drum along a mangrove shoreline lined by seagrass, I often use my imitation of a juvenile blue crab.

Midwater Baitfish

The Clupeidae (herring) family includes larger, schooling baitfish that are best imitated with three- to seven-inch-long Deceivers. In the tropics, these species are present year-round; in the subtropics, they are seasonal. The species in this family that you are most likely to encounter near mangrove shorelines and mangrove lagoons include redear sardine *(Harengula humeralis)*, scaled sardine *(Harengula jaguana)*, and species of similar coloration and shape. These fish have silver sides and gray to green shaded backs, with a high body profile. Their size varies seasonally, especially in the subtropics. For example, juvenile scaled sardines found in seagrass beds near mangrove shorelines are most abundant in late spring. They've grown to larger adult sizes by summer. Mangrove lagoons (or mangrove shorelines adjacent to grass beds) with moderate depths, large areas of open water, and decent water clarity are where you will most often find schools of herrings in association with mangrove habitats.

In the tropics, groups of barjacks *(Caranx ruber)* and blue runners *(Caranx crysos)* often strafe schools of small herring in the open-water sections of these mangrove lagoons, whereas crevalle jacks *(Caranx hippos)* are the primary marauders in the subtropics. Tarpon, snook, red drum, spotted seatrout, ladyfish, barracuda, and even the occasional large bonefish will also feed heavily on herrings found near mangrove habitats. It is quite a sight to watch tarpon herd a school of herring along a mangrove shoreline and take turns charging open-mouthed through the panicked baitfish.

Silversides and anchovies can spend all or a significant portion of their lives in the vicinity of mangroves. You will most often encounter silversides among the mangrove prop roots and anchovies in more open waters. Species from these families are often collectively referred to as glass minnows and always occur in schools. Within each family, individual species are often hard to distinguish; it may even be difficult to distinguish between anchovies and silversides that occur in the same locations. Fortunately for anglers, the similarities in size and coloration of anchovies and silversides mean we can imitate these prey with the same flies.

Silversides and anchovies have large eyes relative to body size. A silver stripe runs the length of the body. The lower half is generally pale, and the distinct silver of the abdominal cavity lining shows through the pale flesh. The dorsal (top) half is a darker shade of tan to olive. Anchovies and silver-

Silversides and anchovies are similar in size and shape and are common in most coastal habitats.

sides can grow as long as four to six inches but are often found in smaller sizes. Species of silversides you will most likely encounter are inland silverside *(Menidia beryllina)* and tidewater silverside *(Menidia peninsulae).* Common anchovies include striped anchovy *(Anchoa hepsetus),* dusky anchovy *(Anchoa lyolepis),* bay anchovy *(Anchoa mitchilli),* and Cuban anchovy *(Anchoa cubana).*

While fishing in the Caribbean, I have often watched barracuda suspended in the shadows among the mangrove prop roots suddenly dart out and engulf a mouthful of silversides from a school as it passed along the outer edge of the mangroves. In the subtropics, snook lie in wait and are the prime consumers of glass minnows among the mangrove prop roots. Small tarpon can be found feeding on large schools of these baitfish in backwaters of the tropics and subtropics.

You will potentially encounter as many as six species of mullet along mangrove shorelines, in shallows adjacent to mangroves, and in mangrove lagoons. All of the mullet species are similar in shape and coloration, so they can be imitated with any generalized mullet pattern. Mullet are bullet-shaped and silvery gray, lighter on the belly with darker shades on the back. In the subtropics and warm-temperate areas, you are most likely to encounter the striped mullet *(Mugil cephalis),* although white mullet *(Mugil curema)* can be found in the same areas but usually in lower abundance. In the tropics, liza *(Mugil liza)* replaces striped mullet, and white

Juvenile mullet enter estuaries in late winter and spring.

They become "finger mullet" size by summer and fall.

mullet is often the most abundant species. Fantail mullet *(Mugil gyrans)* are found most abundantly in the tropics. While adult mullet can reach over two feet in length, it is the juveniles that are best imitated with a fly and are often targeted by gamefish in mangrove habitats. In general, juvenile mullet occupy the shallow water near mangrove roots, while adults venture farther from the shoreline and use a wider variety of habitats.

LOCATION MATTERS

Numerous studies of mangrove habitats have revealed that the composition of fish and invertebrate communities depends in large part on three factors: where the mangroves are located (semienclosed lagoons, on shorelines exposed to open sea, on flats, along a backwater estuary, or lining a creek); what habitats are adjacent to the mangroves (seagrass, sand, or mud); and the depth of water near the mangroves. Although there is natural variation even among similar habitats, some generalizations can be made about prey species most likely to be found in these different areas.

Mangroves adjacent to creeks often have more total species and a greater number of individuals of resident and seasonal species than shallow areas. In part, this is because many species follow the flooding tide

Holes *(dark area in center)* at the mouths of mangrove creeks offer safe places for gamefish to rest during low tide and to wait for prey. Shallow flats at the entrances to these creeks are excellent sight-fishing locations on a rising tide, especially on a warm winter day when gamefish come onto the flat to warm up in the midday sun.

into the mangroves to feed on the rich and diverse communities in these intertidal areas and then retreat as ebbing tides drain the mangroves. The creek provides a deep-water refuge close to the food source for these species.

In turn, the greater number of organisms and the behavior of the species that use this strategy attract gamefish, which often can be found at the edges of these creeks opportunistically feeding on prey that is washed out of the mangroves with the dropping tide. The spring tides that are associated with new and full moons are especially good for fishing the edges of mangrove creeks because increased volumes of water being moved by these tides create stronger currents that force more prey from the mangrove shallows to the creeks.

Areas with seagrass adjacent to mangroves generally support more species than areas with mud or sand. Small juvenile fish prefer locations with seagrass adjacent to mangroves, but as they grow, juveniles often move to areas where open bottom is adjacent to mangroves. This change in habitat occurs because larger juveniles are able to avoid more predators, feeding opportunities are better for their changing diets, and the shelter of mangrove prop roots is nearby as protection from larger predators. You may want to vary the size of your flies with the habitats you are fishing—smaller flies for seagrass and larger flies for areas of open bottom next to mangroves.

However, you are more likely to find large gamefish, like snook and red drum, feeding along mangroves where no seagrass grows into the prop root habitats. Areas with open bottom next to mangroves are easier places for gamefish to find and capture prey, and a deep open bottom may hold more large fish than a shallow open bottom. Gamefish can wait in the shadows of the mangroves and ambush passing prey more easily.

In the tropics, mangroves that are exposed to open water are likely to harbor high numbers of juveniles of the same coral reef fish found in seagrass beds that surround coral reefs. In contrast, mangroves that are more removed from the ocean, such as in lagoons that are connected to the ocean by only a narrow channel, or those that are deep within estuaries will be dominated by the core group of resident species that are primarily associated with mangrove habitats.

This pattern also holds in the subtropics. In general, mangroves closer to the ocean environment have more marine species and more seasonal species. The farther upstream you go in a tidal mangrove creek, the fewer seasonal fish you will find, and the communities of baitfish and other prey will be dominated by residents. Numerous gamefish, such as tarpon and snook, are able to travel from salty ocean areas to mangrove habitats that are almost fresh water. Understanding how the species of prey available to gamefish change as they travel among mangrove habitats from the ocean toward fresh water will aid in your fly selection.

TIME OF DAY

Many species of fish use mangrove prop roots as shelter during the day and then venture out at night to feed in adjacent open areas of seagrass, sand, or mud. This is especially common for juvenile grunts of two to five inches. Grunts form large schools along the edges of mangrove prop roots just prior to dusk and venture out into lagoon feeding areas once darkness falls. This period, from sunset to approximately thirty minutes after sunset, has been termed the "quiet period" because there is little activity relative to daytime. Most fish have either retreated to nighttime shelters or are waiting to venture out under cover of darkness. The quiet period is somewhat of a misnomer, however, because it can actually be a time of peak predatory activity. Large mutton snapper *(Lutjanus analis)*, barracuda *(Sphyraena barracuda)*, and other species focus on the juvenile grunts that aggregate along the edges of the mangroves, especially as the grunts begin to move out into adjacent habitats. If you find a section of mangroves that harbors a large number of grunts during the day, you may want to make a mental note and return just prior to dusk. There are no guarantees, but you may find yourself witness to a flurry of feeding by large predators. Yellow-over-white Deceivers are suitable imitations of these small grunts.

Anglers who have witnessed the sudden surge in feeding activity by snook in estuarine mangroves also know the potential of the dusk feeding period to provide great fishing. Snook have an advantage over their prey at dusk, so they tend to be more aggressive in their feeding behavior. They might also feel less threatened by potential predators under cover of low light and may wander farther from their prop root shelters. In any case, snook that might have been tentative toward a fly during the day will be more likely to have shifted into feeding mode at dusk.

SEASONS IN THE MANGROVES

Although not as drastic as in temperate latitudes, seasons do occur in the tropics and subtropics, and these seasons influence gamefish and their prey living in mangrove habitats.

The tropics and subtropics experience two major seasons. The wet season generally runs from May or June through October or November, and the dry season from November or December to April or May, with actual months varying among locations. Some regions, such as the Caribbean coast of Costa Rica, might receive heavy rains throughout most of the year. In contrast, some islands in the Caribbean, such as Curacao, don't receive much rain at any time of year. The extent to which gamefish respond to changes due to wet and dry seasons varies, depending on how much seasonal variation there is in their area.

During the dry season, less fresh water flows down rivers into the estuaries, so the salinity of the estuaries increases. In some years, the salinity can be nearly the level of the open ocean far into the estuaries and river mouths.

During a dry winter period in south Florida, red drum might be found much farther up in an estuary than you would normally find them in summer, or they might be more abundant in areas where you might not normally find them. One recent winter, I found large red drum in a river mouth at the head of an estuary, as far from the ocean as they could be before entering the river. Part of the reason these large adult red drum were exploring this area was because the salinity was twenty-five parts per thousand (ppt), almost the same salinity as the Gulf of Mexico.

In the wet season, salinity in the rivers and estuaries drops as more fresh water flowing from rivers and creeks mixes with salt water from the ocean. The same area where I found the large red drum in winter had a salinity of less than ten ppt the following summer wet season, and those fish had left for waters lower in the estuary with more stable salinities.

Knowing how wet and dry seasons influence the salinity and clarity of water in mangrove estuaries can help you create a strategy for where and when to fish and what type of flies might be best. During the wet season, you are more likely to find large red drum in areas with medium to high salinity, so you should concentrate your efforts where salinity is higher. During the dry season, red drum will be more widely dispersed and may be farther into an estuary, so you are likely to find them in a wide range of locations.

Snook spawn in summer, and in order to spawn successfully, they need salinities greater than twenty ppt. As the amount of fresh water coming out of rivers and creeks increases during the summer wet season, larger mature snook migrate to areas closer to the open ocean to spawn. This may cause a sudden decrease in the number of large snook you see along a mangrove shoreline near the head of an estuary as the wet season progresses. So if you are in search of large snook, the wet season is not the best time to search for them along mangrove shorelines in the upper reaches of the estuary.

Seasonal changes in temperature also influence gamefish. This is particularly true in the subtropics. In winter, mangrove creeks, especially those with deep holes, are great places to find snook. Snook, a tropical species, is near the northern extent of its range in the subtropics and can't tolerate cold temperatures. Snook find refuge in deeper waters of creeks sheltered from cold winter winds, and these are great places to find hungry snook in winter. Many of these winter refuge areas also have a source of fresh water, which may provide a more consistent temperature during winter than do many open-water marine locations. As the water warms in spring and into summer, snook will move out of the creeks and feed along mangrove shorelines and adjacent flats.

Warm spells in winter can trigger a brief change in the distribution of snook. Shallow, muddy bottoms near creeks used by snook as winter refuge areas can be good places to fish in the afternoon during warm spells. The shallow water over the dark bottom will have been warmed considerably by the sun. Snook move to these areas to warm up in midday and afternoon, when the water is warmest. Since snook generally feed less during winter, these basking fish can be pretty aggressive toward a well-cast fly.

Whereas winter is probably the best time to fish for tailing red drum in subtropical grass beds, during summer days they feed in the shade of mangroves. I can think of two possible explanations for why red drum habitat use changes seasonally. First, on average, in much of the red drum's subtropical range, daytime tides are generally lower in winter than in summer, when the lowest tides tend to be at night, so access to mangroves is more limited than in summer. Second, in winter the water is cooler, and the sun-warmed flats are a more comfortable temperature for red drum. Since red drum, like other fish, are cold-blooded, the warmer waters of the shallow flats are more desirable for them in winter. During summer, the water warms considerably, and although red drum can be found feeding in grass beds, often in the morning and evening, you will also find them feeding in mangrove habitats. The high daytime tides of summer in much of the red drum's subtropical range help them in several ways. These tides allow the fish access farther back into the red mangrove prop roots, and even into the flooded roots of black mangroves, to feed on marsh and fiddler crabs, and the shade of the mangroves provides cooler water. Mangrove edges are also great places to find snook and even spotted seatrout and crevalle jacks on hot summer days.

The gamefish you find along mangrove shorelines in summer will be ready to pounce on flies that imitate any of the small baitfish that can be abundant during this time of year. Small mojarra in the tropics and subtropics, as well as pinfish in the subtropics, can be especially abundant along mangrove shorelines in summer.

Seasonal changes in temperature can also affect tropical gamefish, such as bonefish and permit. This is especially true in the northernmost portions of their range, where seasonal changes in temperature are greatest, such as in the Florida Keys and even the Bahamas. In Florida, it seems that bonefish are abundant in Florida Bay during warm months but move to the Atlantic side of the Keys during summer. Florida Bay is very shallow, and shallow waters can be cooled or warmed more rapidly by the air than deeper water, making them more susceptible to dropping temperatures brought on by cold fronts. In contrast, the Atlantic side of the Keys has more stable water temperatures, and bonefish have quicker access to deeper waters as a refuge from dropping temperatures.

APPLYING WHAT YOU'VE LEARNED:

Gamefish in the Mangroves

There are three basic approaches to fishing red mangrove shorelines. The standard approach is to wade or pole a boat some distance from the mangroves and cast into the shadows. "Some distance" means as far away as you can comfortably cast, because it's important to stay away from the mangroves to remain unseen by the fish. If you don't occasionally snag a mangrove branch, you aren't casting close enough to the prop root habitat. For this approach, I generally use streamer patterns with weedguard.

Snook are ambush predators, sitting in the shadows of the mangroves waiting for an unsuspecting prey fish to swim by or for a school of resident silversides to move within striking distance. This ambush strategy and their body shape are probably why some people call snook "saltwater pike." Red drum also take advantage of unsuspecting small fish, and crevalle jacks cruise the mangrove edges chasing just about any small fish they can find.

Low tide is my favorite time to fish for snook along mangrove edges. Near high tide, snook can hide way up under the mangrove branches, but as the water drops, they are forced to leave the shelter of the mangrove overhang. Often the fish will remain near their favorite spot, as close to the mangroves as the water depth allows. It takes some practice to pick out the motionless form of a snook lying perpendicular to the shoreline, sometimes so shallow that the top of its tail or dorsal fin is exposed. If you don't see a snook laid up as you pole along a shallow shoreline, you'll know as it explodes out of the shallows that you've gotten too close. It's important to cast to these laid-up fish from far enough away that the fish can't see you or your fly line on your false cast. A sidearm cast is a good idea. A quiet boat is also important as you pole along the shoreline—any noises out of the ordinary will send the snook to deeper water.

A second approach is to wade or pole close to the mangroves and look for fish either cruising or resting in the strip of open bottom that is often between the mangrove shoreline and seagrass bed, or in open-bottom potholes if seagrass grows all the way to the mangroves. It's important that you see these fish from a long way off; they are especially wary because they are lying on exposed bottom. A long cast, soft landing, and patient presentation are also helpful. Resting fish may seem like they are asleep. It may take a few casts—each one closer than the last—to move the fish, either to strike the fly or to move away.

A third, more difficult approach, but one that often results in more strikes for me, is to cast the fly into the shadows among the prop roots under overhanging mangrove branches. This takes practice and can be frustrating even for crusty old veterans, but it is the standard approach of anglers experienced in the ways of fishing mangrove shorelines. You will snag your fly on the mangroves, even with a weed guard, but that's okay. If you don't hang your fly on the mangroves on occasion, you aren't casting your fly up far enough into the prop roots.

While fishing mangrove habitats, expect numerous break-offs. Hooked fish often head into mangrove prop roots, where your line may be cut on oysters, barnacles, mussels, or other sharp edges. A heavy bite tippet is a good idea for these conditions. I like a relatively short leader, 7 feet, with 12-pound test tippet and a bimini twist to a 20- or 25-pound shock tippet. Weedless flies are a must along mangrove shorelines because of the many roots and branches.

My favorite fly for casting into mangrove shadows is a red and white or red and grizzly Seaducer, as this fly sinks very slowly, remaining in the strike zone longer than most streamers with only twitches to give the fly motion. I like this pattern in size 2 for red drum, even though it doesn't imitate the crabs the red drum are usually feeding on. A crab fly would quickly get lost or tangled in all the roots and debris, and the Seaducer is a midwater fly that stays off the bottom. Plus, it works. Deceivers, glass minnows, Muddlers, and Divers are also good patterns for casting into red mangrove prop root habitats.

One of my greatest frustrations in fishing these shorelines is trying to track and cast to fish that are feeding far into the mangrove forest at high tides. These fish can be snook, tarpon, red drum, or bonefish. Except for bonefish, I've had occasional success casting small poppers along the outer edge of the mangroves. I think the feeding fish hear the popper and come out of the mangroves to investigate.

When fishing for bonefish feeding in the flooded mangrove forest at high tide, listen for the telltale swashing sounds they make. It's worth your time to pinpoint the location of the feeding fish and to find indentations in the shoreline where you might intersect the bonefish as it moves through the mangroves. Often a fish will zigzag in and out of the mangroves as it moves along in search of food. If you are able to intersect these hungry fish, you have a good chance of hooking up. One not-so-elegant catch I made proves it's worth tracking bonefish feeding in mangroves.

A friend and I were wading along a flooded mangrove shoreline at dawn. High tide had pushed the water well into the mangrove forest. Eighty feet ahead of us, we heard a ruckus deep within the mangroves. A feeding bonefish? We worked our way slowly along the mangrove edge toward where we thought the fish was feeding, listening for more signs of the feeding fish. We heard nothing, but as we reached the spot where the noise had come from, a bonefish tailed halfway between us.

I made a quick roll cast in case the fish hadn't already spooked, and as the fly dropped toward the bottom, I stripped twice. A wake appeared as the fish bolted toward the fly. The wake bulged as the fish turned on the fly. The fly line jumped, and I set the hook.

Catching that bonefish was pure luck. It tailed between two anglers, and then ate the fly. But we were in the right place at the right time because we had made the effort to find the fish we heard feeding deep within the mangroves, and then came across it during its zigzag search for prey.

Numerous species of jacks will cruise the edges of mangrove prop roots at high speed, picking off unwary glass minnows as they go. Even if you can't see the jacks, you can sometimes follow their path by watching for the telltale sign of schools of glass minnows jumping from the water to escape the jacks. When jacks are in this rapid-fire mode, cast ahead of where you think they might be rather than at the spot where you just saw the minnows jump out of the water. By the time you make your cast, the jacks will probably be another ten feet farther along the shoreline. Sometimes, however, the schools of glass minnows will be sufficiently large to keep the jacks in one spot long enough to get a cast to them. In such a situation, be ready for a strike as soon as the fly hits the water.

The escape behavior of glass minnows will also give away the location of snook that ambush them along mangrove shorelines. A shower of glass minnows along the edge of mangrove prop roots, along with the *slurPOP* of air being sucked in with a mouthful of water and glass minnows, is a sure sign of a feeding snook.

Among the largest snapper you will find feeding along mangrove prop roots is the mutton snapper. Large adult mutton snapper forage along the mangroves much like permit or bonefish, feeding on crabs, lobsters, and smaller fish. Because mutton snapper feed on the same prey as bonefish and permit, the same shrimp, crab, and juvenile lobster flies are appropriate for all three species. Unlike bonefish and permit, however, mutton and other kinds of snapper that live among mangrove prop roots in deeper water will also chase poppers. So if you find yourself in a lagoon or creek with deep water, it's worth some casts of a popper along the mangrove edge. If not a snapper, a jack, snook, or small tarpon may strike this fly.

Although you have a good shot at finding large fish feeding along shallow, protected mangrove shorelines and lagoons, I've found that most often the fish associated with these areas in the Caribbean are in the medium size class. Since wind is usually not a problem in protected lagoons, flies are often small, and fish are generally not very large, I often use a 6-weight fly rod to fish the mangrove shorelines. If I'm in a boat, I always have a heavier rod rigged in case larger fish make an appearance, but a 6-weight rod makes for good sport in many situations.

Wade with caution when fishing around mangroves. Because the roots trap sediments and dampen currents, the bottom in and around mangroves can be rather soft. This is not always the case—there are some great hard-bottomed wading opportunities along mangrove shorelines—but it is a possibility you need to take into consideration when fishing an area for the first time. Some areas are so soft that you can become permanently stuck unless you go fishing with a friend.

Finally, mangroves are home to many insects. The mosquitoes and no-see-ums can be brutal and can sour an otherwise productive day of fishing, so take along a some strong bug repellent.

STEWARDSHIP

Threats to mangroves are extreme and warrant immediate attention. Like wetlands worldwide, these critically important habitats have declined significantly and continue to be under stress. Diversion of fresh water from mangrove areas, filling in these wetlands for development, cutting the trees for wood products, and pollution all are immediate threats to these habitats and to the communities that depend on them. Without these fragile habitats, many species will not be able to survive, and we will lose a fantastic habitat for fly fishing.

As in all of our coastal environments, the connections between diverse healthy habitats are essential to the success of gamefish populations. Juvenile fish such as tarpon and snook require shallow, protected, low-salinity areas during at least the first year of life but must be able to move to somewhat deeper areas with higher salinity as they grow. Eventually adults use the various habitats provided by estuaries and the coastal ocean, but even they have specific habitat requirements. A fish's chances of survival are much greater if it can move from one habitat to another without having to negotiate large inhospitable areas, such as seawalls, where mangrove shoreline used to be. This is especially true for the juvenile and subadult stages of the life cycle, which depend on the mangrove shorelines.

Sadly, coastal habitats are under increasing stress, and poor-quality habitats are bad news to the fish that depend on them. Despite some changes in environmental laws, development continues to eradicate important mangrove habitats. In many areas, only small sections of mangroves remain where once the entire shoreline was a continuous stretch of undisturbed habitat. In other areas, poor water quality from too much sediment or pollution, or from too much or too little fresh water due to channelization, has eradicated seagrass beds next to mangroves, leaving only open bottom. Such conditions also may alter the communities associated with existing mangrove prop roots. In addition, dredging to allow more boat access removes the shallow habitats that are essential to both juvenile and adult gamefish. Often these destructive forces act in tandem, resulting in sparse coastal landscapes.

To fragment these important fish habitats into ever smaller, low-quality parcels is to invite disaster for coastal gamefish. This is an outcome we should try our best to prevent.

There are two simple things that you as an angler can do. First, fish responsibly. If you break off your leader, for example, don't leave it dangling in the mangroves. Birds often become entangled in monofilament left hanging from mangrove branches. Second, as a responsible steward of gamefish habitats, it is important to report any destruction of mangroves. Enforcement agencies aren't able to be in all places at all times, so if you observe the destruction of gamefish habitat while you are on the water, it is your duty to report it.

Chapter 4

Oyster Bars

My favorite series of oyster bars lies in knee-deep water along the deep edge of a large, shallow grass bed. The oyster bars protect the grass bed from waves that build under south winds whipping across two miles of open water. These disconnected patches of oyster bar also break up incoming tidal currents whose diversions have carved small sand potholes, about five feet across, at the ends of the bars. Baitfish temporarily congregate in the shelter provided by the oyster bars, taking refuge from the forceful currents and seeking escape from foraging gamefish.

Unfortunately for the schooling baitfish, the oyster bars render a false haven. At low tide, the shallow oyster bars provide shelter from gamefish, but the baitfish are at the mercy of wading birds such as blue heron. At high tide, when water covers the bars, they are easy places for gamefish to corral and feed on the baitfish because of the bars' proximity to deeper water. I have witnessed snook, tarpon, red drum, and spotted seatrout feeding on sardines, mullet, and anchovies that have sought shelter in the shadows of these oyster bars. An appropriate-size streamer cast into the mix almost certainly results in a strike.

A whole community of potential gamefish prey lives permanently among the oyster shells and takes advantage of food and shelter provided by an oyster bar's many crevices. These residents seem to live a less frantic existence than the baitfish. When gamefish feed on the resident prey, their feeding is more methodical, and your fly-fishing approach must follow suit.

Oysters can grow in many locations—on mangrove prop roots, pier pilings, rocky shorelines, and many other hard surfaces. The communities of organisms that live among these oysters can attract feeding gamefish. But oysters growing on prop roots, pilings, or rocks are merely components of the habitats where they are growing. In contrast, oysters also occur on a scale large enough to constitute a unique type of habitat all their own: oyster bars.

Intertidal isolated oyster bars are great focal points for red drum and spotted seatrout, especially on changing tides. Look for current-carved channels or holes as likely feeding and resting spots for these gamefish on dropping and low tides, respectively.

Some people make a distinction between oyster bars and oyster reefs, a bar being a smaller structure than a reef. It seems to me too subjective a definition—what constitutes a bar in a location with extensive oyster growth may be considered a reef in an area with relatively minor oyster coverage. In addition, many local nuances tend to further confuse the issue. Therefore, I use the terms interchangeably to describe natural structures made entirely of oysters.

A fly angler might encounter six species of oysters while in pursuit of gamefish in coastal habitats in our coverage area, yet only one species, the eastern oyster (*Crossastrea virginica*), forms oyster bars or reefs. Other oyster species grow only on mangrove prop roots or rocky shores and don't form reefs, or occur in very low abundance on oyster bars composed almost entirely of eastern oysters. In the tropics, oysters are mostly found growing on mangrove prop roots and rarely, if ever, as oyster reefs because in most locations there isn't enough plankton to support large reefs. In the subtropics and warm-temperate climates, however, where the eastern oyster is abundant, oyster bars are common and important estuarine habitats that are used as feeding areas by gamefish.

Even in subtropical and warm-temperate environments, the importance of oyster bars to gamefish varies. In areas with abundant seagrass or
mangrove habitats, oyster bars are just one of three major habitats where
gamefish find prey and shelter. But in areas with no mangroves and little
or no seagrass, oyster bars provide the best habitat for gamefish prey and
are very important.

What gamefish are you most likely to find around oyster bars? The
short answer is, any gamefish worth catching. In the subtropics, gamefish
that are common on or near oyster reefs include red drum, spotted seatrout, snook, ladyfish, and gray snapper. Tarpon, cobia, and crevalle jacks
occasionally show up around reefs near deep water. In North Carolina,
you will commonly find gulf flounder, red drum, spotted seatrout, black
drum, weakfish, bluefish, gray snapper, and juvenile gag.

ECOLOGICAL REQUIREMENTS

Oysters follow a life cycle typical of many marine organisms, employing
the broadcast spawning strategy. After hatching, the larvae float as plankton for a few days before they must find a good place to settle. The oyster
larvae require a hard surface to settle, with oyster shell the most preferred
surface. The time period for settlement is short, and if oyster larvae don't
find a hard substrate in a few days, they will die. Once settled, the tiny
oysters, called spat, cement themselves to the hard surface and begin
to grow. Thus oyster bars are generations of oysters built one upon the
other.

How an oyster bar gets started in a soft-bottom estuary is anyone's
guess, but once it is established, the subsequent generations are able to
build upon that initial success and provide valuable habitat for gamefish
and their prey. But because their life requirements limit where they can
grow successfully, oyster bars won't form in just any location. One such
requirement is that oysters need a constant source of new water to survive. Oysters are filter feeders, filtering plankton and particles out of the
water they pump through their gills, so they need a constant supply of
new water to bring them food. This is why oyster bars grow in areas
where new water arrives with each rising tide or where tidal currents or
flows from creeks and rivers continually bring new food for the filter-
feeding oysters.

The filter feeding of oysters is an essential component to the health of
the estuaries where oysters grow. An individual oyster is able to filter
plankton and organic particles from as much as fifty gallons of water per
day, and the clearer the water, the better the conditions for the growth of

seagrass. Plus, the more water that oysters can filter, the less likely there are to be plankton blooms, which have negative effects on the ecology of the estuaries, including fish kills.

While currents are essential for carrying food to the oysters, and oysters are efficient filter feeders, it is essential that currents don't carry too much sediment. Too much sediment will smother and kill the oysters, resulting in a dead reef. Over time, a heavy sediment load will entirely cover a once-living oyster reef, and since oyster larvae need a hard surface on which to settle, the habitat is buried forever.

Currents can also help mix surface and bottom water, and areas with a lot of mixing can produce healthier oyster bars. This is because in deep areas, bottom water can become low in oxygen, which can either slow the growth of, or in severe conditions kill, oysters living at the bottom of oyster bars in deeper water. These low-oxygen conditions are most common during summer months and are worsened by high nutrients (mostly nitrogen and phosphorus) from fertilizers used on farms and lawns and sewage from urban areas. In general, the upper portions of oyster bars in deep water have the healthiest oysters. This is important to gamefish, because healthier oyster bars host larger prey communities.

Oyster bars tend to grow across the prevailing currents, with a higher mound forming in the middle and the reef tapering at each end, often into deeper water. In areas with optimal growing conditions, oyster bars can form massive reefs and can deflect and reroute currents. In less-than-perfect growing conditions, scattered oyster clumps or patchy bars form instead. These patchy oyster bars have a less dramatic effect on currents but can provide great gamefish habitat. And like the advantage gamefish get from feeding in open patches in seagrass or along the outer edges of mangroves, gamefish feeding along the edges of oyster bars have a better chance of capturing prey than those pursuing prey hiding among the oyster shells, so patchy reefs have their advantages.

TYPES OF OYSTER BARS
Oyster reefs can be always submerged, even at low tide, which is known as subtidal, or exposed at low tide and submerged at high tide, which is termed intertidal. In general, intertidal and shallow subtidal reefs are the most important to fly anglers. Regardless of whether they are intertidal or subtidal, there are three types of environments where oyster bars are found.

One type of oyster bar I call a point bar begins at the shoreline, often a point on the edge of a marsh, and extends outward over open bottom into current-swept waters. The growth of these reefs occurs on their outer ends that extend into the currents, because the outer part of the reef receives the most plankton-filled water. Over time, these reefs can get very large, and the seaward growth may choke off currents to the landward part of the reef. In many cases, the inner portion of the reef is colonized by marsh plants or mangroves, creating more wetland.

A second type of oyster bar, an isolated bar, grows on sandy or muddy bottom without any association to land or marsh habitats. Isolated oyster bars often form on a large expanse of open bottom. Sometimes the reef will be surrounded by a ring of open bottom separating the oyster bar from seagrass, and on occasion seagrass will grow right to the edge of the oyster bar. Over time, some intertidal bars will be colonized by mangroves or marsh plants, but the tidal range is often too great or currents too strong for mangroves or marsh plants to become established.

A fringing bar, the third type of oyster bar, grows parallel to a shoreline or marsh fringe (bounded by land, marsh, or mangroves), with seagrass or open bottom on the outer edge. Fringing oyster bars are especially important at stabilizing shorelines, and the deeper edges provide refuge for many marsh organisms at low tide. Fringe oyster bars provide complex habitat to an otherwise open, muddy marsh bottom, which results in a concentration of gamefish prey seeking shelter among the oyster shells.

Fringing oyster bars, as along this red mangrove shoreline, often indicate edges with good water flow and thus typically hold gamefish on dropping tides. The added structure the oyster bar provides to the shoreline can be a collecting point for prey and gamefish at high tide.

CURRENTS

Because they are solid structures rising off the bottom, all oyster bars that are exposed to currents influence those currents. Depending on their size and orientation, oyster bars might produce small eddies, concentrate water flow through narrow channels, or completely deflect currents onto a different path. In each case, the resulting water movement affects the species living on or near the oyster bar. Whether this influences gamefish is partly a matter of scale. At one extreme, large bars can influence the course of large volumes of water, diverting the flow of creeks draining a marsh, for example, which can have notable effects on distributions of gamefish. At the other extreme, very small oyster bars affect only their immediate surroundings, much like a rock in a stream, and their influences on marine gamefish are less dramatic.

When large bars of any type block currents, they often create an area of slow water on the upcurrent side. Upcurrent stillwaters are usually areas of slow, swirling water, and baitfish drifting downstream often get confused by these slowly whirling currents and collect in these eddies. And upcurrent stillwaters that hold baitfish often hold gamefish.

More common and easier to fish than upcurrent stillwaters are downcurrent eddies. Large point oyster bars that extend far from shore can significantly affect currents, even to the detriment of the oysters growing closest to shore. Large bars can deflect currents so that most water passes over the outer, growing end of the bar, leaving only a very slow downcurrent eddy near shore. The very slow currents at the shoreline end of the bar bring little food, so these areas often have few live oysters and tend to hold fewer prey for gamefish. This is not always the case, however. Some of these backwaters can be good collecting places for baitfish and may hold concentrations of killifish and sheepshead minnows, so they are worth checking out.

On point bars extending from shore, the strongest currents flow over and around the outer portions of the bar. These are usually the best spots for fishing. At low tide, most of the bar may be exposed, so any moving water will pass over the bar's outer edge. At high tide, much or all of the bar might be covered, so currents may sweep over most of the bar. Where the strongest currents occur depends on the shape of the bar and the orientation of the bar to the current. In addition, some bars experience the best flows for fishing during an incoming tide, others on an outgoing tide. When fishing during an incoming tide, the best fishing in the early part of the tide will likely be at the outer edge of the bar; as the tide rises, you should shift your position shoreward; by high tide, you might be fishing where the bar meets shore. Follow the reverse path when fishing during a dropping tide, starting at the shoreward end and working your way toward the outer edge of the bar. It will take some observation on your part to figure out which tide is best for each bar.

Spots with the strongest currents are most likely to harbor sleek gamefish, species built for speed. Crevalle jack, bluefish, ladyfish, and spanish mackerel all have small scales, a streamlined body shape, and a forked tail—characteristics that decrease drag so these species can feed in faster flows. Species that aren't as hydrodynamic, such as weakfish, spotted seatrout, red drum, and snook, will be more abundant in the slower flow and will either dart from behind an obstruction into the faster current to pick up wayward prey or wait in the slower water for prey to come to them.

Except near high tide, when the whole bar is covered, isolated intertidal oyster bars situated in currents will have water racing around the ends of the bar. Isolated subtidal bars will likely have currents at the ends and over the top of the bar throughout the tidal cycle. In either case, currents may dislodge and wash away sediments from around the edge of the bar, creating deeper holes that are attractive to gamefish. Where to look for deeper holes depends on the depth of water where the bar is located and on the bar's configuration. On bars that have little water flow over the top, you are likely to find deeper holes on the ends of the bar or in the cuts between adjacent bars. These holes aren't necessarily large, but they often hold fish. Oyster bars that have strong water flow over the top often have deep holes on the downcurrent side of the bar. These holes are best fished when water is flowing strongly enough to sweep small fish and other prey over the top of the bar. This includes prey that are being swept downstream, such as silversides, and prey that live on the oyster bar, such as shrimp, crabs, and gobies, that are dislodged by strong currents.

Fringing oyster bars often experience currents that run parallel to the shoreline, so they tend not to produce large eddies and deflections of currents. Oyster shells protrude into the currents, however, creating small-scale turbulence along the surface of the oyster bar—miniature eddies that are used as shelter from the current by small fish, crabs, shrimp, and other prey. Gamefish often forage just above fringing bars, hoping to find prey that gets dislodged from these small eddies.

TIDAL RANGE

Oyster bars are three-dimensional structures, so they add complexity to the bottoms where they grow. Even in areas with slower currents, the holes that form next to and between oyster bars often hold gamefish, because gamefish that forage on the edges of oyster bars at high tide wait out the low tides in the deeper holes. As the tide turns and begins to rise again, these fish become more active and renew their search for food along the edges of the oyster bars.

Many of the small, mobile species associated with oyster bars move with the tides to feed and find refuge. These species—crabs, shrimp, and especially small fish—move up and down the slope of an intertidal oyster bar in order to remain in shallow water. Given the mobility of prey in relation to tides, you might expect gamefish to use tides to their feeding advantage, and they do. This is one reason the best locations for searching for gamefish are along edges rather than on top or in the middle of oyster reefs.

SALINITY

Salinity is also an important component in the formation of oyster bars. Oysters can tolerate a wide salinity range, but overall, they do best in the brackish waters of estuaries. It's all about growth and predation.

On one hand, oysters grow fastest in higher-salinity water and slower in low-salinity water, and they will die if exposed to fresh water for more than twelve days or so. This might lead you to search for the largest and greatest number of oysters in the portions of the estuary with high salinity.

On the other hand, oysters in high-salinity water fall victim to predators and diseases to a much greater degree than oysters in low salinity. A major oyster predator, the oyster drill, is found mostly in high-salinity water and can really do a number on oysters. A type of snail, the oyster drill is aptly named—it actually drills a hole in the oyster's shell and eats the oyster while the oyster is still in its shell. In addition, diseases that affect oysters are only active at higher salinities.

So the tradeoff is that oyster growth rate is higher in saltier water but so is oyster death rate, whereas oysters in low-salinity water don't grow as fast but are less likely to die from predation or disease. The best of both worlds seems to be medium-salinity water. The planktonic oyster larvae from adults in medium- and low-salinity areas are able to recolonize reefs in high salinity areas where predators or disease have reduced the numbers of live oysters, and thus maintain the oyster bar habitat throughout the estuary. This is why you will often find high-salinity areas dominated by younger, smaller oysters, with the largest oysters in medium-salinity areas.

Salinity also influences the organisms that live on oyster bars. In general, there are more total organisms on upstream than downstream oyster bars, but the total number of species is higher downstream. So gamefish feeding on oyster bars have fewer choices of prey upstream, but if they like to eat what they find on upstream bars, they are in luck because prey abundance may be higher.

Exploring Oyster Bars

When you put the ecological requirements of oysters together, you get a good idea of where you will find the healthiest oyster bars and what types of fishing situations you are likely to encounter. The first locations to eliminate when searching for large, healthy oyster bars are areas that are either completely fresh water or full ocean salinity throughout the year. In contrast, locations that have medium salinity, or experience fluctuations in salinity that reduce the occurrence of predators and disease while not killing oysters with low salinity, should have the best oyster bar habitats. Backwater areas that receive little flushing are also poor locations for oyster bars, whereas locations that receive frequent tidal flushing or are regularly exposed to currents—from either tides or rivers—are your best bets for finding healthy oyster bars. So if you come across healthy oyster bars while exploring new waters, you can be sure the location receives current and/or significant tidal flushing.

Exploration of a new area at low tide will show you where the intertidal oyster bars are located. Looking for eddies and changes in current direction during incoming or outgoing tides will help you pinpoint the locations of shallow, subtidal oyster bars or intertidal bars covered at high tide. Large point oyster bars will probably give you the most varied fishing conditions in a single location—from slack water near shore to strong currents near the end of the bar—and the location of the best currents for fishing will change with the tide.

Fringing oyster bars provide the best conditions for casting along the shoreline for gamefish feeding along the confluence of marsh, oyster bar, and open bottom. Depending on the depth, fringing bars can provide good fishing at different tidal stages—shallow areas will be best at high water, and deeper areas may hold gamefish at low water. Fringing bars offer great opportunities to cast flies right to the edge of the shoreline and fish the fly from the marsh edge down the slope of the oyster bar. In many ways, it is similar to casting streamers along rocky shorelines for smallmouth or striped bass.

Sometimes fringing bars grow out from the shoreline, or perhaps the shoreline erodes, leaving a shallow lagoon between the bar and shore. These lagoons are often used as shelter by small fish and even large mullet. Gamefish sometimes venture into these areas to feed, making quick charges into the lagoon before heading back to deeper water. Even if you can't catch up to a fish you see feeding in the shallows, you'll likely find gamefish resting along the outer edge of the bar.

Isolated oyster bars, my favorites, often present opportunities to fish upcurrent or downcurrent eddies during moving tides and holes between bars during low tides. It may take a little investigation to figure out whether an isolated bar is best on an incoming or outgoing tide, and on which side the deepest holes are located. But once you find an isolated bar that is productive on a particular tide, it should be productive under similar conditions much of the time.

It's worth exploring networks of isolated bars to chart where the best holes between bars are located. Sometimes you will find that bars are separated only by shallow mud that would never hold a gamefish at low tide. But you will sometimes find at least a few spots where isolated bars are separated by open bottom deep enough to hold gamefish at all but the lowest tides. I explore these areas in two ways, depending on how much time I want to invest. The strategy that takes the most time but can also yield fish is to methodically work my way from spot to spot, casting to areas between oyster bars that might have deep holes. A sudden swirl and a tight line are the rewards for taking this patient approach. If I am in more of an exploratory mood, I move from spot to spot and examine each to determine whether it is deep enough to hold gamefish. Although you have the potential for spooking gamefish holding in the deeper holes, this is an efficient method for scouting areas that you can later add to your list of fishing locations.

APPLYING WHAT YOU'VE LEARNED:

Basic Fishing Tactics

Now you can use the points in this chapter in your fishing—to find the largest and healthiest oyster reefs, to know what types of reefs to expect in different locations, to understand the conditions for different types of oyster bars in various locations, and to recognize how the health of the reef influences the number and types of prey and how the habitats adjacent to oyster bars influence gamefish and their prey.

When deciding on what fishing tactics to use for an oyster bar, the first consideration is currents. I like to approach upcurrent stillwaters from the upstream side and cast streamers to the edges of the eddy where the swirling water meets the downstream-flowing current. I always cast to these upcurrent stillwaters from as far away as possible, often angling the cast across the current and letting the fly swing into the slow water of the eddy.

I cast from a distance because I've found that gamefish holding on upcurrent sides of bars are more wary of approaching anglers than their counterparts on the downcurrent sides of bars. My sometimes less-than-stealthy approach from the upstream side of an oyster bar has resulted in more than a few large wakes made by gamefish heading off to safer waters. Perhaps the fish on the downcurrent sides of bars can't see or hear anglers approaching from upstream, while the fish on the upcurrent side of the bar can. Whatever the reason, make your casts to upcurrent eddies from a distance before moving close to the bar.

Once you've fished the edges of the eddy to your satisfaction, it's worth a few casts with a sinking fly, such as a Clouser Minnow, to the slower water right along the front of the bar. This area often contains the deepest hole, scoured by currents, and can hold large fish in its depths. I've pulled some large spotted seatrout from these deep spots.

In areas with strong currents, take the time to fish the holes on the ends and backside of the oyster bar just as you would rocks in a stream. Cast across and just upcurrent from the bar, and let the fly wash over the bar and swing through the deeper water of the hole. Start by casting to the area nearest you, and make your casts progressively longer until you've sufficiently covered the hole.

The strength of the currents, size of the hole and eddy, and whether you see fish actively feeding can help you determine the best fly to use. A strong current that sweeps into a large hole probably requires a sinking fly, such as a Clouser Minnow. With a slow current, a shallower hole, or fish actively feeding on the surface, I prefer an unweighted streamer or even a popper.

In areas with slow currents, you are likely to find gamefish feeding along the edges of the bars on a rising tide and resting in the deeper holes next to, between, and behind oyster bars at low tide. Red drum, for example, will take advantage of higher tides to feed along oyster bars that are not accessible for much of the tidal cycle, and then either rest or continue feeding in the deeper holes around the bars during low tides.

In clear water, you will be able to see where the holes between bars are located and will often see the fish. Even so, your best bet is to cast well before you are close enough to spot fish resting in the holes. Very often the fish will spot you at about the same time you see it, and it will swim off. Even if the fish remains in the hole, it will usually refuse your fly. More frustrating is when a large gamefish darts out

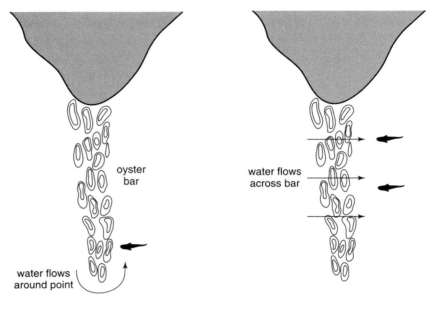

NEAR LOW TIDE   **NEAR HIGH TIDE**

The best locations to fish a point bar will vary with the tide. Near low tide, the outer point of the bar will probably have the best currents and will hold the most gamefish waiting for prey to be washed over the bar. Closer to high tide, the better currents are going to be closer to the land-based portion of the bar.

from the shadows on the edge of a hole as you approach after you were sure the hole was empty.

The holes between oyster bars and the deep water behind bars are good places to find red drum and spotted seatrout in warm-temperate areas like Louisiana. In these murky water areas, it is often difficult to see where the deeper holes are, and any fish resting in these murky holes will be impossible to see. Making a couple casts into each of the spots where you suspect holes are located is your best strategy in this situation. In such conditions, flies that can be heard or detected by a gamefish's lateral line system can be productive. Crab and shrimp patterns with small rattles tied into their bodies are good for bouncing over open bottom. In holes that might have snags on the bottom, a fly that pulsates and sends out vibrations but stays in midwater, such as a Seaducer, is a good bet.

In both clear and murky water settings, after you've covered the water to your satisfaction, head in for a closer look. You might find that the holes weren't oriented quite the way you thought, or that fish were holding differently than you anticipated. Or you might find there were no holes decent enough to hold fish. In any case, you can learn from what you find.

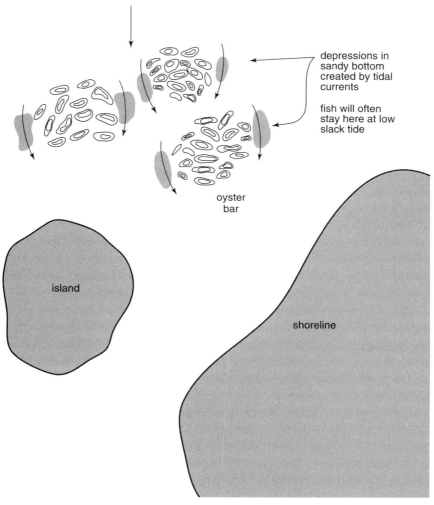

depressions in sandy bottom created by tidal currents

fish will often stay here at low slack tide

oyster bar

island

shoreline

Isolated bars often have deeper holes or depressions along one or more edges. These depressions have been scoured out by currents. Those next to isolated bars that are swept by current or between bars deep enough to hold gamefish at low tide are good places to target.

OYSTER BAR HABITATS

Oyster bars provide complex habitats for many small organisms that are prey for gamefish. In the tropics, gamefish and their prey can choose from seagrass, mangroves, coral reefs, rocky shorelines, and other coastal habitats that provide shelter and places to feed. In the subtropics, seagrass and mangroves are still available, but coral reefs are not, and rocky shorelines are rare, so oyster bars are an important component of coastal habitats. Even in locations with man-made jetties, the jetties are often in locations with strong currents or waves that are not hospitable for many organisms typical of an oyster bar community. In warm-temperate latitudes, mangroves are no longer present and seagrass occurs less frequently than in the subtropics, so gamefish and their prey are even more reliant on the shelter provided by oyster bars.

Oysters provide a complex, three-dimensional habitat that is full of crevices—perfect hiding and feeding locations for small fish, crabs, shrimp, worms, and a host of other organisms that seek shelter between shells or within empty oyster shells. In addition, many organisms, including mussels, sponges, and anemones, attach directly to the shells. Though not directly important to most gamefish, these attached organisms are food for gamefish prey. More importantly, they add to the three-dimensional structure of the oyster shell habitat, so an oyster reef with more attached organisms can support more gamefish prey. Some fish that feed directly on the mussels, such as sheepshead (*Archosargus probatocephalis*), are potential fly-rod targets. Although difficult to catch on the fly, sheepshead do eat crabs and shrimp and can be caught on crab flies.

At first glance, all oyster bars might appear the same. But like grass beds and mangroves, not all oyster bars are equal quality habitats. Even oyster bars that are close to one another can differ in the quality of habitat they offer to their inhabitants, and these differences can affect how oyster bars are used by gamefish. Two major reasons for these differences are the health of the oyster reef and where it is located in relation to other habitats.

Health refers here to the proportion of oysters and attached organisms that are alive. Oyster bars composed of live oysters tend to house more prey than ones with few live oysters. Though still home to more prey than open bottom, a dead-shell oyster bar is not as good a habitat as a live bar. In general, the healthier the oyster reef, the more prey available to gamefish.

More complex habitats provide better shelter and hiding places for gamefish and prey, and oyster bars are no exception. As in complex seagrass and mangrove habitats, gamefish can have a hard time catching prey that remain within the small crevices of the oyster reef. This is one reason gamefish often feed along the edges of oyster bars rather than search for prey within the bars.

The habitats that surround an oyster reef help determine the amount and types of prey a gamefish will encounter and influence where it is likely to feed. In areas of otherwise open bottom, oyster bars provide the most complex habitat for gamefish prey, and the diets of gamefish are often dominated by prey associated with oyster bars.

In contrast, when an oyster bar is surrounded by seagrass or is adjacent to marsh, gamefish diets tend to be a more even mix of prey from the oyster bar and adjacent habitats. Here gamefish are able to feed among a variety of habitats over a large area rather than have only a single habitat surrounded by bare bottom, and their feeding efforts will likely be more evenly distributed among the available habitats.

Interesting research in southern North Carolina provides some insight into the extent to which gamefish diets reflect whether a gamefish has been feeding on an oyster reef or on nearby habitats like seagrass, open bottom, or marsh. The general patterns are true of gamefish in other locations as well. Some gamefish, such as gulf and southern flounders appear to have little variety in their diets regardless of where they feed. The flounder examined in the North Carolina study fed mostly on small fish, whether they were caught on an oyster reef or in another habitat. Spotted seatrout ate mostly fish, regardless of habitat, but were also opportunistic and ate shrimp and polychaetes. In contrast, red drum varied their diets depending on where they were feeding. When feeding on or near oyster reefs, crabs and shrimp were common in their stomachs, whereas fish were the most common prey for red drum feeding in nonreef habitats. Surprisingly, although bluefish ate mostly fish, those feeding on oyster reefs also ate shrimp and crabs. At the very least, this stomach content data should emphasize that many gamefish vary their diet according to the habitat where they are feeding, and these diet differences should be reflected in your oyster bar fishing strategies.

Regardless of the surrounding habitat, an oyster reef can be a crowded place, and many organisms must venture away from the reef in search of food. When small fish, shrimp, and crabs venture from the shelter of oyster bars onto open bottom in search of food, they are easier targets for gamefish. Gamefish are aware of the abundance of prey living on oyster reefs, and they are also aware of the need for many of these potential prey to venture onto open bottom surrounding the reef. Often, rather than try to capture prey hiding among the oyster shells, gamefish such as red drum, black drum, weakfish, and spotted seatrout cruise along the edge of a reef hoping to surprise a crab, shrimp, or fish that is out over open bottom.

Many oyster bar inhabitants use the bars as shelter during the day and venture into the surrounding habitats to feed at night. This is especially true of oyster bars on open bottom, where the abundance of fish and crabs on the bottom surrounding the oyster bar is low during the day and increases dramatically at night. Many of the species that hide during the day and feed at night start their movements around dusk and return around dawn, one of the reasons my favorite times for fishing for tailing red drum around oyster bars are dawn and dusk.

SEASONALITY

Since oyster bars occur in subtropical and warm-temperate climates, the associated communities display a rather distinct seasonality. In warm-temperate areas, juvenile fish are most abundant from late spring to summer, peaking in June to July. Timing is similar in the subtropics, but juveniles of some species, such as pinfish, arrive in late winter, and juveniles of other species, such as some mojarra, mullet, and ladyfish, arrive in fall and winter.

Other species also show seasonal changes in abundance. In southern North Carolina, peak abundance of both juvenile and adult fish associated with oyster bars occurs in late summer to early fall, with medium abundances in late spring and late fall. Lowest abundances occur in winter when water temperatures are lowest. Patterns in abundance of small fish are similar in the northern Gulf of Mexico.

Gamefish also show changes in their association with oyster bars. In South Carolina, oyster bars are good places to find large schools of red drum in winter. Because of the low number of prey species that remain through the winter, flies that imitate the mummichog (Mud Minnow) are your best bet. Trout, which prefer cooler but not cold water, also hang in deep holes around oyster bars in winter.

In the subtropics, seasonal changes in abundance tend to be less dramatic than in warm-temperate latitudes. Fish abundance usually declines later in the fall and increases earlier in the spring than in warm-temperate climates. Crabs and shrimp show similar regional differences in seasonality, with more dramatic seasonal differences in warm-temperate than in subtropical areas.

GAMEFISH PREY

A gamefish that forages around oyster bars can depend on the resident prey species throughout the year, especially during periods when seasonal or transient prey are absent, but may switch its diet almost entirely to take advantage of temporary abundances of seasonal and transient prey species. Since a gamefish's behavior differs depending on the prey it's pursuing, this information is an essential component of any strategy for fly-fishing oyster bar habitats.

Crabs and Shrimp

As in seagrass beds and mangrove habitats, a large portion of the resident community of gamefish prey is made up of crabs and shrimp. One of the most abundant groups of potential prey on subtropical and warm-temperate oyster bars is mud crabs. In fact, mud crabs usually outnumber shrimp and other crustaceans on oyster bars by a sizable margin, so crab flies should be a staple in your fly selection for fishing oyster bars.

In many cases, the species of mud crabs you find on oyster bars are also found in seagrass beds. Even when the species are different between habitats, they are similar in appearance, so the same crab patterns you use in seagrass beds may also work on oyster bars. And because of the many potential snags on oyster bars, the weedguards you tied into your mud crab fly patterns for seagrass are just as necessary here.

The most common species of mud crabs are similar on subtropical and warm-temperate oyster bars. In North Carolina, the common mud crab

Mud crabs are often the most abundant species in seagrass, oyster bars, mangrove shorelines, and subtidal salt marsh bottoms.

(Panopeus herbstii), Say's mud crab *(Neopanope sayi)*, depressed mud crab *(Eurypanopeus depressus)*, and juveniles of the closely related and similar-looking stone crab *(Menippe mercenaria)* are the most common species. In the northern Gulf of Mexico, the Say's mud crab is replaced by the Texas mud crab *(Neopanope texana)*, but the species are similar in appearance. In the subtropics, the depressed mud crab, numerous species in the *Panopeus* genus of mud crabs, and juvenile stone crabs are the most abundant.

Mud crab carapace colors range from brown to olive and are often mottled, and all of the species listed here prominently feature black tips on their large claws. Behind the black tip, the dorsal (top side) portion of their claws is similar in color to their carapace, while the ventral (underside) portion is pale or white. Most mud crabs range from one-half to two inches across, with the common mud crab growing the largest of the species listed. The typical size of mud crabs I have found in red drum stomachs in southwest Florida is one-half to one inch across. Stone crabs grow much larger than mud crabs, but the juveniles found on oyster reefs are similar in size to mud crabs. As they grow, stone crabs move to other habitats.

Mud crabs on oyster bars, like mud crabs in seagrass beds, tend to hide during the day and venture out at night to feed. However, the habitats—oyster bar versus seagrass—force a different feeding behavior by gamefish in search of a mud crab meal. In seagrass, a red drum can move slowly with its snout in the bottom. As the red drum finds mud crabs hiding at the bottom of the grass blades, it can easily push aside the grass blades and capture some of the crabs. I have examined the stomach contents of many red drum caught while they were tailing in seagrass beds, and most were dominated by mud crabs.

In contrast, oyster shells provide mud crabs a solid shelter that is not easily breached by red drum or other gamefish. The edges of oyster shells are sharp and deter much grubbing by gamefish in search of prey. And since many of the shells are cemented together to form clumps, even if the shells weren't sharp, the clumps would be too heavy for a fish to move.

Only so many crabs can feed on an oyster bar, however, and many crabs emerge from hiding at the end of the day to feed on the surrounding bottom. Even those that remain on the oyster bar to feed are often exposed on the edge of the bar rather than hiding in the crevices that extend deep beneath the shells. This is another reason why the edges of oyster bars are the best areas to find feeding gamefish.

Although mud crabs are usually the most abundant type of crabs, many other species also inhabit oyster bars. In North Carolina, in addition to the four species listed above, researchers have found seven other species, of which blue crabs and spider crabs *(Libinia dubia)* are the most common. These two crabs are also found on subtropical oyster bars, as are hermit crabs. In general, blue crabs are more abundant in the habitats surrounding the oyster bar than on the bar itself.

You might find a couple mud crab species living in burrows between the high- and low-tide lines in the marsh mud adjacent to fringing oyster bars. Harris' mud crab *(Rithropanopeus harrisii)* is brown, grows to one-half inch wide, and is most active at low tide. The mangrove mud crab *(Eurytium limosum)* grows to one inch wide, is dark in color, ranging from dark gray to black, and is most active at high tide.

Although not as abundant as crabs, numerous species of shrimp inhabit oyster bars and are important prey for gamefish. Brown, pink, or white shrimp (family Penaeidae, the type of shrimp we generally eat) are present on oyster bars and nearby marsh habitats as juveniles. Grass shrimp (mostly the genus *Palaemonetes*) are also common in these habitats and are very similar in appearance to juvenile brown, pink, and white shrimp but reach a maximum size of only two inches. Each of these shrimp is clear or may take on a translucent tan or gray coloration to blend into its surroundings. Grass shrimp are residents, but the juvenile brown, pink, and white shrimp move away from the oyster habitats as they grow.

Snapping shrimp are also common oyster bar residents, especially in the subtropics. The most common species is the slow-moving common snapping shrimp *(Alpheus heterochaelis)*, which can grow to about one and a half inches long and is usually dark green with pale, often reddish legs and an orange-fringed tail fan called a uropod. On South Carolina oyster bars, the striped snapping shrimp *(Alpheus formosus)* is also abundant. Snapping shrimp are common prey for red drum on subtropical and warm-temperate oyster reefs but are also eaten by spotted seatrout and weakfish.

Despite their almost constant presence, crabs and shrimp do undergo seasonal changes in abundance. Mud crabs are present in similar numbers throughout the year; blue crabs show seasonal pulses of juveniles in late spring and summer. Peak crab abundance is from late spring to late summer, with more dramatic seasonal differences in warm-temperate than in subtropical areas. Similar seasonality occurs for juvenile shrimp, with differences among regions. Pink shrimp *(Penaeus duorarum)* juveniles are present throughout the year in subtropical estuaries but are most abundant from summer through fall. In warm-temperate regions, juveniles are present in both spring and fall but are most abundant in fall. In the western Gulf of Mexico, juvenile brown shrimp *(Penaeus aztecus)* are dominant.

Brittle Stars

Oyster bar residents that are often overlooked as gamefish prey suitable for imitating with a fly are brittle stars. Among the species you might find on oyster bars are the smooth brittle star *(Ophioderma brevispinum)* and the angular brittle star *(Ophiothrix angulata).* Brittle stars have a round, flat, coin-shaped body called a disc. Radiating from the body are five long arms that are either smooth or covered in short spines and taper to a point. Unlike the stereotypical sea star, brittle stars can move rather quickly, using their arms to crawl across the bottom like a spider. Brittle stars found on oyster bars are usually green to tan and may be mottled or striped. The central body disc is about a half inch across, with arms extending five or more disc widths from the body. Though never the most abundant prey item in gamefish stomachs, brittle stars are eaten by numerous species, including red drum.

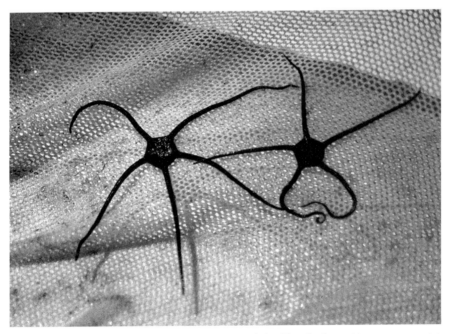

Brittle stars vary in color, but all have a similar shape and size. They live in most low-energy coastal habitats and come out to feed at night.

Fishing at Dawn and Dusk

Like mud crabs, many resident crabs, shrimp, and brittle stars on oyster bars hide during the day and are most active at night. You don't have to fish at night to take advantage of this behavior. Instead, you can use a number of strategies to take advantage of the behaviors of prey and gamefish.

First, by fishing at dusk, you will catch the beginning of nighttime feeding activity by these prey species. The timing is very similar to the dusk "quiet period" for small fish in mangrove prop root habitats. As dusk approaches, the resident crabs, shrimp, and brittle stars become active as they ready for a night of feeding. If the tide is right, you may find gamefish cruising along the edges of oyster bars or in the surrounding habitats in search of prey beyond the safety of shelter. Many times I have fished through dusk and into darkness, casting to tailing red drum and spotted trout in the fading light. In the early minutes of dusk, flies with a lot of flash attract the attention of feeding gamefish. As light fades, flies that create vibrations in the water that can be detected by the gamefish's lateral line system seem to work best.

Second, limit the parts of an oyster bar that you fish. A major mistake many fly anglers make is casting to the middle of an oyster bar. The middle, or top, of the oyster bar is not where you are likely to find gamefish. And if you do find gamefish feeding over the top of an oyster bar, flies imitating crabs or other bottom-dwelling prey are not the best choice. When a weighted fly falls into the crevices between oyster shells, it's out of view of the gamefish. To fish these flies naturally, you have to get the fly on the bottom, which can result in hooking oysters rather than fish. You can combat this somewhat with a weedguard, but there are so many nooks and crannies for a fly to hang in that it's easy to get frustrated. In this situation, use an unweighted streamer instead.

Rather than becoming frustrated by casting to an area of an oyster bar that is full of snags and devoid of gamefish, focus on the gamefish that are cruising along the edges of the bar in search of crabs, shrimp, and other prey that have left their shelter to feed. You don't have to limit this strategy to dusk. Although mud crabs are most abundant at night, there will always be a few that dare to venture out during the day. This is especially true on a rising tide. Crabs often follow the rising water as it covers the bar, and you will sometimes find gamefish following suit, hoping to catch crabs that linger too long along the deeper edges of the bar.

Third, focus your efforts on the best tides. My favorite time for chasing tailing red drum along oyster bars is the first hour or so of incoming tide. I think the best time is as soon as the tide has raised the water level enough to allow the red drum to come in to feed. Focus on the deeper holes between or near oyster bars in case red drum have been waiting out the low tide in these deep spots. As the water rises, these fish will move to the oyster bars in search of prey.

In the event you don't find red drum tailing on a rising tide, don't hesitate to do some blind-casting along the edges of oyster bars. Bouncing a size 1 or 2, dark-colored, olive or brown crab fly or similarly colored Clouser Minnow across the mud bottom next to oyster bars might catch the attention of gamefish you didn't spot—including red drum, spotted seatrout, weakfish, or gray snapper. Better yet, try the old standby Seaducer worked slowly along the edge. Regardless of the fly you choose, it doesn't get much better than when it all comes together—an early incoming tide at dusk, with hungry gamefish prowling the edges of an oyster bar.

RESIDENT PREY FISH

A typical oyster bar in a subtropical or warm-temperate estuary will have a dozen or more resident species of small fish. Species from four families— gobies (family Gobiidae), clingfish (family Gobiesocidae), toadfish (family Batrachoididae), and blennies (family Blenniidae)—rest on oyster shells or on the bottom and dart out to capture prey or ward off competitors. Most of these species are medium to dark brown, but some are olive, with mottling and markings on their sides. If you pick up enough oyster shells from a shallow oyster reef, you will eventually find some of these fish. Since these species are closely associated with the bottom, your flies should be also, and because of all the possible snags, your flies should be weedless.

Common goby species include the frillfin goby *(Bathygobius soporator),* code goby *(Gobiosoma robustum),* and naked goby *(Gobiosoma bosci),* each around two inches long. These species are found on oyster bars in the subtropics and into the warm-temperate northern Gulf of Mexico and can also be found in nearby seagrass and mangrove habitats. The skilletfish *(Gobiesox strumosus),* a clingfish that grows to three inches, is found on oyster reefs throughout the warm-temperate and subtropical regions. You will find the gulf toadfish *(Opsanus beta)* in subtropical waters and the very similar-looking oyster toadfish *(Opsanus tau)* in warm-temperate waters. Both species can grow quite large, to twelve inches or more—too

Toadfish aren't pretty but they must taste good, as they are eaten by many gamefish, including bonefish and red drum.

large to be gamefish prey or to imitate with a fly—but the smaller juveniles are common prey for gamefish on oyster reefs. Among the blennies, the Florida blenny *(Chasmodes saburrae)* inhabits oyster reefs throughout Florida and into the northern Gulf of Mexico; the feather blenny *(Hypsoblennius hentzi)* and crested blenny *(Hypleurochilus germinatus)* reside on oyster reefs throughout subtropical and warm-temperate climates. All three blennies grow to approximately four inches long.

Within each family, the species listed here and other related species look similar enough that one or two fly patterns will be sufficient for a decent imitation. Gobies are round-bodied, tapering from a large head to a pointed tail. My favorite fly for imitating gobies is a Muddler Minnow variation: size 4 long-shank hook; a head of spun brown or tan deer hair, trimmed short; a body of gold braid wrapped around the hook shank; and a tail of brown bucktail tips, uneven so they taper to a point. I tie in a small cone ahead of the deer-hair head for deeper reefs and use a weedguard for both weighted and unweighted versions.

The skilletfish and toadfish are similar to one another in shape, with a large, wide head and a body that tapers to the tail, much like a sculpin you'd find in fresh water. Brock Apfel of Punta Gorda, Forida, showed me a size 2 or 4 Dahlberg Diver variation with a brown head, tan body, and

Blennies are common prey for gamefish feeding in most coastal habitats.

artificial material tail with vertical bars that is a reasonable imitation of these bottom-dwelling, troll-like fish. I have done well with this pattern— weedless and either unweighted or weighted with a conehead—for red drum on oyster bars.

Like gobies, skilletfish, and toadfish, blennies have large heads and tapered bodies. However, that's where the similarities end. Blennies are higher-bodied than they are wide, so they have a larger profile from the side view. They have steeply sloped foreheads and are almost square-fronted when viewed from the side. The dorsal fin runs the length of the body, and the anal fin from midbody to the tail. Flies imitating blennies require a higher profile than those imitating gobies, skilletfish, or toadfish.

A handful of species from two families—killifish (family Cyprino-dontidae) and mollies (family Poeciliidae)—are found in schools above and around oyster reefs in shallow areas near shore. These species are mostly associated with oyster reefs that are in or near marshes. They are among the most abundant and important fish in subtropical and warm-temperature marshes. Among the most common killifish associated with oyster bars are the gulf killifish (*Fundulus grandis*), goldspot killifish (*Floridichthys carpio*), mummichog (*Fundulus heteroclitus*), striped killifish *(Fundulus majalis)*, and sheepshead minnow *(Cyprinodon variega-tus)*. The gulf killifish is mostly limited to fresh and low-salinity waters; the other four species can tolerate a wide range of salinities. Within Poe-ciliidae, the sailfin molly *(Poecilia latipinna)* is the most common near oys-ter reefs, but mosquitofish *(Gambusia holbrooki)* will also inhabit oyster reefs in protected backwaters with frequent freshwater input.

Killifish and mollies are similar in size and shape, so even though species may vary among locations, the same flies should work for all. In fact, many of the species are similar enough that anglers confuse them and lump them all together as "mummichogs." In general, killifish and mollies are small, from one to as much as seven inches long, though most are on the smaller side of the size range, and tan to medium brown in color. A good, standard imitation for these species is a Muddler Minnow variation or brown-over-tan Clouser Minnow.

A species of fish you might not think of as typical gamefish prey is the blackcheek tonguefish *(Symphurus plagiusa)*. The tonguefish (family Cyno-glossidae) are flatfish that are similar to small, elongated flounder but have a teardrop shape. The blackcheek tonguefish is dark to medium brown and grows to seven inches long. Tonguefish don't actually live on oyster bars, but they inhabit soft or sandy bottoms that surround the bars. They have been found in stomachs of red drum and spotted seatrout, among others.

Mojarra (family Gerreidae) are everywhere. They are prey fish in grass beds, along mangrove shorelines, and in association with oyster bar habitats. In the subtropics, the most common species near oyster reefs are the silver jenny *(Eucinostomus gula)* and tidewater mojarra *(Eucinostomus harengulus)*. Both species are silver but often have mottled gray sides. Both grow to seven inches but are usually much shorter, and the tidewater mojarra has a slightly higher body profile. They are associated with soft or sandy open bottoms around oyster bars. Three-inch white Deceivers are good imitations of these two species.

SEASONAL PREY FISH

Many gamefish prey use oyster bars on a seasonal basis. Some species use these habitats only as juveniles; others migrate from oyster bars to deeper habitats to escape the cold water temperatures in winter. Gamefish may change their feeding behavior to take advantage of seasonal changes in prey, so knowing what changes may occur in your area should be an important part of your fishing strategy.

A large pulse of juveniles arrives on oyster reefs in spring and early summer in both subtropical and warm-temperate estuaries. Among the species with juveniles on oyster reefs that are appropriate for imitating with a fly are pinfish, pigfish, spot, croaker, spottail pinfish, mojarra, and gray and lane snappers. In general, abundance of these juveniles peaks in June and July. As the summer progresses and the juveniles grow, they move away from the reefs onto other habitats.

Though not as abundant on oyster reefs as in seagrass, juvenile pinfish can be among the most abundant prey fish on oyster reefs. This is especially true in areas that have little or no seagrass. As in subtropical grass beds, juvenile pinfish arrive in late winter through early spring, and they grow throughout the summer before migrating to deeper water in late fall. This puts the arrival of pinfish slightly earlier than that of the other species mentioned above, so early-season gamefish may concentrate their feeding efforts on juvenile pinfish.

Pigfish also are present during summer. They are similar to pinfish in coloration and size—in fact, many find it difficult to tell the juveniles apart—so they can be imitated with the same patterns.

Spot, croaker, spottail pinfish, and mojarra vary somewhat in shape, but all are silvery white and are well imitated with white Deceivers, Clouser Minnows, and similar patterns.

The biggest challenge when imitating these juveniles is in matching their size. Since many larvae enter the estuaries at the same time, you will find large groups of similar-size juveniles, which makes it easier to select the right size fly. But as pulses of larvae may arrive weeks or months apart, you may have a wide range of juvenile sizes to choose from, so it might not be the case that one fly fits all scenarios. Because fish larvae ride currents into estuaries, and these currents vary, different oyster bars may receive different numbers of fish larvae at different times. This means that the size of juvenile fish may vary among different locations in an estuary. Thus, it's worth examining the size and species of juvenile fish when you first arrive at an oyster bar.

For some species, the peak juvenile season occurs at the same time adults are abundant in the estuary, which might add to your confusion in selecting the correct fly size. But in general, adults use different habitats, have different diets, and exhibit different feeding strategies than juveniles. Spot are a good example of such a species. In spring, adults migrate into the estuary from winter grounds either offshore or in deeper waters at the mouths of estuaries, so they are in the estuary at the same time as juveniles. But adults are found in somewhat deeper, more open-bottom areas than the juveniles' preferred habitats of shallow marshes and oyster bars. In most situations where juvenile fish are the most abundant prey, small flies are your best choice.

Midwater Baitfish

Transient prey species can be found near oyster bars throughout a season, but they are not present throughout the year, and although they might be common at certain tides, their presence can be unpredictable. This group of species is generally what we are imitating when we cast baitfish imitations into currents that sweep past and over bars. Silversides (family Atherinidae), anchovies (family Engraulidae), and herrings (family Clupeidae) are the most common members of this group. The baitfish species that gamefish key on vary with location and time of year, but within each family, the species are similar enough to be imitated with a couple basic patterns. Clouser Minnows, bucktail streamers, and Deceivers are the classic imitations of these baitfishes.

In my experience, the best time of year to cast and swing baitfish imitations across sandbars and oyster bars is from midsummer through fall. Mid to late summer is when many species are in greatest abundance, and fall is when the migratory baitfish species begin to leave the estuaries and migrate to winter locations. The abundance and migration of baitfish combine to make these species a common diet item for gamefish in late summer and fall. This is one reason that when you drift a size 1 chartreuse and white Clouser Minnow over an oyster bar on an outgoing tide, the weakfish that sees the fly might mistake it for a silversides lost in the currents. Drifting flies into the holes around sandbars and oyster bars can bring in a grab bag of gamefish, including crevalle jack, speckled trout, and red drum, on successive casts.

Several species of mullet can also be found near oyster bars. This is probably due to mullet's association with shallow, protected areas and the presence of oyster reefs in these same shallow areas rather than an association with oyster reefs. Mullet feed on detritus and algae, so they don't feed in oyster reef habitats but likely feed on the surrounding bottom. However, when pursued by gamefish, mullet will seek shelter in the shallows that surround oyster bars. The oyster bars provide false hope to the cornered mullet but an opportunity to the fly angler in the right place at the right time.

APPLYING WHAT YOU'VE LEARNED:

Fly Selection

Spotted seatrout and a host of other gamefish hide in the current shadows and eddies of oyster bars and dart out to pick off prey caught in the currents washing over or around the bar. In winter, spotted seatrout and small red drum may be the only gamefish feeding in the currents. Then the selection of prey washing over the bar will be slim, with killifish, often the mummichog *(Fundulus heteroclitus)*, the dominant prey. Fly selection is easy during winter. In summer, ladyfish, bluefish, and jacks often join the fray, and so do a whole host of baitfish, including mullet, anchovies, silversides, and juvenile menhaden, spot, and croaker.

While any streamer may be the right fly on some days, on other days the fish will be focused on one particular species of baitfish, so keep an eye out for which baitfish is dominant on any particular day. As the summer progresses, the baitfish grow larger, and this increase in size should be reflected in your fly selection. It is true that larger gamefish eat larger prey, so although smaller flies will likely result in more fish, every once in a while it's worth starting out with a large fly just in case that big fish is lurking behind the oyster bar.

APPLYING WHAT YOU'VE LEARNED:

Be Ready for Baitfish

Because a sinking line can get snagged on the shallow part of the bar, I prefer floating lines for fishing oyster bars. A floating line also allows me to drift an unweighted fly over the far side of a bar without worrying about hanging the fly line on the bar during the drift. If I am fishing a deeper hole next to an oyster bar, I prefer to use a sinking fly such as a Clouser, with a slow retrieve to get the fly deeper. Since many of the baitfish associated with oyster bars are also found in seagrass beds and along mangrove shorelines, they can be imitated with the same flies, but the transient nature of their association with oyster bars means you have to be on the lookout for when these baitfish are present.

One August day, my strategy of keeping a second rod rigged with a white Deceiver while I cast Muddler Minnows into holes between bars paid off. The small creeks I was fishing drained a large marsh, and on outgoing tides, moderate currents flowed out of the creeks onto grass beds that stretched across the creek mouths. Snook often waited at ambush points where the creeks narrowed and picked off small silversides that were caught in the currents. Situated near the mouths of the creeks, and spilling over into the seagrass, lay scattered isolated oyster bars. I began the day fishing the mangrove creeks early in the falling tide and then switched my attention to the oyster bars

as the tops of the bars became exposed. I'd had limited success finding small snook in the creeks and caught only an occasional spotted
trout in the holes next to the oyster bars.

As I poled to the next in a series of small oyster bars, I noticed
plumes of white spray erupting from the water about a half mile
down the shoreline. My first thought, that a group of brown pelicans
had just hit the water en masse, was immediately negated because the
eruption continued. Since it was late summer, my second thought,
that it was marauding crevalle jacks, seemed a reasonable explanation. Ready for some fast action, I stowed the push pole and motored
the boat toward the chaos.

As I made my way along the shoreline, I could see that the school
of feeding fish was moving toward me. I shut down the engine and
pulled out the rod rigged with a white Deceiver. Whatever the gamefish were, I knew what they were feeding on: Scaled sardines *(Harengula jaguana)*, an abundant baitfish (family Clupeidae) in subtropical
grass beds in late summer, erupted from the surface as large fish
chased from below. The school of gamefish was easy to spot by the
large wake they pushed ahead of themselves as they moved through
the grass bed from oyster bar to oyster bar. As the marauding school
came upon each small bar, their pace quickened and their bow wake
became larger and more pronounced. I watched as they sped toward
the oyster bar in front of me, the water exploding as they attacked sardines that were trying to hide in the shallow water surrounding the
bars. I caught my first glimpse of color as a large fish broke the surface
and rolled through the panicked sardines. The copper hue told me
these were red drum.

I threw a cast into the mix, and as the fly darted forward with my
second strip of the line, the water boiled with the ferocious charge of a
red drum. The fish fought with an energy born from the bedlam of
a marauding school in the midst of a feeding frenzy. As I fought the
fish, the school continued their plunder along the line of disconnected
oyster bars.

I was able to get in front of the school of red drum two more
times, hooking three large fish and landing two, before a line of strong
thunderstorms came through and sent all of us packing. All three fish
were caught on a four-inch, white Deceiver. It didn't take much more
than being in the right place at the right time, knowing that gamefish
might be keying on the sardines that were hiding among the oyster
bars, and being ready with a rod rigged with a white Deceiver just in
case.

STEWARDSHIP

Numerous threats to oysters exist, and because oyster bars made up of live oysters support more prey than those made up of dead shells, any threats to oyster bars will negatively affect associated gamefish. Too much sediment can bury oysters, and many estuaries are inundated with sediment-laden water draining from farmland, housing developments, and urban areas. Too many nutrients can cause plankton blooms that create hypoxia (low oxygen) or anoxia (no oxygen) lasting for periods long enough to kill oysters. Runoff heavy in nutrients comes from farms and suburban lawns, from urban sewage outfalls, and from livestock. The often accompanying herbicides and pesticides can also stress oysters. Boat wakes from channels that border oyster bars can prevent juvenile oysters from colonizing reefs, thus dooming a reef to eventual death. Too much physical disturbance from tonging, dredging, or frequent boat groundings can damage or even destroy reefs as well.

Since oysters and their predators and diseases are so affected by salinity, changing the flow of fresh water into estuaries can have dire consequences. If the release of water from dams causes long periods of high freshwater flows, salinities may drop enough to kill oysters in the upper portions of an estuary. If much fresh water is diverted from rivers by cities or agriculture, salinities in most of an estuary may become high enough to allow predators and disease to become established farther into the estuary than they would under natural conditions. In both scenarios, which are already realities in some areas, the health of oysters and oyster bars declines.

Oyster bars influence water current patterns, so changing their location, size, or orientation—by dredging, for example—can have unpredictable effects on the flow of water and sediments, in turn causing problems for gamefish and prey. Currents may become stronger and carve deep holes in the bottom or wipe out areas of seagrass that had previously been protected by a removed bar. Or currents may be completely blocked, creating a stagnant area behind an altered bar that holds few prey and gamefish.

Oyster bars are an essential component of a healthy coastal ecosystem, creating important habitats for gamefish and their prey. In some areas, they are arguably *the* most important gamefish habitat. Once an oyster bar is gone, it's probably gone for good, because oyster larvae need the hard substrate provided by adult oysters to survive. Effective stewardship means making sure these habitats remain viable parts of our coastal ecosystems.

Chapter 5

Salt Marshes

In the tropics and subtropics, mangroves are the dominant wetland vegetation, providing crucial habitat for gamefish and their prey, protecting shorelines from erosion, and serving many other valuable functions. In temperate regions, salt marshes fill these vital roles. Although they do occur rarely in the tropics and are a bit more common in northern subtropical areas, salt marshes become the dominant type of wetland from mid-Florida north, so they are important gamefish habitats for the entire warm-temperate region. In the Gulf of Mexico, salt marsh habitats are dominant north of Cedar Key, Florida, on the east and Port Isabel, Texas, on the west. On the Atlantic coast, salt marshes dominate north of Cape Canaveral, Florida. The border between salt marsh and mangroves is not static; it fluctuates with changes in temperature. A series of warm winters will allow mangroves to encroach northward, but a winter freeze will quickly wipe out the mangroves, and the salt marsh plants will return.

Salt marshes are vital gamefish habitats in temperate regions because they are host to a suite of resident organisms and visiting juveniles that are prey for larger gamefish. In addition, many gamefish juveniles use the protection provided by salt marshes, so these habitats are important nurseries. Like mangroves to the south, salt marshes stabilize shorelines; filter sediments from land that would otherwise inundate other nearby habitats, such as oyster bars, and their organisms; and form the base of a food chain that supports many gamefish.

Salt marshes form in intertidal zones of temperate climates with abundant rainfall and in locations where mud and silt can accumulate. The most common sites for salt marshes are along the shorelines of estuaries that lie on the coastal plain, on the back sides of bars or barrier islands that separate an estuary from open ocean, and on coastal shores that are protected from wave energy. The first step in the development of a salt marsh is the deposition of fine-grained sediments by slow-moving currents. Salt-tolerant marsh grass then takes root in these areas, and as the grasses grow, they baffle the currents, much like seagrass. This causes more sediment to be deposited, which is soon mixed with the remains of dead marsh plants. The original colonizing grasses spread outward via an underground root system, and if these plants are able to spread fast enough to keep pace with sediment deposition, a salt marsh is established. The spreading plants stabilize the surrounding sediments and cause more sediments to be deposited, slowly expanding the marsh.

Stabilization of sediments is an important function of salt marsh plants. Without stabilizing marsh plants, sediments would be constantly displaced and relocated by runoff from rains, storm waves, and even strong tides. Such an unstable habitat would not support many prey to attract gamefish. Among others, the stable sediments allow burrowing organisms such as fiddler crabs and marine worms known as polychaetes to live in the marsh, and these types of organisms are important prey for salt marsh gamefish. Eventually enough silt and plant material accumulates to raise the surface of the marsh above sea level, which allows plants less tolerant of salt water to become established. In the meantime, sediment deposition often continues on the outer edge of the marsh, allowing seaward migration of the intertidal portion of the marsh.

Because salt marshes are found only in areas protected from strong waves, they are dominated by fine-grained, soft sediments. Despite the stabilizing effect of marsh grasses, salt marsh sediments are easily eroded in high-energy areas because the grass root systems are not strong enough to hold the sediments in place. The protected nature of salt marshes makes them especially nice places to fly-fish on windy days, when more exposed areas might be unfishable. An added bonus is that gamefish also know the value of protected salt marshes during windy periods and often take shelter in these areas.

Since salt marshes are intertidal, they are inundated by high tide and quickly drain on the dropping tide. Often the water deposited on the upper marsh by the high tide has a harder time draining off the marsh by the same path as the incoming tide. Instead, much of the water on the dropping tide flows out of the marsh through the creeks that crisscross the marsh. The creeks are also important for draining the fresh water that runs onto the upper marsh from land.

Sediments stabilized by marsh grass are essential to the formation of the creeks that drain the marsh. In a new marsh, areas that were naturally low soon become collecting areas for water draining the marsh, and creeks and drainage channels are born. Stable sediments held together by the roots of marsh grasses form the walls of the creeks, and once established,

Continuous seagrass beds are full of a variety of gamefish prey and offer excellent wading opportunities. However, precision casting is essential to avoid having the fly get lost among the grass blades and never seen by the fish. Healthy seagrass beds are essential to sustainable gamefish and prey populations and offer challenging areas to fish.

Patchy seagrass offers the advantage of high numbers of prey and plenty of open space to cast a fly without snagging seagrass.

Patches of open sand bottom, called potholes, that
dot continuous seagrass beds offer excellent
feeding stations for gamefish.

The completely exposed black mangrove pneumatophores indicate a low tide. All the prey that hide in these aerial roots during high tide are concentrated in the creek during low tide, easy pickings for any gamefish in the creek.

Mangrove flats are great places to find feeding bonefish and permit, especially during a spring high tide. Barracuda, snapper, and jacks also come into these areas at high tide to feed.

Fishing along a medium-energy beach. Note the
angler standing on the beach rather than in
the water. With the sun at his back, he's able to
spot gamefish cruising the shallow dropoff
(indicated by the change in water color) at the
low-tide line.

A snook *(at center)* waiting for prey to pass by just off the beach.

A semiprotected beach in the Caribbean. Note the mixture of seagrass *(dark area in foreground)* and open sand bottom adjacent to this shallow-sloping beach.

The large size of the cobbles on this beach
indicates a high-energy shoreline under typical
conditions. This shoreline is unlikely to harbor
bonefish or permit but is good for jacks and
barracuda.

Low-energy beachrock shorelines that border sand
and seagrass flats are good places to search for
bonefish and permit tailing at dawn and dusk.

Medium-energy beachrock shorelines are best for fish-eating gamefish that are usually on the move, like jacks, barracuda, and tarpon.

Steep, rocky shorelines provide shorebound fly anglers access to larger reef fish, like snapper and grouper, as well as large jacks that cruise the shoreline edge in search of prey.

A backreef rubble flat that is well protected from waves by a shallow reef. The seagrass growing along the rubble *(foreground)* and the open rubble bottom *(center)* probably indicate differences in wave energy during high-wave periods. Note the barracuda *(center of picture).*

An angler searching for fish on a backreef rubble flat with less protection from ocean waves. The waves present a new challenge to an angler casting to tailing permit.

A spacious sand flat with patches of sparse shoal
grass. The seagrass and numerous animal burrows
indicate a "live" flat that should be inviting to
bonefish and permit.

Flats of open sand don't often hold gamefish but are home to enough prey that gamefish, such as bonefish, cruise these habitats in search of a meal.

Backreef rubble flats such as this one are good locations to find many species of gamefish, especially permit. They are protected from wave energy by the coral reef and often have deeper channels on the shoreward side that can be travel avenues for large fish.

Protected beaches have gentle slopes and little wave action and make for easy wading. In the tropics, bonefish are common travelers along protected beaches.

Because they are exposed to moderate wave action, semiprotected beaches tend to have slopes that are not as shallow as protected beaches. Snook like to cruise these beaches in the tropics and subtropics.

Rocky points often protect sand beaches from the
heaviest of wave action, and the deeper water that
is adjacent to these points can be a productive
fishing area, especially with larger flies.

High-energy beaches have steeper shorelines and deeper water close to the beach than protected and semiprotected beaches. During calm conditions, you may find great fishing when gamefish have pushed schools of baitfish against the beach.

the course of a creek is slow to change. The creeks also allow more water to enter the marsh with a rising tide, which helps maintain good tidal flushing essential to sustaining a healthy marsh.

Because sea level has been rising since the last ice age, estuarine salt marshes that are nearer the coast are older than those near the head of the estuary. When sea level was lower, salt water encroached only on the outermost coastal areas, so this is where salt marshes first formed. As sea level has risen, salt water has intruded farther inland, allowing new salt marshes to become established. Mature salt marshes have deeper sediments and more intricate patterns of creeks and drainage channels, which often translate to more diverse prey communities and more gamefish.

How far inland salt water penetrates is also a factor influencing the type of marsh you will find as you travel from the ocean into the estuary. Marshes closest to the ocean or Gulf experience the highest salinities and are dominated by salt-tolerant marsh grass. Farther inland, where tides mix with fresh water, the marshes are dominated by brackish water species. Beyond the reaches of salt water, you will find freshwater swamps. There is no set distance of saltwater influence, so how far inland you will find salt marshes varies with the location. In coastal Georgia, the transition from salt water to fresh occurs over a relatively short distance. In contrast, the saltwater influence travels farther inland along the Louisiana coast.

You can use the dominant species of marsh plants as a general guide to finding the inland boundary of salt marshes. Low-salinity marshes are dominated by waterhyssop *(Bocopa monniere)*, camphorweed *(Pluchea camphorata)*, and various species of the genus *Spartina*. Dominant marsh plants in salt and brackish areas are black needlerush *(Juncus roemerianus)*, smooth cordgrass *(Spartina alterniflora)*, seashore saltgrass *(Distichlis spicata)*, saltmeadow cordgrass *(Spartina patens)*, and other *Spartina* species. As you explore new areas, you can use the distribution of marsh plants to help you determine salinities and tides so you can focus your energies on the salt marshes most used by saltwater gamefish.

HIGH AND LOW MARSH ZONES

Tide, rainfall, and salinity are major structuring forces of a salt marsh, resulting in the formation of two zones: a high marsh and a low marsh. Each zone is dominated by different marsh plants. You can use your knowledge of marsh zonation to figure out the most promising spots for finding gamefish.

The portion of the salt marsh that abuts land is called the high marsh. This zone is inundated by salt water only during spring high tides. It does best with a mixture of runoff from rain and occasional salt water from high tides. Thus, rainfall is an essential component of a healthy high marsh.

The high marsh is often dominated by saltmeadow cordgrass, but black needlerush can dominate in some areas, especially in brackish water, and seashore saltgrass is also common. Under most circumstances, tides won't be high enough in these areas to allow gamefish to enter, but recognizing where these species of marsh grasses occur will help you focus on the most productive fishing areas of the marsh and get a better handle on water movement.

The low marsh is fully intertidal and occupies the area between mean sea level and the mean high-water mark. This zone is subject to daily incursions of the tides, so it is an area of high salinity and the sediments remain wet. Plants in the low marsh have special adaptations enabling them to tolerate salt water: They are able to exclude salt water from their tissues and excrete salt from the water they do take in.

Rainfall influences the extent and robustness of salt marshes, especially the high marsh and upper portion of the low marsh. As a general rule, areas with low rainfall have wetlands only in the portion of the intertidal zone that is frequently flooded by tides. Such a salt marsh mostly consists of only a narrow section of low marsh, with few if any high marsh plants present. In extremely arid areas, wetlands may be very sparse or completely absent. In regions with high rainfall, wetlands usually cover the entire intertidal zone. Even in wet regions, however, you may find barren areas in normally healthy salt marshes during prolonged dry spells. In most cases, these open areas are recolonized by marsh grasses once normal rains return.

But not all open spots in a salt marsh are caused by low rainfall. Even salt marshes that receive sufficient rainfall can have areas of open bottom. Large mats of floating dead plant material can be carried well into the low marsh, and even to the high marsh, by a rising tide. When the dead plant material isn't carried away by another high tide, it can smother the marsh grass that it covers, creating a bare spot in the marsh. These bare spots often become a little lower than the surrounding marsh, forming depressions, and salt water brought in by high tides can collect here. If high tides only occasionally reach the bare spot, the evaporating water will leave behind salt deposits, which may inhibit the recolonization of marsh grasses. If, on the other hand, tides frequently flood these spots, small fish may collect in these pools at low tide, and they can be stops on the rounds of a gamefish following a rising tide into the low marsh.

Sediments of the low marsh tend to be oxygen-poor, or anoxic. This would kill most plants, because the roots need oxygen to survive. Salt marsh plants don't have prop roots or pneumatophores to obtain oxygen from the air like the mangroves. Instead, they are able to transport to their roots some of the oxygen they assimilate through their leaves, allowing them to remain firmly rooted in the anoxic sediments. Healthy roots, in turn, help stabilize the marsh sediments.

The marsh grass species in our warm-temperate region that is best adapted to dealing with the stresses of full salt water, low-oxygen sediments, and daily inundation by tides is smooth cordgrass. This grass is so superior at handling these stresses that it is the overwhelmingly dominant plant species in high-salinity low marshes. In fact, in many locations it is the only plant in the low marsh. In areas of brackish water and low tidal range, like much of the northern Gulf of Mexico, black needlerush can be the dominant marsh grass. These grasses are good indicators of where in the salt marsh you will most likely find gamefish.

Although smooth cordgrass is best adapted to the low marsh, even it has limits, and some areas of the low marsh have better growing conditions than others. The varying quality of growing areas is revealed by the height of the cordgrass. Better growing conditions result in taller smooth cordgrass, and less-than-optimal conditions produce shorter plants.

Black needlerush *(shown here)* and other salt marsh plants provide small fish, crabs, and shrimp with protection from gamefish.

The same conditions that provide better growth for smooth cordgrass also provide better habitat for gamefish and their prey, so finding areas with taller cordgrass will generally put you in the best places to find gamefish. Understanding why this is the case will help you better read a salt marsh in order to get the most out of your fishing time.

An important factor that creates the best growing conditions for smooth cordgrass is tidal flushing. Sediments in areas of the low marsh that are frequently flushed by tides have a greater percolation rate, and marsh grass roots are bathed with new water with each tidal cycle. This means the sediments are better aerated and thus have a higher oxygen content, which results in better plant growth. Although smooth cordgrass and black needlerush can tolerate sediments with low oxygen, they grow best in aerated sediments. Another factor contributing to the growth of smooth cordgrass is the type of sediment. Fine-grained sediments are more densely packed and have higher nutrient levels than sandy soils, resulting in better growth. Tides help deposit fine-grained sediments in the low marsh, another reason why areas with frequent tidal flushing are good. Finally, smooth cordgrass grows best in medium salinity, again relating to the importance of rainfall or other fresh water input to a healthy salt marsh.

You will find the best growing conditions along the edges of creeks that receive frequent tidal flushing, and perhaps some fresh water as well, and in the most seaward portions of marsh that benefit from daily incursions of tides. Outer portions of the low marsh that abut deeper water are often better than those adjacent to expansive intertidal mudflats, because much of the fine-grained sediments are deposited on shallow mudflats and never reach the marsh grass. Mudflats are indicative of low-energy areas, so although they may be intertidal, they don't experience the stronger tidal currents associated with creeks. In addition, deeper water provides gamefish with safe holding places to wait out low tide and quick access to the marsh once the tide begins to flood. Once again, stable sediments are key, allowing the growth of smooth cordgrass right to the edges of the creeks and low marsh fringe and helping create great habitats for gamefish prey.

Some of the best salt marshes you will encounter while fishing for gamefish seem to go on forever. The low marsh extends along the shoreline as far as you can see and reaches far out into the estuary. Behind the low marsh, the high marsh rolls slowly landward into the distance. In other locations, a slender high marsh gives way to a low marsh that is only a narrow strip along the shoreline, which drops abruptly at its seaward edge. Both types of marshes are in areas protected from waves and strong currents, so why are they different?

All other things being equal, the best explanation is that they differ in slope. A marsh that slopes gently from its landward edge to sea level will cover the greatest area and have the widest high and low marsh zones. This is because the slope affects how far a tide can flood a salt marsh. The shallower the slope of a marsh, the farther a typical high tide will penetrate. In a shallow-sloping marsh, even just a vertical foot of tide can flood a very large area of marsh. Since the low marsh is defined by the area between sea level and mean high water, the farther the high tide penetrates, the wider the low marsh zone. And because the high marsh often covers the area where the low marsh used to be, it also covers a wide, shallow-sloping terrain. In contrast, steeply sloping marshes don't provide much horizontal surface area for the tide to cover, so the low marsh is limited to a narrow zone. The high marsh is similarly narrow, if it exists at all.

APPLYING WHAT YOU'VE LEARNED:

Finding Gamefish in Salt Marshes

The general environmental conditions required by salt marshes—low energy, protected areas with tidal flow, and fine-grained sediments—add up to great backwater locations that are out of the wind and are well suited to fly angling. The older, more mature salt marshes are closer to the ocean or Gulf and tend to be firmly situated in the salinity range preferred by coastal gamefish, providing a transition from marine to brackish water realms. These older marshes also tend to be crisscrossed by creeks that create a diverse habitat rich in gamefish prey.

Within these marshes, the grasses provide many clues to help you locate the best spots to find gamefish. Although the high marsh is unlikely to hold fish, even during spring high tides, recognizing the high marsh zone gives you the inland boundary of the area in which to look for gamefish. Red drum may travel across the low marsh almost to the high marsh in their search for food, as illustrated in the story in the next section.

Once you've learned to recognize the plants of the high and low marshes, a marsh that in the past would have seemed a featureless sea of grass will appear complex. You'll now note that the low marsh doesn't necessarily parallel the shore, but tends to grow as a network of patches and gaps, with the edge between high and low marshes weaving in and out. Small embayments often interrupt the low marsh and may even graze the high marsh. Deep embayments may be good places to find gamefish waiting out the low tide. Shallow ones are great places to search for gamefish feeding along the marsh edge in the hours around high tide.

In situations where the low marsh stretches across wide areas from the water's edge to the high marsh, the inlandmost reaches of the low marsh will probably never see a gamefish. But where creeks traverse the low marsh, gamefish will use the deeper ones as avenues to gain access to the numerous species of prey that live well into the low marsh. You can easily find these creeks amid the endless grass, because it is along them that the tallest grass grows.

Because they drain the salt marsh, current is associated with marsh creeks, and creeks with currents are great places to find game-fish on the dropping tide. The creeks with the strongest flows usually have a deep hole at the mouth and may even have undercut banks at creek bends. This is because the currents are strong enough to sweep away fine-grained marsh sediments.

Deeper holes and creek beds with strong currents are often lined with shells or even live oysters or mussels. Spots where shells have been swept into a pile are favorite places for weakfish and spotted trout to wait for a meal to be delivered by the currents. And because of frequent tidal flushing, the mix of fresh and salt water, and good currents, these creeks are great places to find oyster bars. In contrast, although gamefish feed over mudflats, these areas don't receive the currents and exchange of water that the creeks do, so they tend to hold fewer prey. But some of the prey species that live in marsh grass may venture onto adjacent mudflats in search of food, so mudflats next to healthy low marshes may be good places to look for gamefish that feed on these wandering marsh prey, again pointing out the importance of adjacent habitats of varying complexity.

With a little exploration, you will discover that some of these creeks lead to ponds hidden deep within the marsh. Some of the ponds are too small and shallow to hold fish, while others are large enough to be considered lakes. As long as these stillwater areas are deep enough at low tide and are connected to open water through creeks, there is a decent chance they will hold fish when weather conditions are right. Louisiana is a great example of an area where these backcountry ponds and lakes can afford fantastic fishing in relative peace and quiet.

Red Drum in the Salt Marsh

It was late afternoon on a midsummer day under clear skies. The air hung heavy and still—a perfect day for fishing in the low-country salt marshes of South Carolina. The slick surface of dark backcountry water slid into a green sea of waist-high marsh grass. The bright green of early-season growth was gone, and the grass stood strong to the horizon. As the flooding tide crept into the marsh, the pace of the fiddler crabs become more frantic as they hurried to finish their meal of mud and detritus before retreating into their burrows. Small blue crabs scurried about in preparation for the advancing tide. Some of the crabs abandoned the flight altogether and climbed the stalks of grass to sit out the high tide above the fray. The marsh was electric with anticipation of what the crabs hoped would not happen, but what I was planning on—hungry red drum invading the shallow marsh with the rising tide.

My friend Joe Cronley had brought me to this spot. I was midway through an extended drive up the East Coast, from Florida to New England. The drive could be made in three easy days, but I was stopping to fish along the way, and it turned into a two-week trip. Joe was kind enough to take me in for a few days and guide me through the world of low-country red drum.

Now, however, I was standing in this spot alone. I had followed Joe from his house, and after a few minutes' drive, we parked our trucks along the side of the road. Joe waited while I grabbed my rod and gear bag, and then we walked off the road and into the marsh. As we made our way through the marsh grass across the hard-packed mud, Joe pointed out where the tide first entered the flat and where the red drum might first appear. Although it was tough to see some of the spots because of the higher grass, I nodded in understanding. While I scanned the marsh to get my bearings, Joe bade me good luck and headed off. He had a full schedule that afternoon and evening that didn't include fishing.

I don't think Joe had made it back to his truck before I started seeing signs of red drum entering the marsh. The first sign was the parting of the grass, as if by an unseen hand. The red drum were forcing their way through the heavy grass without hesitation, their paths marked by the tips of grass swaying in the still air. The second sure sign of advancing fish was the telltale splashing of a red drum as it turned on a crab. Using the thick grass as cover, I was soon close enough to see the glint of bright copper as a red drum worked its way across the flat in water so shallow its back was partially exposed.

I had tied on a size 4, copper and brown yarn crab fly, which seemed a fair imitation of the local fiddler crabs. After a few false casts, I sent the fly toward the feeding fish. Although the distance was right and the placement was good, the fly never hit the water. The line and leader were draped across the rough-edged cordgrass, the fly dangling ten inches above the water as the fish passed below. I cast again with the same result. I brought in the line and clipped my leader to four feet of 20-pound test. Hadn't Joe said something about this?

It didn't take me long to find the fish again, since it hadn't moved far. It was rooting in the bottom intently as it moved in a small circle in search of another crab. I made another cast, and although the line hung across the marsh grass, the short, stout leader slid through the grass to the water. The splat of the fly hitting the water caught the fish's attention. I barely had time to take the slack out of the line before the fish surged forward to investigate and slurp in the fly. I had no idea a red drum could move so quickly and so far through marsh grass that was so thick it made for tough walking. But the fish was well hooked, and a red drum the color of a new penny eventually came to hand.

I was fortunate to capitalize on Joe's local knowledge, which put me in the right place at the right time. But my experience serves to illustrate many of the characteristics of salt marshes, which you can use to your advantage when fly-fishing in these productive habitats.

The first clue to why that flat at that particular time and place was such a hot spot for red drum is that it was an incoming tide. If red drum were going to feed on the flat that day, they would have been riding the rising tide into the marsh. Second, the tide was rising late in the day, and a rising tide at dusk or dawn often translates into the best fishing of the day. This is especially true during the heat of summer, when dawn and dusk offer cooler temperatures. Third, the presence of smooth cordgrass meant I was fishing in the low marsh, and fiddler crabs were in abundance because it was a frequently flushed intertidal area. Fourth, the areas Joe pointed out in the low marsh where I would first see the rising tide flooding the flat, and soon after see red drum, weren't creeks, but low-lying areas that were frequently flushed by tides. Because they were lined by the tallest cordgrass, they were easy to spot. Finally, the hard-packed sediments indicated that this was a healthy marsh of long standing, so it was likely to have a diverse prey community. All of these factors combined to make this a good time and place to be fishing.

TIDES

Tides are especially important factors to consider when devising a strategy for fishing a salt marsh. In the typical situation, fish gather along edges of the low marsh or in holes near creek mouths during low tide. Often you can cast to these fish in the hours around low tide, just as you would to fish holding in holes between oyster bars. Blind-casting to steep edges, whether an outer marsh edge or the edge of a wide creek, especially those lined with oysters, can be a productive way to fish during the hours around low tide. Many fish, shrimp, and other gamefish prey that reside in the low marsh in high water find themselves evicted from the marsh for the hour or two around low tide. These prey collect along the edges, waiting for the rising tide to allow them back into the marsh. Although gamefish may seem inactive when they are waiting out the low tide in these deeper holes, they often pounce on small fish and shrimp that venture too far from the safety of the marsh edge.

As the tide begins to rise, the prey that have been waiting along the edges are the first to head into the shelter of the marsh grass or across the shallows of the mudflats. Their arrival in the low marsh signals the arrival of a new tide to the fiddler crabs and marsh crabs that have been feeding on the exposed mud. If the tide is strong enough (a spring tide), gamefish will come into the marsh grass in search of crabs and shrimp. If the tide is weak (a neap tide), you may find gamefish mostly restricted to the edges and to creek beds.

Because of differences in tidal range, marsh slope, number of creeks, and other factors, each salt marsh has its own optimum feeding times and zones for fish, so it may take some research to figure out specific marshes. A salt marsh with a wide-reaching low marsh but no creeks may see red drum venture only a short distance into the marsh, since they don't want to get too far from the safety of deeper water. A similar-looking marsh with numerous creeks or shallow sloughs may provide avenues for red drum to venture farther onto the flats in the same amount of time.

Once the tide turns, you can again focus on the edges of the marsh and on the creeks. Some of the prey that were so eager to get into the marsh on the rising tide are swept off the marsh flats with the ebb, falling over the edges and into creeks. Red drum, spotted seatrout, weakfish, ladyfish, and bluefish are some of the gamefish that collect in these areas to pick off prey caught in the currents. Creeks with obstructions that break

Creek edges in salt marshes are good places to find gamefish on the prowl at low tide. The small fish that hide in the marsh grass during high tide are forced into the creeks at low tide.

up the flow, such as oyster bars, are especially good places to find gamefish waiting for an easy meal. The same strategies that work for fishing oyster bars are applicable in these situations.

Fishing the Tides

At high tide, many species of small fish and shrimp invade the grass of the low marsh to feed and to escape predators. The rising tide drains the low marsh and forces these prey into creeks that drain the marsh and to the deeper edges of low marsh exposed to open bays. So your first thought might be that low tide is the best or only time to fish the marshes—with all the prey that should be available, gamefish will certainly be foraging along the edges and in creeks at low tide. Yes, this is true, but gamefish will also feed in these areas on rising tides, high tides, and falling tides, and putting yourself in the right place at the right time is half the battle.

Creeks are the avenues gamefish use to enter and exit salt marshes with the tides. Mouths of creeks are good spots on both rising and falling tides. On rising tides, gamefish that have been waiting out the low tide in the creek mouth or in deeper water nearby pass through the mouth on their way into the marsh. On falling tides, gamefish pick off prey that are swept off the marsh and out of the creeks. Each creek has its own exact timing because of variables such as depth, width, and length, but in general, early in the rising tide and late in the dropping tide are good bets. Fish that are eager to feed in the marsh will enter the creek early in the rising tide in order to get as far into the marsh as they can in the limited time before the tide turns. Gamefish feeding in the marsh retreat into the creek as the tide begins to fall, but they may continue to feed as they move toward the creek mouth and not take up a feeding station until later in the tide. If, however, gamefish are not traveling into the marsh to feed but are remaining in the creek or in deeper water, early in the falling tide may be the best time to drift flies through the outgoing current at the creek mouth.

As the tide rises, it is well worth exploring the larger creeks that disappear into the low marsh. Keep an eye out for small fish becoming airborne as they flee gamefish; for tails of red drum, black drum, or even spotted seatrout feeding in the bottom for crabs; and for swirls and wakes from fish that you spook as you move silently up the

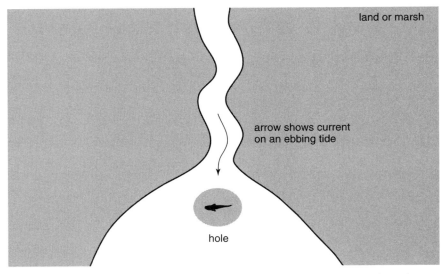

Salt marsh creek mouths are great places to intercept gamefish as they head into and out of a marsh. In addition, gamefish will hold in the holes scoured by currents. A creek with a straight course through its mouth will most likely have a deeper hole in the middle.

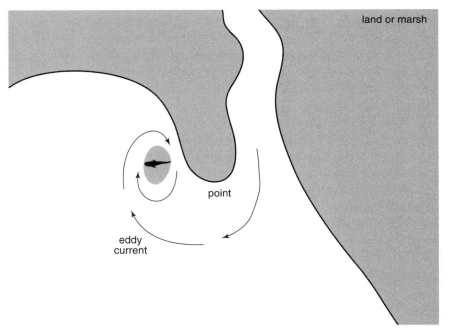

A creek that curves as it reaches the mouth will have its deepest spot on the side of the creek that receives the strongest current.

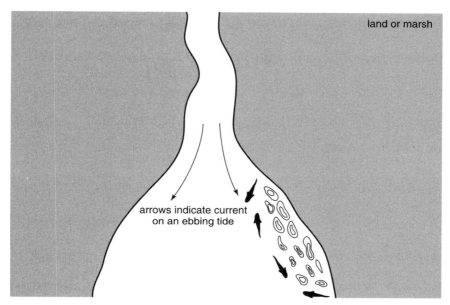

Longshore oyster bars create turbulence as water flows past. Gamefish like to feed on the small fishes, shrimp, and crabs that can be dislodged from the oyster bar by this turbulent water. At low tide, gamefish often concentrate along the deeper edge of the bar, but they may move closer to the shoreline at high tide.

creek. If you see fleeing baitfish or a tailing drum, cast to it. Even the spooked fish are worth a cast. If the fish is not too badly spooked, a cast that leads it by six feet or more may prompt a strike. If not, no big loss. In all cases, it pays to be ready to make a cast quickly. Even if you spot no signs of fish, casting ahead of the boat—along both shorelines and in the middle of the creek—is worth the effort, because gamefish don't always reveal themselves, even if they are feeding. Areas where smaller creeks dump into the large creek you are navigating are worth special attention, as these junctures often have a deep hole that holds fish.

GULF VERSUS ATLANTIC COASTAL SALT MARSHES

The ecological processes, dominant plants, and most of the gamefish and prey are the same in Atlantic and Gulf of Mexico salt marshes, but each coastline has some unique features that are worth examining. The differences are mostly in sediment type and marsh orientation, but understanding them will help you get the most out of fishing in each area.

In oceanographic terms, the continental shelf of the Atlantic is relatively wide and shallow, but not so much that wave energy is dissipated before it reaches shore. This is why southeastern Atlantic coasts are sandy beaches: There is too much wave energy to allow the deposition of the fine sediments necessary for marshes to become established, so Atlantic coastal salt marshes are limited to estuaries or the back sides of barrier islands. The ocean's energy combined with runoff from land creates marsh sediments that are best described as muddy sand. This means the sediments are relatively well aerated, and the growth of marsh grasses is good. In North Carolina, salt marshes are limited to the edges of the sounds that lie behind the Outer Banks and the mouths of the rivers that feed them. In much of South Carolina and Georgia, the long string of barrier islands and the supply of new sediments from numerous rivers and creeks create good conditions for salt marshes along much of the coast. The salt marshes of northeastern Florida rest behind a series of mostly connected barrier islands that have melded with the coast in many locations, creating lagoons.

A consequence of the separation of the Atlantic Ocean from the estuaries by barrier islands is that salt and brackish water are limited to narrow coastal areas. This is quite a contrast to the coast of the northern Gulf of Mexico, where salt marshes fringe much of the shoreline and spread far inland.

Another difference that contributes to the extensive coverage of salt marshes along the Gulf of Mexico is that the tidal range in the Gulf is very small. The large tidal range of the Atlantic means that an area exposed at low tide might be under four to six feet of water at high tide. Salt marsh plants can't tolerate water that deep, so salt marshes are limited to the upper portion of the intertidal zone. In contrast, the combination of the Gulf's very shallow slope and the small tidal range means that large areas of the coast are intertidal, and thus exposed to salt or brackish water, so they are suitable for salt marsh plants. The salt marshes of Louisiana are a great example of such wide salt marsh coverage.

The small tides of the Gulf are also more notably influenced by weather—atmospheric pressure and wind—than their Atlantic coast counterparts. During periods of low barometric pressure, when there is less pressure from the atmosphere pressing down on the water, tides can rise higher than predicted. When barometric pressure is high, more pressure on the water surface can prevent the water from rising as high as predicted. Wind can have similar effects. Strong onshore winds can make high tides higher than predicted and in extreme conditions can even prevent low tides from occurring—in effect creating a ghost tide. In contrast, offshore winds can make both high and low tides lower than predicted. While atmospheric pressure and wind influence tides everywhere, the effects are especially notable in the Gulf of Mexico. The shallow continental shelf, shallow coastal bays and marshes, and small tidal range allow wind and atmospheric pressure to have a greater influence than they do in areas with deeper water and a greater tidal range.

Therefore, you should pay special attention to the weather when fishing the Gulf coast. And you can take advantage of typical weather patterns to plan the best times to fish different areas. In conjunction with the spring and fall equinoxes, typical weather patterns create periods of the highest water levels of the year in April and May and again in September and October, and the best chance for low water is from December through February. This is because typical onshore winds of spring, summer, and fall combine with the spring tides to push water well into the shallow marshes and bays. During winter, strong offshore winds combine with the lowest tides of the year to drain many shallow marshes and bays, which may concentrate gamefish in deeper holes and sloughs. Fish are keyed in to weather and tides and can change their behavior and distribution to take advantage of these periods. If you are in tune with the same conditions as the gamefish, you are more likely to be in the right place at the right time.

For our purposes, we will divide the salt marshes of the Gulf of Mexico into four zones. The three zones from the Mississippi Delta east are dominated by sand, mud, and silt from the Mississippi River. In the first zone, from northern Florida to Mississippi, much of the coast is fringed by salt marshes. These marshes are protected by low-lying barrier islands or by extensive shallows that break up much of the wave energy long before it reaches shore. The second zone, the Mississippi Delta, is famous for its extensive marshes, which extend from far inland to direct contact with the Gulf of Mexico. These marshes are relatively well protected by extensive mud shallows on the seaward edge, but the outer edges are subject to forces of erosion during storms. The third zone, the western side of the Mississippi Delta, boasts salt marshes that thrive on and lie behind low-lying, relatively stable, sandy islands called chenier islands.

The salt marshes of the Texas coast, which make up the fourth zone, are protected by extensive barrier islands that create vast, shallow lagoons. In fact, the barrier island that protects the Laguna Madre is the longest in the world. In addition to the seemingly endless shallow habitats of grass, mud, sand, and oyster bars in these lagoonal systems, the landward portions grade into extensive salt marshes and backcountry lakes that hold gamefish, especially from spring through fall. The shallow lagoonal marshes of Texas are especially vulnerable to the influences of weather.

They are so shallow and experience such a minor tide that portions can become unfishable in windy conditions. Winter winds out of the north are especially bad, pushing much of the water out of the marshes and piling it on the back sides of the barrier islands. So it pays to keep an eye on the weather when fishing the salt marshes and lagoons of Texas.

The Gulf's small tidal range also means that many of the inland ponds and lakes of the coastal marshes, and the creeks that connect them to the Gulf, hold fish throughout the tidal cycle. There just isn't enough tide relative to water depth to influence the behavior of fish. This is great news for anglers, because these waters provide vast protected areas that are perfect for fly fishing. You'll often hear reliable reports of dozens of red drum on the fly in a day of fishing on these backcountry lakes.

In these backcountry salt marsh habitats, weather and season are often more important than tide in finding gamefish. In general, you'll find the greatest numbers of gamefish in these backcountry areas beginning when water temperatures warm in spring and ending when they start to drop in fall. The exception is shallow areas that become too warm in the heat of summer. These locations are best in spring through early summer and later summer to fall. During midsummer, many of the larger fish may move to deeper coastal habitats, such as beaches.

In late fall and winter, the shallow waters in these areas can quickly drop in temperature when a strong cold front passes through, which can spell trouble for gamefish. Every so often a particularly strong cold front causes a rapid drop in temperature that kills fish trapped in the shallows. So once again, locations that are very shallow are unlikely to hold fish. During winter, marshes that are adjacent to deeper water or have deep holes where gamefish can wait out the cold periods hold the most gamefish.

SALT MARSH FOOD WEB

The richness of the salt marsh supports many gamefish and prey species in the warm-temperate region. Because of the toughness of salt marsh grasses, few animals graze directly on them. Instead, the salt marsh food web is fueled by nutrients from decaying marsh grass that has died and fallen to the ground. The fine-grained sediments and detritus from fallen marsh grass combine to make the perfect home for countless bacteria that cause the grass to decay. These nutrients are used by benthic diatoms, small, planktonlike algae that live on the sediment surface rather than in the water column like most plankton, and other algae that grow on marsh sediment surfaces. The benthic diatoms, other algae, and detritus are then eaten by numerous marsh organisms.

Many species of worms eat the detritus, either by filter feeding like oysters and mussels or by ingesting the detritus much like an earthworm ingests soil. Numerous species of fish—killifish and mullet among them— also eat the detritus, and most of these species are prey for gamefish. Fiddler crabs, marsh crabs, shrimp, and other crustaceans also feed on detritus. Fiddler crabs emerge from their burrows at low tide to scoop up morsels of mud and clean it of nutritional material. The small balls of mud you see around fiddler crab burrows are the crabs' way of setting aside the sediments they have already cleaned of food material. The next high tide will bring a fresh supply of detritus-laden sediment and diatoms to be gleaned for food.

In addition, nutrients resulting from decay of plant material support phytoplankton, which in turn supports zooplankton that can be abundant in waters around salt marshes, especially in summer. Oysters and mussels filter plankton and detritus particles that are swept into the water column, and they in turn are eaten by crabs and some fish. Numerous species of fish, including menhaden, sardines, and anchovies, also feed on zooplankton emanating from the salt marsh. Gamefish eat these baitfish as well as the crabs, fish, worms, and other organisms that feed directly on detritus or on smaller detritus-feeding organisms.

Understanding the salt marsh food web is important to fly anglers because the same forces that influence the growth of smooth cordgrass in the low marsh also influence the types and numbers of prey, which influence when and where you can find gamefish. The process of bacterial decay of marsh plants uses oxygen and creates sulfur, so the amount of oxygen available to organisms living on and near the bottom can be a serious issue. But currents bring in oxygenated water, so the greater the tidal flushing, the greater the abundance of prey. This in turn creates more hospitable conditions for marsh organisms. The changing tides also help deliver new detritus to organisms like fiddler crabs, which are able to take advantage of the intertidal zone by feeding on detritus delivered by each high tide. In addition, the three-dimensional structure provided by creek edges, bottoms, and associated mussel and oyster communities, which do best with moderate water exchange, provides more shelter for small organisms, which increases the number of gamefish prey.

GAMEFISH PREY

Salt marshes in both the Atlantic and the Gulf of Mexico host a variety of residents that are eaten by gamefish. Many of these species are also found in warm-temperate seagrass and oyster bar habitats, and most of the families are represented in tropical mangrove and seagrass habitats as well.

Some of the species have been described in detail in previous chapters; others deserve a more detailed description here because it is in the salt marshes that they are highest on the list of gamefish prey.

Crabs and Shrimp

Fiddler crabs are arguably the signature animals of warm-temperate salt marshes, where you may cross paths with as many as eight different species. They are exceptionally adept at using the salt marsh habitat to their advantage and seem to cover every square inch of marsh in some locations. These crabs live in burrows in the intertidal zone of salt marshes and come out at low tide to feed on detritus and diatoms deposited by the previous high tide. Though they usually retreat into their burrows during high tide, enough fiddler crabs remain active at high tide to be targeted by salt marsh red drum.

Like the species that inhabit mangrove habitats, each fiddler crab species in salt marshes prefers a different type of habitat, based on sediment and salinity, so you will encounter different species depending on where you are fishing. Since fiddler crabs are similar in size, you can use a couple crab fly patterns of different colors to imitate them when fishing for red drum in the salt marshes. Typical body sizes for fiddler crabs range from one-half to almost one inch. They have square carapaces and come in a variety of earthy colors, including olive, green, brown, mottled brown, tan, and orange-brown. So casting a fiddler crab fly of your choice to a red drum feeding in the low marsh is a good, simple strategy. Though the enlarged claw is the most notable characteristic of fiddler crabs, it is not a necessary component of a fiddler crab fly, since only the males have this appendage.

Habitat preferences of different species of fiddler crabs tend to cause clumped distributions of fiddler crab colonies, so you will find that some areas of a low marsh are loaded with fiddler crabs while other areas appear empty. A walk through the marsh at low tide will tell you where the biggest groups of fiddler crabs are located. You will likely hear them skittering across the marsh mud and see them retreating to their burrows as you approach. You can be assured that the red drum know where the best areas are, so it is worth exploring an area at low tide to determine where fiddler crabs are most abundant, and then fishing there on the incoming tide.

Knowing what type of habitat each species of fiddler crab prefers also will give you clues to the best locations to fish at different tides. Red-jointed fiddlers *(Uca minax)*, dark-colored crabs with red bands around their leg joints, live mostly in brackish water in association with black needlerush marsh grass and are most common in Atlantic salt marshes. Because black needlerush is mostly in upper portions of a brackish water low marsh, areas with red-jointed fiddlers are accessible to gamefish only during spring high tides. If the needlerush is separated from open water or a creek by a wide, low marsh, it is unlikely that red drum or other gamefish will ever reach the spot. But if a creek provides close access, this spot may be worth checking during a spring high tide.

The red-jointed fiddler is largely replaced by the Gulf freshwater fiddler *(Uca spinicarpa)* and Ive's fiddler *(Uca speciosa)* along much of the Gulf of Mexico. As its name implies, the Gulf freshwater fiddler, present only from the northern to the western Gulf, prefers low-salinity areas. Ive's fiddler prefers brackish water.

The mud fiddler crab *(Uca pugnax)* is widespread in mudflat areas of salt marshes and is common along the banks of intertidal marsh creeks. It is brown to pale gray, with white-tipped claws, and often has a spot of turquoise between the eyes. The front edge of the Gulf mud fiddler *(Uca virens)* has a white fringe, and the front half of its carapace is green. It lives in habitats similar to those of the mud fiddler but is limited to the northern Gulf.

The Caribbean fiddler *(Uca rapax)* is the most common fiddler crab in muddy bottoms of Texas marshes. The sand fiddler *(Uca pugilator)* is common on sheltered sandy shores of Atlantic salt marshes and is pale tan to white to match its surroundings. The panacea sand fiddler *(Uca panacea)* replaces the sand fiddler in the western Gulf, where it is found only from west Florida to Texas. It has a signature orange or red edge to its claw. The long-wave gulf fiddler *(Uca longisignalis)* is also limited to the western Gulf, but it lives in mud bottoms and has a blue-green carapace.

Closely related to fiddler crabs, marsh crabs also live in salt marshes. Species you may encounter include purple marsh crab *(Sesarma reticulatum)* and gray marsh crab *(Sesarma cinereum)*. The purple marsh crab is common along the banks of intertidal marsh creeks. It is dark purple, brown, or olive in color and reaches one inch across. The gray marsh crab is light-colored and less than one inch across and lives in the upper intertidal zone in burrows often in association with layers of dead grass and detritus.

Mud crabs are common residents of the oyster reefs and mudflats that lie within salt marshes and are high on the menu of red drum, spotted seatrout, and weakfish. They have been discussed in detail in previous chapters.

One caveat to your selection of flies to imitate crabs in salt marshes and to your strategy for fishing these flies is that the waters of salt marshes are often rather murky. The fine-grained mud, clay, and sand that make up marsh sediments are easily disturbed by currents and waves and take a long time to settle back to the bottom, so the water of salt marshes is usually turbid. During summer, plankton adds to the murkiness of the water. In these conditions, exact imitations of different crabs are probably less important than getting the fish's attention with a reasonable facsimile and giving the fly the appropriate action to imitate the real thing.

In particularly murky water, flash, bright colors, vibrations, and even noise may be useful methods of attracting the interest of a feeding gamefish. Appropriate for these conditions are flies with a lot of flash (I like a small, brown, bucktail bendback with copious copper flash), bright colors (orange, white, yellow, chartreuse, and white are good attractor colors), materials that create waves in the water from their undulating motion (flies with palmered hackle or marabou move a lot of water), and noise (crab patterns with a rattle). How you fish these flies is also important. Sometimes you really have to splat the fly onto the water to get the fish's attention, and then fish the fly slowly to avoid spooking the fish. Other times the fish are wary of heavy-landing flies, so casting well beyond the fish and bringing the fly in front of the fish is the best approach. In either case, you'll know when the fish detects the fly because it will either suddenly surge toward the fly or turn and hightail it out of there.

Grass shrimp (usually *Palaemonetes pugio*) that occur in salt marshes are the same as or similar to the species that occur in seagrass beds and oyster bars. In salt marshes, grass shrimp can be found feeding in shallow water among smooth cordgrass and along edges of creeks. Sometimes you will find large aggregations of grass shrimp trapped in small pools left by the falling tide. These can be hotspots once gamefish are able to reach these pools at high tide or when grass shrimp decide to leave pools on a dropping tide.

Mud shrimp *(Upogebia affinis)* and ghost shrimp (*Callianassa atlantica, Callianassa major, Callianassa trilobata,* or *Callianassa jamaicense,* depending on location) live in burrows on open bottoms in the mid to upper intertidal zone within and near salt marshes. Each species prefers a different sediment type: Mud shrimp prefer the fine sediments of mudflats, whereas ghost shrimp are found only in clean sand. All of the species are white and similar in size, at two to four inches.

A few species of hermit crabs also live in salt marshes, often on open-bottom flats, and are susceptible to gamefish when they are caught out of their shells. As hermit crabs grow, they have to find larger and larger shells, so they are always on the lookout for a new home. Appropriate-size shells in good shape are rare enough that hermit crabs often fight one another for a suitable shell. Gamefish occasionally surprise a hermit crab that is trying on a new shell or is homeless because it has lost its shell in a battle with another hermit crab. Common salt marsh hermit crabs are long-clawed *(Pagurus longicarpus)* and green-striped *(Clibanarius vittatus)* in the Atlantic and flat-clawed *(Pagurus pollicaris)* in both the Atlantic and Gulf. The long-clawed hermit crab is small, only three-quarters of an inch, and tan with white and brown markings. The flat-clawed hermit crab is also tan but grows to three inches, as does the green-striped, which has green and white stripes along its legs.

Worms
Numerous species of worms, called polychaetes, live in salt marshes, and many species are eaten by gamefish. The most common worms in the diets of gamefish are sandworms (family Nereidae). These segmented worms, which look like earthworms with small jaws, live in burrows in intertidal bottoms of mud and sand and feed along the bottom. The large sandworm *(Nereis succinea)* grows to seven inches and the small sandworm *(Nereis limbata)* to six inches. Both are earth-toned.

Resident Prey Fish
Mollies, mosquitofish, and killifish occur in shallow, low-energy areas of marsh that are protected from strong winds. Mollies are especially abundant in tidal creeks, mostly in the subtropics. They are pale to dark gray or brassy, with rows of fine, dark spots so closely aligned they look like stripes running the length of the body. During the summer mating season, males become very colorful: The long, sail-like dorsal fin can be iridescent silver and black, sometimes with an orange fringe. Although mollies may reach five inches in length, two to four inches is the typical size in salt marshes. The related mosquitofish are brown to brassy in color, reach a maximum size of about one and a half inches, and prefer vegetated brackish areas in the marsh.

Killifish are perhaps the most abundant group of resident fish in warm-temperate salt marshes, so they are important prey for gamefish. They occur in schools in shallow, protected backwaters, flats, and creeks of salt marshes. Within the warm-temperate region, you might come across eleven species of killifish, each preferring a slightly different habitat or salinity. Though species may vary among locations, they are similar in size, shape, and color, so the same flies should work throughout. In general, killifish are small, from one to seven inches long, though most are between one and a half and four inches, minnow-shaped, and medium to dark-brown.

Species you may encounter in both Gulf and Atlantic warm-temperate salt marshes are sheepshead minnow *(Cyprinodon variegatus)*, marsh killifish *(Fundulus confluentus)*, striped killifish *(Fundulus majalis)*, and rainwater killifish *(Luciana Parva)*. Species mostly limited to the Gulf of Mexico include Gulf killifish *(Fundulus grandis)*, diamond killifish *(Adinia xenica)*, saltmarsh topminnow *(Fundulus jenkinsi)*, goldspot killifish *(Fundulus carpio)*, and bayou killifish *(Fundulus pulvereus)*. Species limited to the Atlantic are the mummichog *(Fundulus heteroclitus)* and spotfin killifish *(Fundulus luciae)*.

Most killifish spawn in late spring or summer, and males of many species change coloration during spawning season. While females retain their bland, earthy coloration, males display swaths of orange, yellow, or blue, accented by dark bands and spots. During the spawning season, it seems that males can become so distracted during their mating displays that they completely forget about predators.

Two species of silversides inhabit salt marshes: inland silversides *(Menidia beryllina)*, whose range includes both Atlantic and Gulf salt marshes, and tidewater silversides *(Menidia peninsulae)*, found in salt marshes of Florida and through much of the Gulf of Mexico. Both species reach about four inches in length and are difficult to tell apart. Silversides spawn in late spring or early summer, resulting in an abundance of small juveniles, known as glass minnows, from summer through fall.

Seasonal Prey
Blue crabs are abundant in salt marshes but become less active during winter months. Juveniles, which are the size most eaten by gamefish, are most abundant during summer.

It seems that shrimp are on the diet of just about any gamefish. Juvenile pink and white shrimp (family Penaeidae, common shrimp) are present seasonally in salt marshes. These species use warm-temperate salt marshes as juveniles and migrate to deeper water as adults. Most juvenile common shrimp in salt marshes are from one to four inches long, but most are less than three inches. The possible colors of juveniles include clear and translucent shades of green, gray, and brown, depending in part on the type of bottom where they are living. Juvenile shrimp are most abundant in Gulf salt marshes in fall and spring, and in Atlantic marshes in late summer through fall. Brown shrimp *(Penaeus aztecus)* is the most common species in western Gulf of Mexico salt marshes.

Mullet are also important prey in warm-temperate salt marshes. The most common species are striped mullet *(Mugil cephalus)* and white mullet

(*Mugil curema*). Mullet larvae enter salt marshes in winter and grow to large juvenile size by fall, which is when juveniles are most abundant. Juveniles often undertake migrations out of salt marshes and shallow coastal bays toward warmer areas in fall, inciting rather dramatic feeding frenzies by gamefish. Mullet leaving Louisiana marshes in September fall victim to gorging tarpon, which is when tarpon are close enough to shore to be within reach of small boats. This is in contrast to the long runs necessary to reach schools of tarpon feeding on menhaden ten miles off the coast of Louisiana in summer. Likewise, the fall southward migration of tarpon from the southeast Atlantic coast coincides with the evacuation of salt marshes and southward push by white mullet.

Juvenile fish of many species begin arriving in warm-temperate salt marshes in early spring and continue arriving through summer, when they peak in abundance. Common species with spring arrivals include spot, croaker, and pinfish. Silver trout arrive in summer. Red drum arrive in late fall and early winter. Juveniles that use other shallow coastal habitats will also use salt marshes, particularly if those other habitats are uncommon. Many juveniles that survive the summer migrate out of marshes in the fall, which can induce gamefish to collect along marsh edges and creeks that drain marshes to take advantage of this seasonal bounty.

APPLYING WHAT YOU'VE LEARNED:

Strategies for Murky Water

Because of the often murky waters of the salt marsh, flies that move water, make noise, or are tied with bright colors or flash can be productive, especially during wet times of year. When fishing marshes, I use all-white streamers or throw in some chartreuse, yellow, or orange. Flash can certainly help, especially in the most turbid waters, but sometimes it seems that too much flash scares fish away. When I do use extra flash, I always select a color that enhances the local water color: gold flash in tannin-stained water, and pearlescent or silver flash in clear water.

Small poppers can also be productive flies in the salt marsh, especially in the early and late parts of a summer day. I enjoy moving from hole to hole along the edge of a marsh or a creek bed in the evening, casting a popper a few times into each good-looking spot. The commotion of a fish hitting the fly and the ensuing battle often shut down the remaining fish in that hole, but the excitement makes it worth it. And there is always another hole a little farther along.

Bright flies and flies that move water are also good for blind-casting at creek mouths on a falling tide. Casting across the creek and swinging the fly through the current is a good strategy. Be careful not to fish the fly too quickly. In turbid water, it may take a bit longer for a fish to find the fly because the fish can't rely as much on sight as on its lateral line system. When a fly (or baitfish) moves through the water, it creates small vibrations that travel through the water in waves, much the same way that sound travels through water. At distances of twenty feet or less, the fish's lateral line system picks up the waves as changes in pressure. So a fly pulsating through murky water is detected by a fish long before it can see the fly. As the fish gets closer to the fly, the bright colors stand out more and may elicit a quick strike before the fish gets close enough to give the fly a good look. For this reason, slowly fished, bright flies that move water are the top flies for casting to tarpon rolling in creek mouths in summer.

It is important to approach fishy-looking areas quietly, even when the water is murky. Given the speed and distance of sound travel in water, gamefish are able to detect even the slightest sound over a considerable distance. So in addition to detecting prey, the lateral line system and inner ear can also detect sound waves from careless anglers.

APPLYING WHAT YOU'VE LEARNED:

Seasonal Strategies

Since salt marshes occur in warm-temperate climates, they are subject to a wide range of temperatures that are reflected in obvious seasonal changes. Salt marsh grasses grow during the warmer months and become dormant or die back in the colder months. The inhabitants of salt marshes undergo similar seasonal changes. While most resident species don't leave the marshes in winter, they decrease their activity or even become dormant in especially cold periods. Killifish often burrow into sediments and remain there, dormant, until the temperature rises. Fiddler crabs and mud crabs wait out cold periods in their shelters and emerge once the weather warms. Some resident species may occasionally vacate the shallow waters of salt marshes when temperatures drop, waiting out the cold temperatures in deeper, warmer waters adjacent to the marsh. At the other extreme, temperatures can get very warm in shallow waters of a salt marsh in the heat of summer. This often results in less activity by residents during the day and greater activity at night.

During cold months, temperatures in the shallows can rise quickly during the day, as the dark marsh bottom is warmed by the sun, causing a surge in activity. Gamefish such as red drum and spotted seatrout will move onto the shallows to take advantage of increased prey activity and to warm up in these shallow, sun-heated waters. Mid to late afternoon is the best time to find gamefish moving into the shallows, because it often takes a few hours of sun to warm things up.

Gamefish can also take advantage of the warming effect of the sun on the shallows on the dropping tide. After a day of warming in the sun, water falling off a marsh flat with the dropping tide will be warmer than surrounding deep water. Gamefish wait along current-swept dropoffs or at mouths of creeks to warm up in this water and feed on prey that is swept off the flats.

A somewhat different pattern takes shape during the heat of summer. The summer sun may warm the flats beyond the comfort zone of gamefish and some of their prey. When this happens, gamefish take refuge in cooler waters in deeper holes or along dropoffs. As a rising tide moves the cooler water from deeper areas into the shallows, gamefish often follow the cooler water to feed on the flat. Another strategy employed by gamefish in the heat of summer is to take refuge in cool, deep waters during the day and invade the shallow marsh flats during cooler temperatures at dawn and dusk. Here again, an incoming tide occurring at dawn or dusk can be a productive time for fly fishing.

In addition to affecting gamefish behavior, seasonal temperature changes often result in peaks and valleys in the abundance of gamefish in shallow marshes. Red drum abundance and feeding activity in shallow marshes usually peak in the fall, as this is the season when many prey are at peak abundance, and when adult red drum are collecting in large schools prior to heading to deeper water to spawn. Spawning makes for hungry fish, so fall is when you have a good shot at finding large red drum in shallow waters. The best spots to find these prespawn fish are in shallows that are close to deep, well-flushed areas that the drum may be using to spawn. Similar seasonal changes in abundance and behavior occur for other gamefish in warm-temperate salt marshes. Tarpon and spotted seatrout are coming off their summer spawning, so they need to fatten up in the fall in preparation for winter; the trout need the energy to tolerate the cooler temperatures, and the tarpon to migrate south into warmer waters.

STEWARDSHIP

Salt marshes have functioned as excellent protectors of shorelines against erosion for thousands of years. They have also acted as efficient collectors and depositories of sediments that might smother other habitats or quickly fill in estuaries and other coastal areas. Moreover, marsh plants stabilize the transition between land and sea, and by doing so, they provide valuable habitat to both marine and land animals. In fact, many marine species, including gamefish, have come to depend on salt marshes for part or all of their life cycles. In other words, salt marshes are an indispensable habitat in the coastal environment.

With all we know about the importance of salt marshes for sustaining healthy fisheries and healthy coastal ecosystems, you wouldn't think much would be needed to keep salt marshes in a healthy state. Unfortunately, this couldn't be further from the truth. Salt marshes are under continuing threats from many sources, and threats to salt marshes are threats to gamefish.

Development in and around salt marshes and other wetlands has perhaps the most obvious effects on the health of these habitats. Development simply wipes out the marshes by converting them to land, resulting in wholesale habitat loss. This also removes the protection from erosion that the salt marshes naturally provide. The measures that developers have to take to keep their new development from eroding further degrades the coastal habitats. Also, some government agencies are using salt marshes as disposal areas for spoil from channel dredging, which has the same effect on the salt marsh as development—covering and filling in, and thus destroying, the salt marsh habitat.

Less obvious, but also damaging, is the digging of drainage ditches and canals to drain the water from the marsh, either for control of mosquitoes or for flood control of neighboring areas. Salt marshes depend on tidal flushing and the mixing of salt and fresh water, and draining the marsh prevents this. It is doubtful that apparent benefits of drainage ditches outweigh long-term negative effects on the salt marsh communities and associated gamefish. In fact, drainage ditches may convert low marsh into high marsh, completely removing gamefish habitat.

The diversion of freshwater flows and the sediments they carry also threatens salt marshes. Without fresh water, the high marsh deteriorates. And without the infusion of sediments to maintain the marsh's structural integrity, the marsh begins to erode. The shrinking of salt marshes of the

Mississippi Delta has been linked to diversion of freshwater flow resulting from channelizing of the Mississippi River. In the past, the river deposited most of its sediments in the delta's marshes, but now the channelized flow is so strong that sediments are carried far into the Gulf. Without new sediments to replace portions of salt marshes that are eroding, the marshes are shrinking.

What's more, many of the species of animals that use the salt marsh, including some gamefish and their prey, depend on the mix of fresh and salt water or on the supply of new sediments. A possible explanation for the decline in abundance of tarpon along the Louisiana and Texas coasts, for example, is the diversion of fresh water from the salt marshes. Small juvenile tarpon require low-salinity backwaters of marshes, and without the juvenile habitats, the entire population suffers. Other activities that cut off normal flow of both fresh and salt water, such as impounding or damming, may have similar effects.

While salt marshes can act as good filters of pollutants and keep pollutants from reaching the estuaries, pollutants can harm or even kill some of the organisms that live in the salt marsh. Chemicals sprayed to kill mosquitoes also kill invertebrates that are food for juvenile gamefish in these marshes. Housing developments that use septic systems inject far too much nitrogen into the groundwater that flows into adjacent salt marshes. The excess nitrogen creates blooms of algae and phytoplankton, which can cause severe depletions of oxygen when it dies and decays. Lack of oxygen can cause rather severe die-offs of marsh organisms, including juvenile gamefish.

Saltwater gamefish in the warm-temperate region have an intricate relationship with salt marshes, and the degradation of salt marsh habitats has negative effects not only on the gamefish species that we pursue with a fly rod, but on the health of entire coastal ecosystems. The decisions we make now about these important coastal habitats will affect many generations of saltwater fly anglers.

Chapter 6

Beaches

In many ways, beaches offer a different experience for anglers than the habitats discussed so far. In some cases, they will simply be avenues for you to reach other habitats, like seagrass or mangroves. Even in these situations, however, beaches can allow a close, land-based approach to actively feeding gamefish. In other cases, the beach creates its own environment—a dynamic mosaic of habitats that challenge both angler and gamefish. Fishing along beaches requires your attention to subtle details that can make the difference between success and failure. The gamefish available along beachfronts are mostly the same suspects you've been chasing in more protected waters of seagrass beds, mangroves, oyster bars, or salt marshes, but a few other species are especially abundant along beaches.

The sediment composition of beaches varies among regions. Atlantic beach sediments change as you move from warm-temperate to subtropical locations. The sand of warm-temperate beaches is composed mostly of fine-grained quartz eroded from continental rocks. Calcium carbonate becomes more common once you reach Florida, where carbonate sands dominate the subtropical beaches of the southern part of the state. There, beaches on the barrier islands are dominated by calcareous sands. Much of the sand is from the limestone that makes up the lower Florida peninsula; it has been reworked by waves for thousands of years. But you'll also notice fragments of shells that have been washed shoreward from the abundant bivalves (mostly clams) and gastropods (snails) that live in coastal waters, and bits of coral on southern beaches.

Along the Gulf of Mexico, southern beaches are mostly calcium carbonate, with the influence of sediments from the Mississippi River and from terrestrial erosion increasing as you move north. In the Caribbean, beaches are mostly calcium carbonate, but some consist of land-based sediments as well. Sediments say a lot about a beach's environment: The more coarse the sediments, the higher the wave energy. With a bit of investigation, you'll soon note differences in sediment types and sizes, not only among beaches, but also along a single shoreline. This information provides clues to where you'll find gamefish.

Another variable is tidal range, which influences the width of beaches. Along the Atlantic coast, much of North Carolina and Florida experience relatively small tidal ranges and thus have mostly narrow beaches. In contrast, South Carolina and Georgia tend to have wider beaches because of their larger tidal ranges. In some locations along the Gulf of Mexico, moderate tidal ranges combine with shallow-sloping coasts to create wide beaches, such as those of the microtidal barrier islands of Texas and the chenier islands of Louisiana.

A dominant structuring force of beaches is waves. Most warm-temperate and subtropical Atlantic and Gulf coast beaches form the seaward edges of barrier islands that protect estuaries and shorelines from onslaughts of the open ocean, so they are frequently exposed to high wave energy. Because of the ocean's energy, these barrier island systems are very dynamic and always on the move. The nearly constant bombardment of waves means the sands are constantly in motion, so it is almost impossible for seagrass or other live bottom habitats to become established. On the Atlantic coast, North Carolina's Outer Banks tend to be the highest-energy beaches, with less dramatic conditions farther south. Most Gulf of Mexico beaches experience moderate to low surf conditions throughout most of the year.

WAVES

As anyone who has spent time on the beach knows, waves crashing on the beach move sand. The energy from breaking waves and the rush of their wash up the beach displaces grains of sand. As the wave's energy dissipates, the sand settles back to the bottom. An individual sand grain is moved only a short distance by a single wave, but the accumulation of many small movements by many grains of sand results in large-scale changes in beach formations and offshore sandbars.

Waves generally approach beaches at an angle, so instead of simply moving sand up and down the beach, they also transport it along the beach. As the wash from one wave retreats seaward, carrying a load of sand, it is met by another incoming wave. While some of the water continues its seaward flow along the bottom, some of the wash and the sand it carries become entrained in the wash from the next incoming wave. And since waves are approaching the beach at an angle, accumulation of water in the wash zone creates a current that moves along the beach. This is called a longshore current.

Every once in a while, the volume of water pushed against shore by so many successive waves becomes large enough that it's able to break through the surf zone and head seaward. This seaward rush of water that interrupts the longshore current is called a rip current. You can recognize a rip current by the discoloration of the water, because it carries so much sediment, or by the change in the appearance of the water's surface due to conflicting currents of the seaward flowing rip and incoming waves. Strong, consistent rip currents cut through longshore bars. Rip currents provide feeding areas for gamefish in much the same way as do current edges around oyster bars. Baitfish and other prey get caught in the rip current and are transported offshore, and gamefish wait along edges of the rips to pick off discombobulated prey.

In some cases, conflicting forces of incoming wave energy and seaward-flowing rips cause a sorting of sediments into a pattern of cusps and bowls along the beach. Cusps are small ridges of coarse sediment that rim bowls composed of fine sediment. These formations often continue into the water. When they do, they act like miniature bars and troughs that lie across the longshore current. Baitfish will try to escape the current by collecting on the downcurrent sides of submerged cusps, making for good feeding stops for cruising gamefish.

The movement of sand by waves and longshore current forms longshore bars—underwater sandbars lying parallel to the beach. Sometimes longshore bars become so large they're exposed at low tide; they are then known as ridges. Some beaches have only a single longshore bar; others sport a series of parallel bars off their shores. Between the beach and the first bar, and between parallel bars, troughs of deeper water form. Although still high-energy, the deeper water of troughs provides a refuge from the turbulence of waves breaking over the bars, so they attract baitfish and other prey that live along the beachfront. Gamefish travel the edges of troughs looking to pick off baitfish that get caught in the turbulence of waves tumbling over the bars.

Longshore bars and troughs often reveal their location to an observant angler. Incoming waves rise up, and even break, as they travel over shallow bars, and subside as they travel over troughs. If there are no waves, look for changes in water color—generally a lighter shade marks bars and darker water marks troughs—or for breaks in currents marking the edge of a bar.

Wave action can quickly change the shape of beaches. This is most dramatic after storms or during winter and occurs because of differences in wave energy. In summer, the dominant wave type is low-energy. These low-energy waves deposit sand onto the beach and create a gently sloping shoreline. Check these summer beaches for a short but steep dropoff, or lip, at the low-tide mark—anywhere from six inches to two feet deep. The lip is a good area to spot cruising gamefish in search of a meal especially on an incoming tide.

The large, high-energy waves associated with winter and with storms cause beach erosion and transport sand offshore. The result is a steeper beach with waves often crashing right along the shoreline. The sand generally doesn't go far and is usually redeposited inshore during summer in this natural seasonal cycle, so as the calmer seas of summer return, the beaches are slowly built up again. The constantly changing nature of beaches means that it takes some study and frequent exploration to really know a beach and the best places to find gamefish.

APPLYING WHAT YOU'VE LEARNED:

Basic Strategies for Fishing the Surf

The crashing surf and roiled water of beaches can be intimidating to the uninitiated, leading to confusion in what approach to use when fly-fishing these areas. The most common mistake of fly anglers new to fishing beaches is that they try to cast as far off the beach as they can. I can't tell you how many times I've watched fly anglers wade out to waist-deep water and put all their strength into casting as far offshore as possible. After all, big fish want to be in deep water, right? Nope. Most of the time, by wading off the beach, they bypass most of the fish, which are close to shore. You'd be surprised by the number and size of gamefish that cruise along the beach in water barely deep enough to keep them wet. There are times when the fish are feeding off the beach and casting offshore is necessary, but more often than not, you will find good numbers of gamefish within easy casting distance from the beach. And why throw out your arm trying to cast across the ocean if you don't have to?

My general approach toward beach fishing is to walk along the beach edge or perhaps just a step into the water. Many fish feed in the roiled water right next to the beach. By staying on the beach, I have a good vantage point for seeing fish if the water is clear and then casting to the fish I spot. But even if the water is too murky for me to see fish, chances are they're still in these same areas. When blind-casting, the best strategy is to cast on a line that runs between parallel to the beach and at a forty-five-degree angle to the shoreline.

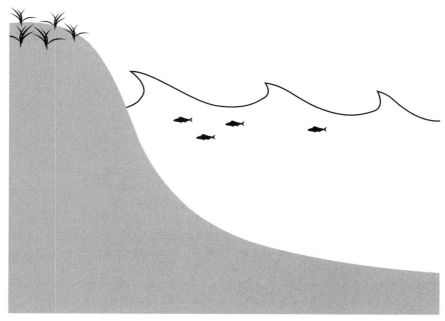

A high-energy beach, or a beach during winter or after a strong storm, has a steep slope and few underwater formations to hold fish. Along these beaches, gamefish are always on the move.

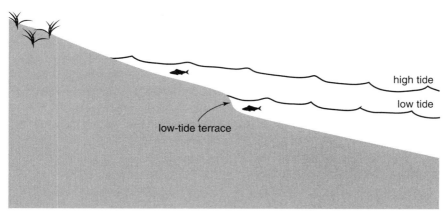

A low-energy beach has a shallower profile and often a lip at the low-tide mark. This lip is a good spot to find gamefish cruising in search of food at both high and low tides.

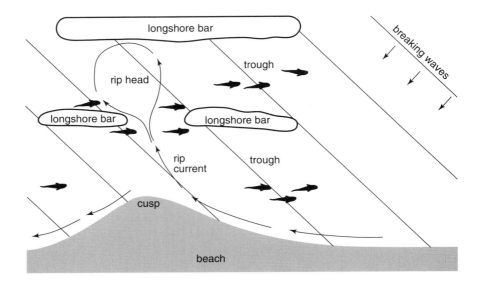

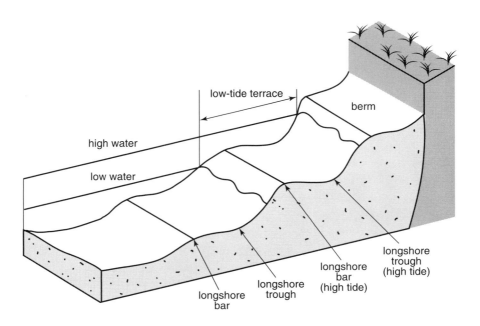

This wide beach has a series of longshore bars and troughs extending offshore. At low tide, some of the bars may be exposed, and you may find gamefish concentrated along the outer bar. At high tide, the troughs between bars become flooded with baitfish, which attract gamefish closer to shore.

There are two schools of thought for what fly line to use for this type of beach fishing. Some prefer an intermediate line to get under the surf. They feel it is easier to maintain a straight line and gives them a more direct connection to their fly. Others prefer floating lines and maintain a connection to their fly by mending the line over the surf. It's a personal preference; use whichever works for you. Regardless of the fly line you choose, it is important to keep enough tension on the line to feel a fish take the fly. If you are using a floating line, you can also detect strikes by keeping an eye on the end of your fly line. Sometimes gamefish will really slam the fly, but often a strike in the surf will be more subtle. And although there are times when a rapidly stripped fly garners the most strikes, unless fish are actively feeding I've found it best to fish the fly slowly. I like to let the fly bounce around in the turbulent water of the surf zone like a disoriented baitfish. The challenge with this strategy is to keep enough tension on the fly line to be sure you can detect the strike while allowing the fly to roll around just inside or outside the surf zone.

SHIFTING SANDS

Although many think the Gulf Stream is the dominant current along the southeastern Atlantic coast, it is too far offshore to influence the movement of sand along the coastal beaches or to directly influence coastal gamefish in most circumstances. Instead, the northward-flowing Gulf Stream forms the outer boundary to the warm-temperate coastal system. Inside the Gulf Stream, the off-colored water reflects the influence of coastal rivers and beach sediments, while the clear water of the Gulf Stream to the east speaks of tropical influence. Closer to the coast, the dominant coastal current flows from north to south, and this current slowly moves sand southward. The currents of the Gulf of Mexico are a bit more complex, but the general flow is in a counterclockwise direction. The direction of sand transport influences where bars and shoals form, which affects where you will find gamefish.

The dominant longshore current, in concert with the dominant coastal current, transports sand along the coast. I'll use the Atlantic coast as an example of how these currents transport sand along the outer beaches, but the same processes are at work in the Gulf. As this sand moves southward, it builds up against the barrier islands and extends seaward as shoals. These shoals act as reservoirs that maintain a ready supply of new sand for beaches farther south. Because of the wave and current action, longshore bars often radiate southward from these shoals. The longshore bars, which are really trails of southward-moving sand, eventually wrap around the southern tip of the barrier island in the form of a spit. In many cases, sand is transported behind the islands, forming large sand flats on the back side of the inlets. These shoals provide shelter for small baitfish looking to escape gamefish lurking in the deep water of the adjacent inlet. Outgoing tides sweep unwitting baitfish to the waiting mouths of gamefish cruising the edges of these flats, but sometimes gamefish become impatient and swim forays into tightly packed schools of baitfish in the shallow water. Drifting a streamer the size and color of the dominant bait over the edge can be productive on the dropping tide. During the shallow-water feeding frenzies, just getting a fly in the path of a gamefish is usually enough.

Many shallow-sloping beaches have extensive sand deposits extending seaward that allow an angler to wade a considerable distance off the beach at low tide. The sand flats that remain a constant depth for a considerable distance tend to hold fewer prey and fewer gamefish. The best fishing on these flats tends to be along the edges, where you may find gamefish moving along the dropoff hoping to surprise prey, hanging in a current waiting for prey to wash off the flat, or perhaps cruising across the flat on a rising tide.

In contrast, shallows that roll away from shore as bars and troughs hold considerably more gamefish, even if they possess only minor contours. These types of shallows are especially common in the Gulf of Mexico. Although the bars and troughs tend not to be of the magnitude of many of their higher-energy Atlantic coast counterparts, the change in bottom from bar to trough collects and holds baitfish just the same. And as along higher-energy beaches, gamefish prowl the edges of the bars in search of prey.

If surf is moderate or low, many of these beachside flats are wadable on either side of the low tide. These areas are most common off sandy points and where normal wave action is moderate to minor. Even on Gulf beaches with relatively minor tides, be careful not to get stranded on an outer bar on an incoming tide. The larger tides of South Carolina warrant extreme care and attention to tide tables. Sight fishing is a good challenge during calm, clear-water days, and casting into troughs can be productive when the water is turbid. Often baitfish are scattered across these shallows, especially when the water is murky. Under such circumstances, you won't find gamefish attacking tightly packed schools of panicking baitfish. Instead, keep an eye open for swirls from gamefish feeding on the scattered schools of loosely packed baitfish. Rather than focusing on a single baitfish school, these gamefish are cruising through the shallows picking off a baitfish or two as they come across the schools.

Spotted seatrout can be especially abundant along sandy beaches in spring and fall. Deceivers and Clousers are productive flies.

Along subtropical and warm-temperate beaches, Spanish mackerel, ladyfish, red drum, spotted seatrout, snook, bluefish, crevalle jacks, and leatherjackets are typical gamefish roving these shallows from late spring through early fall. Tarpon can be abundant along Gulf coast beaches in summer but require stealthy techniques to get close enough for a cast. You might even come across a cobia, especially in the spring or fall, which is also when pompano run along the beaches.

Large spotted seatrout can provide some fantastic action along subtropical and warm-temperate beaches in late summer and fall. The trout hang out in deeper sections of troughs and dart out to grab small fish that pass along the edges of bars or even right next to shore. Unlike their green or bronze back coloration when they are feeding in the grass beds, these trout are a radiant pale silver that allows them to blend in well to the background of light-colored sand.

In contrast to beaches with extensive sandy shallows, other beaches slope quickly to deep water. These beaches are often associated with the inner portions of embayments and shorelines exposed to moderate surf. Rather than slope evenly from the beach berm into the water, these beaches often have a steep, one- to two-foot dropoff marking the low-tide line. The shallow, sandy bottom then tends to slope gradually deeper away from shore. While it might seem the least likely of places to find gamefish because it's so shallow and close to shore, the little ledge at the edge of a beach is my favorite beach-fishing area—numerous gamefish can be found there.

Summer Beachside Snook

In summer in the subtropics, snook cruise back and forth along beach edges in search of mojarra, scaled sardines, juvenile permit, small Gulf kingfish, mullet, and any other small fish unlucky enough to cross their path. I think the edge gives snook a place to corner the small fish, with the safety of deeper water easily reachable. Though snook are available along these beaches throughout summer, the fishing is best around new and full moons.

These are the best times because snook gather along beaches during summer not only to take advantage of abundant prey fish but also to spawn. In southern Florida, snook spawn in aggregations in passes and inlets from late afternoon into evening on days around

Mojarra *(the four fish at the top)* and juvenile permit are common along low- to moderate-energy sandy beaches in warmer months. Numerous species of mojarra, all of similar shape and coloration, are common in most coastal habitats.

new and full moons. Individual fish probably spawn every few days. All that spawning takes a lot of energy, and beachside snook can be especially voracious as they replenish their energy stores. I imagine snook behavior on the other side of the Gulf is similar. It certainly is on the Atlantic coast of Florida.

Snook along beaches seem to be most aggressive in the low light of dawn and dusk. I've spent many dawns searching for large snook along south Florida's outer beaches near inlets and passes. In the early dawn, snook give themselves away as they chase baitfish onto the beach or explode through a school of sardines. As the sun lights the water, this becomes a sight-fishing opportunity. Depending on the action, it may be sufficient to stand in a spot with the sun at my back and wait for the snook to cruise by. If the fish are more scattered or not as much on the move, I slowly walk along the beach and cast to fish that I spot cruising the shoreline or hanging in troughs between bars. Whether I stick to one spot or move along the beach, I'm sighting and casting to snook within a couple feet of the shoreline.

White Deceivers of three inches or less are the best bets for these snook. Make sure you take a handful because the rough mouth and sharp gill plates of snook will cause a number of breakoffs in a typical day. Similar-size all-white Clouser Minnows are also good imitations of the small, silver-colored fish eaten by snook along these beaches. Though these small flies produce the most action, I always pack a couple of larger flies in my fly box as well. Large, all-white Half-and-Halfs tied on 2/0 hooks do a decent job of imitating the small Gulf kingfish that live along these beaches and are eagerly eaten by larger snook.

Whichever fly I choose, a slow retrieve is best. Lead a cruising fish by a few feet, and twitch the fly to get the fish's attention. A short strip or two may spur a following fish into action. Cast just beyond a resting fish and slowly strip the fly across the fish's field of vision. In either case, I usually need to make only short casts of thirty to forty feet.

Similar snook behavior occurs on Florida's southeast coast, where snook cruise the shoreline between the longshore bar and shore. Similar fishing strategies work there as well. Juvenile pompano and kingfish, mole crabs, and small swimming crabs are among the most abundant prey.

GAMEFISH PREY

The mostly open sand bottom adjacent to high-energy beaches harbors only limited prey for gamefish. Mole crabs and swimming crabs are tops on the list of crustaceans that live along beaches. Pompano, red drum, Gulf kingfish, and spotted seatrout feed on these crustaceans.

Crabs and Shrimp
Mole crabs (family Hippidae), also known as sand crabs, are oval in shape; are generally tan, brown and white, or gray, often with a purplish hue; and grow to one inch long. These crabs live in the swash zone and use the wash from waves to move up and down the beach. They ride the wash either up or down the beach, and then burrow into the sand to feed on detritus among the grains. These crabs are most vulnerable to gamefish when they are moving from place to place. The common mole crab *(Emerita talpoida)* occurs throughout the Atlantic coast, the Cuban *(Hippa cubensis)* and Puerto Rican *(Emerita portoricensis)* mole crabs are limited to Florida beaches, and the purple surf crab *(Albunea gibbesii)* ranges southward from North Carolina. Webster's mole crab *(Lepidopa websteri)* is found in the surf zone from North Carolina southward. Overall, mole crabs tend to be more abundant along Atlantic than Gulf beaches. Mole crabs are a favorite of pompano, which travel the surf zone in large, loosely arranged schools, and of Gulf *(Menticirrhus littoralis)*, southern *(Menticirrhus americanus)*, and northern kingfish *(Menticirrhus saxatilis)*. Pompano are migratory, and along the Atlantic coast they spend their summers along the North Carolina coast, often remaining in small home ranges during the summer season. They head south to Florida in fall and return northward in spring, providing great sport to beachgoing fly anglers in the process. Subadult and young adult red drum also search out mole crabs along sandy beaches.

Numerous species of swimming crabs also inhabit coastal beaches. Among the most common along the Atlantic coast, lady crabs *(Ovalipes ocellatus)* are limited to the warm-temperate beaches north of Georgia. Lady crabs are common just outside the surf zone, often lying buried in the sand waiting to ambush passing prey, and feed mostly at night. Their sand-colored carapaces are covered with dark, purplish dots, so they are well camouflaged on the open sand bottom. The related speckled crabs *(Arenaeus cribrarius)*, present along warm-temperature and subtropical beaches, follow a similar ambush strategy. These crabs are tan to gray with white or yellow spots. The ubiquitous blue crabs or other members of the *Callinectes* genus are also present along low-energy beaches.

In fine-grained sand below the low-tide line on moderate- to low-energy beaches, you may find burrows of ghost shrimp. These shrimp are clear to white in color and can reach three inches in length.

Flies to imitate these crustaceans are best fished on calm days on shallow-sloping beaches in times of relatively clear water. I like to sight-fish for red drum, spotted seatrout, snook, and snapper cruising the beach. If the water along the beach is too deep, or the fish are cruising right along the swash zone, I like to walk along the beach to give myself greater elevation. If I can, I prefer to wade out to a longshore bar and look for fish cruising the edge of the bar, especially at the end of the outgoing and early incoming tide. If you follow this strategy, be sure to retreat to the beach before being trapped by the incoming tide. With the sun at my back and clear water, it's not unusual to get shot after shot at cruising fish. I usually use a floating line because it allows me a quick pickup and recast in case I miss the fish or the fish refuses or doesn't see the fly. If, however, the surf is a nuisance, I'll switch to an intermediate line for more line control.

Prey Fish
Along sandy shorelines, baitfish and other small fish dominate gamefish diets. While red drum, spotted seatrout, and other species that munch on crabs and shrimp in other habitats will continue to do so along beaches, they'll be especially tuned in to the movements of these small fish. Moreover, the larger members of these gamefish species tend to focus more on eating baitfish than on eating crustaceans, so it pays to focus on Deceivers, Clousers, and other fish-imitating flies. So though there are certainly times for crab and shrimp patterns, fish-imitating streamers should be the dominant flies in a beach angler's fly box.

Many of the prey fish that occur along beaches are the same as or closely related to species already discussed in previous chapters. And though the particular species of fish eaten by beachgoing gamefish vary by location and time of year, most of these prey fish are similar enough in size and appearance that they can be imitated with the same flies used to imitate baitfish in other habitats. The only difference may be that when living along sandy beaches, many of these prey fish are pale to match their surroundings, with little or no coloration, so all-white flies are usually my first choice.

Scaled sardines may be the most common large herrings (family Clupeidae) along subtropical and warm-temperate beaches from early summer through fall. Threadfin herring *(Opisthonema oglinum)* are also common warm-weather prey along beaches, though they tend to stay a bit farther off the beach than the sardines and can be especially abundant in the fall. Other herrings found along beaches, especially in the fall, include Spanish sardine *(Sardinella aurita)* and, in the Gulf of Mexico, Gulf menhaden *(Brevoortia patronus)*. Round scad *(Decapterus punctatus)*, a member of the jack family, occasionally run the beach as well but are usually in deeper water.

Scaled sardines are common in many estuaries and coastal habitats during the warmer months.

Threadfin herring also live in estuarine and coastal habitats during the warmer months.

During warmer months, you can find Spanish sardines in estuarine and coastal habitats, too.

While both striped and white mullets are found along sandy beaches, the white mullet is the species of legendary fall runs. Juvenile white mullet flood out of their summer estuarine hideaways in the fall, heading south. Once you've seen and heard the chaos and carnage of large gamefish feeding on schools of panicked mullet right along the beach, the image will be burned in your mind forever.

Anchovies and silversides, often collectively referred to as glass minnows, can also be common along low- to moderate-energy beaches, especially in the fall. Common species are dusky anchovy *(Anchoa lyolepis)*, bay anchovy *(Anchoa mitchilli)*, striped anchovy *(Anchoa hepsetus)*, tidewater silversides *(Menidia beryllina)*, and north of Florida on the Atlantic coast, Atlantic silversides *(Menidia menidia).* It's an amazing sight to see large tarpon rolling through schools of glass minnows. The glass minnows scatter in all directions as tarpon, mouths open, roll through panicked baitfish in what looks like slow motion. Cast to the edges of the schools and the surrounding waters rather than into the schools to give your fly a chance at getting noticed amid the commotion.

Numerous species of mojarra, including mottled mojarra *(Eucinostomus lefroyi)* and silver jenny *(Eucinostomus gula),* are common along sandy shorelines in summer. Species vary among locations but are similar in size and shape.

On more protected beaches, like those outside St. Andrew Bay, near Panama City Beach on Florida's northern Gulf coast, you may find small fish most often associated with estuaries, including Gulf killifish (*Fundulus grandis*), longnose killifish (*Fundulus similis*), and spot (*Leiostomus xanthurus*).

Gulf and northern kingfish are common along sandy beaches. The larger kingfish are good gamefish targets with small shrimp patterns, and smaller individuals are prey for gamefish.

As in other habitats, spring and summer bring juvenile fish to beaches. Pompano, permit, various jacks, yellowtail snapper, triggerfish, and filefish are among the species represented by juveniles during the warm months.

APPLYING WHAT YOU'VE LEARNED:

Seasonality and the Fall Feeding Frenzy

Although in many locations gamefish can be found throughout the year, late spring through fall are the best times of year to target gamefish along beaches. Many of the gamefish found on beaches are migratory, such as Spanish mackerel, tarpon, pompano, bluefish, and jacks, and are most abundant during the warmer months.

Resident species, such as red drum and spotted seatrout, can be found along beaches throughout the year, but even they are most common in beach habitats from late spring to fall. As the water warms in March and April, schools of small red drum cruise the beaches of the Chandeleur Islands, and spotted seatrout show up in number in April. Elsewhere in Louisiana, many of the red drum and spotted seatrout that roamed the backcountry lakes as the water warmed in spring will move to the cooler water along beaches if the shallow backcountry gets too warm in midsummer.

Fall is an exciting season along warm-temperate and subtropical beaches. This is when many fish that have been living, feeding, and growing in coastal waters all summer gather in schools to migrate south or offshore to wait out the cold winter months. The migrating schools of prey fish attract large numbers of gamefish, and the feeding can be frenzied. White mullet leave the protected coastal estuaries where they've summered and head southward along beaches. Tales of broken rods and worn-out anglers from the fall run of mullet along Atlantic coastal beaches are legend and are well founded. Tarpon, ladyfish, snook, crevalle jacks, mackerel, red drum, sharks, barracuda, and other gamefish also take part in this free-for-all. In fact, the south-ward fall migration of tarpon from the Carolinas coincides perfectly with the white mullet migration.

My friend Bob Miller grew up along Florida's southeast coast and has told me some amazing stories of the fall run. He's recounted schools of mullet so thick and so large they stretched across acres of water along and just off the beach. Amazingly, the gamefish can be so abundant and feeding so aggressively that he often hooked a fish on the first cast. He's lamented the long fight when he's hooked into twenty-pound crevalle jack. During the twenty minutes it takes to land that one jack, he's been surrounded by boils and wakes of other gamefish that continue feeding along the beach. I know the gamefish are plentiful when he tells me of losing a hooked fish because another gamefish ran through and broke his leader.

Bob also related a story of a beachside tarpon feeding frenzy. He was fishing along the beach, hoping to find gamefish feeding on sardines. About a half mile down the beach, he heard a tremendous roar and could see commotion in the water just off the beach. He ran to the spot and found six-foot tarpon that had corralled a school of sar-dines against the beach. The tarpon were feeding in a near-continuous explosion, with water and fish flying everywhere. Although he didn't have a heavy enough fly rod to land such a large tarpon, he cast into the fray. It took only that single cast for him to hook into one of those large tarpon. Once hooked, the tarpon headed offshore. Bob hung on as long as he could before grabbing the reel and breaking the fish off at the leader with only a few feet of backing left on the reel.

Throughout their range, red drum move into coastal waters in fall and feed voraciously as they get ready to spawn and between spawn-ing events. They will even stick around after spawning until water temperatures drop and baitfish move off. Spotted seatrout are looking to bulk up after exhausting themselves during a summer of spawn-ing. Bluefish and Spanish mackerel feed with reckless abandon on tightly packed schools of baitfish.

The barrier island beaches of Texas yield their best beach fishing of the year each fall, as monster spotted seatrout, red drum, crevalle jack, ladyfish, tarpon, and other gamefish gorge on schools of mullet, glass minnows, and herrings attempting to slip through the gauntlet. The first light of dawn can bring the best action of the day, so it pays to be early. If you arrive late and miss it, you'll have all winter to regret it. Once the sun is up, you may find that jacks are most active during the midday hours. Tarpon that have spent much of the summer feeding on menhaden in offshore waters will move inshore in fall to feed on schools of dusky and bay anchovies and then schools of finger mullet gathering to head south. Those that feed in early morning may return once light starts to drop in late afternoon, so don't tire yourself out too much on jacks, spotted seatrout, and red drum.

The best strategies for this fall frenzy? Be there early. The first light of day tends to provide the best action. Dusk can be almost as good. Given the choice, incoming tide is best, especially early in the tide. Take binoculars and occasionally search the shoreline for birds, the splashes of feeding fish, or the dark shadows of tightly packed schools of baitfish. Look for troughs, exposed sandbars, or dead-end sand embayments that form in the longshore currents because these are great collecting places for baitfish. Gamefish search out these dead ends, so even if baitfish aren't present when you arrive, you might intercept a gamefish coming in for a look. Pack along plenty of extra leader, some wire tippet, and maybe even an extra fly rod because the variety of gamefish that take part in this fall frenzy can challenge an angler ready for only the basics.

Fish-eating birds, such as brown pelicans and egrets, can be good indicators of gamefish feeding on baitfish. The pelicans feed as the baitfish are chased to the surface, and the egrets and other wading birds feed on baitfish chased onto the beach by gamefish.

BEACHES OF THE TROPICS

Beaches of the Caribbean, as well as those in tropical Florida (mostly the Florida Keys), differ somewhat from the subtropical and warm-temperature beaches of the Atlantic and Gulf coasts. The processes of waves and currents are similar, but the type of sand (mostly calcareous), the protection afforded by coral reefs, and the fact that currents on Caribbean islands are due almost entirely to winds make Caribbean beaches a little different. While living in the Caribbean, I did some wade-guiding on weekends. Most of the anglers who hired me were from the northeastern United States, and most of their saltwater fishing experience had been along ocean beaches from New England to North Carolina. I quickly learned that my first task was to teach these anglers that shoreline fishing on most Caribbean islands was unlike fishing the beaches of their home fishing grounds, and that fishing the habitats found along tropical shorelines required an understanding of these habitats and a different approach than they were used to. Beaches in the Caribbean are of three general types: exposed, protected, and semiprotected.

Exposed Beaches

Exposed beaches are usually on the windward coast and are areas of high wave energy. They are made of coarse sand, coral rubble, shell fragments, rocks, or various combinations of these materials. The stronger the wave activity, the coarser the makeup of the beach. The slope of exposed beaches is often steep, and since so much sand is moved by wave energy and associated currents, the diverse bottom community often found in more protected areas is replaced by a short list of more hardy species. In these respects, exposed beaches of the Caribbean resemble many beaches along the subtropical and warm-temperate Atlantic coast.

Since relatively few bottom-dwelling, or benthic, species are able to tolerate these high-energy environments, baitfish dominate the list of gamefish prey on exposed beaches. Higher-energy beaches tend not to hold schools of baitfish close to shore. Instead, the small fish congregate just outside the surf zone. The numerous species of anchovies and herrings that make up these schools are easily imitated with streamers, which fool the schools of jacks that regularly cruise these shorelines. Tarpon are common visitors to exposed beaches but tend not to hang around for extended periods. Instead, they appear and disappear at irregular intervals, even if baitfish remain, following a pattern I have yet to figure out. In contrast, once snook find a spot they like, they tend to stay put for a while, and prefer murky over clear water. Just inside the edge of clear and murky water can be a hot spot for Caribbean beach snook.

Fishing on exposed beaches can be difficult due to high winds and surf, so choose your days according to conditions. Days when winds are calm or blowing offshore and ocean swell is negligible are when fishing exposed beaches is most enjoyable and when gamefish come closest to the beach. Methods for fishing exposed beaches in the Caribbean are the same as described for Atlantic beaches.

APPLYING WHAT YOU'VE LEARNED:

Tarpon Blitzes

An experience with beach-blitzing tarpon when I lived in the Virgin Islands provides a taste of what can happen if you find yourself in the right place at the right time along an exposed beach on a Caribbean island. In June and again in January, sprat and fry, local names for a type of herring and glass minnows, can often be found schooled up against exposed beaches around St. Croix. I've used a cast net to catch some of the sprat, which were full of eggs and milt and appeared to be schooled together to spawn. The trick is to find where these bait-fish are schooled. There doesn't seem to be a standard pattern. The locations of these schools change from season to season and from year to year.

I found that the most efficient way to search for schools of baitfish under attack was to look for brown pelicans. I usually did this by driving to good vantage points and using binoculars to scan the shoreline. Diving pelicans were sure signs of baitfish schooled below. A lone pelican diving in an area usually meant scattered baitfish, as did a few pelicans flying along a shoreline occasionally diving into the water. Neither was reason to grab the gear and start fishing. What I was searching for was a handful, or more, of pelicans diving repeatedly in the same small area. This invariably meant that a large school of sprat or fry was being corralled by large fish from below and forced close enough to the surface to attract pelicans. Sometimes the pelicans were so full they took some time off, but the sight of a half dozen or so pelicans resting on the water signaled baitfish just as diving did.

Once on the scene, I usually watched the diving pelicans for a few minutes to figure out which type of baitfish lay below, and thus which fly to tie on. If, after diving into the water, a pelican quickly tipped up its beak and swallowed the baitfish, I knew the fish were large—probably sprat. If, on the other hand, a pelican hung its beak to slowly drain the water from its pouch before tipping and swallowing, I knew the baitfish were small—probably fry. The sprat are large enough that a pelican can open its beak an inch or so to let the water quickly drain, but the fry are so small that the pelican must drain the water from an almost closed beak, making a quick way to figure out the dominant bait.

Once a school of baitfish is found, it's a good bet there are large fish along the outer fringes feasting on the trapped baitfish. Barracuda, various jacks, and snapper are the usual predators on these baitfish, but occasionally groups of tarpon will invade the scene. A Deceiver when sprat are the bait of choice or a Clouser Minnow when fry are on tap is all that's needed on most occasions.

The beach near our apartment was part of a long crescent-shaped bay with coral-covered rocky points at each end and sandy shoreline in between. Palm trees and sea grapes fringed the back of the beach but were sparsely located and provided little shade. The road to the apartment passed up and over a hill, which provided a view of much of the bay. On my way out in the morning and returning home in the evening, I usually slowed my truck to take a peek. One evening in June as I drove over the hill toward home, I saw pelicans diving off one of the points. Not one pelican, or even a few, but perhaps a dozen or more. Many were diving into the water just outside the line of small surf that was breaking on shore. Others were sitting in the water, either taking a rest or just too full to fly.

I arrived at the beach at about six-thirty and began the five-minute walk to the point. The pelicans were still working the school of baitfish, flying up and diving back into the water as quickly as they could manage. As I neared the point, I thought to myself that prospects looked good for some fun with a few big barracuda or maybe a hungry jack.

As I got closer, I could see the pelicans were making quick work of the fish they caught, quickly tipping their beaks and swallowing the fish before lurching from the water for another pass. Sprat! Just the same, I made a couple throws with my cast net and netted a few fish to make sure of their size. They were large, up to six inches. As I pulled in the net after the second throw, I saw an unmistakable dorsal fin of a twenty-five-pound tarpon as it rolled through the baitfish about forty feet off the beach. I threw the cast net up on the beach and grabbed my fly rod.

My first two casts were to the deep water just beyond the line of frothing surf. There were no takers. I put the third cast right where I had seen the fish roll when I was throwing the cast net—in the middle of the wild water, where waves rolling in collided with the outgoing wash of previous waves in a fury of white foam. This is no place for a fly, I thought.

The fly hit the water and bounced in the chaotic waves and froth for a few seconds as I hurriedly stripped slack out of the fly line snaking over the white foam. Then the churning water exploded. I didn't see the fish, just the spray of white water erupting from the roiled surface. The line went tight in my hand, and I instinctively set the hook with a strip strike. The hook found its mark, sending the tarpon airborne. It was strange, but because of the "washing machine" effect of water over the reef, the tarpon never really landed in the water, but half rode the bubbling foam and half launched itself again and again. Eventually its leaps carried it away from shore and into deeper water. Once the fish finally was back in the water, I set the hook twice more. With that, the tarpon headed for deeper water at breakneck speed and then jumped three more times, about eighty yards away.

I suddenly realized my situation: I stood waist-deep in the surf, with larger waves breaking at chest level ten feet out before boiling around my midriff and tugging at me from behind as the water rushed back out over the reef. The backing peeled off the reel with amazing speed and disappeared into the white foam before coming into view again outside the surf zone. The line sliced through cresting waves before following the fish into open water beyond the reef.

The fish slowed, and I finally turned it about a hundred yards out. Slowly I began to work the fish back in toward shore. Then came the stalemate—I took in some line, the fish took out a little line.

Just as I thought things were going well, the fish burst toward open water again, as if it had just been hooked for the first time. I briefly lost sight of the fish as it passed behind a wave. My fly line disappeared into the wave's face as the wave rolled toward shore. Then for a brief moment, as it passed through the next wave, I could see the fish clearly. It was suspended motionless as the wave rose to full height before folding forward in crashing white foam. Each large scale on the tarpon flashed silver in the dimming light, the fish framed by the abyssal azure glow emanating from the depths.

And then it was gone. The hook had pulled. As I reeled in the fly line and backing, I felt the adrenaline shakes that so often come with big fish that are lost. I reeled in the line to check the fly and leader, but as I got the fly line to the rod tip, I had another strike. This time I never saw the fish. It never jumped, just headed for deep water at breathtaking speed. I never had a chance. I was unable to set the hook with the fish heading away so fast, and I had no chance at turning this fish, which was even stronger than the last. I held on to my rod and just watched. And then, like with the first fish, the line slackened and it was gone. This time the tippet had parted.

Some light still remained, so I tied on a new tippet and fly and headed back to my spot on the point. Amazingly, the action continued until it was too dark to see. As darkness painted everything in black ink, I felt my way shoreward, gathered my cast net and fly box, and started home. The stiff breeze had dropped with nightfall, but the surf still raced up the beach in fits of hissing foam.

I was sore and tired and had no fish to show for it. But I was happy. I'd been in the midst of a tarpon blitz and had it all to myself. I'd hooked who knows how many fish—eight, ten?—and felt the raw power of them all. None of them jumped quite like the first one, but I saw the reflection of a silver-hued sunset and heard the rattling gill plates again and again as the fish jumped through the dwindling light.

I returned to this spot each evening after work for the next five days. With each evening, the number of pelicans dropped and the sight of tarpon rolling through the surf was less frequent. But on each occasion, I was treated to feeding tarpon—not quite as chaotic as the first evening, but still four or five hookups each time. Then one evening there was just one pelican diving, and I saw no tarpon rolling. I caught a couple of barjacks and lost a barracuda, which are usually fun in their own right, but not the same after the tarpon blitz. A half dozen throws of the cast net netted only a handful of sprat. Most of the bait was gone, and the tarpon with them.

Protected Beaches

In contrast to exposed beaches, protected beaches are sheltered from waves by offshore barrier reefs or wide shallows, tend to be protected from winds, have more stable bottoms than exposed beaches, and tend to hold more gamefish prey. The stability allows the establishment and growth of seagrass and scattered mangroves that support diverse communities. Even if seagrass isn't abundant, the stable sandy bottom supports a rich prey community.

Protected beaches often have lush seagrass beds ending right at the shoreline. These beds provide fantastic habitat for fish, shrimp, crabs, clams, and many other prey items for gamefish. Healthy seagrass beds that reach the shoreline bring this productive habitat right to the feet of shoreline anglers. Although these aren't the kind of beaches that resorts prefer, these types of shorelines are fantastic for fly fishing and provide excellent habitat for gamefish and the prey they rely on for food. In areas with shallow-sloping bottoms, you'll often find a thin strip of sand between the beach and the beginning of the grass bed, especially along semiprotected beaches with small but consistent surf. The lower edge of this strip of sand indicates the low-water mark. In many cases, minor wave action has carved out a slight depression in this sand strip, and this slightly deeper indentation can hold baitfish, juvenile fish, and crabs.

In general, the very shallow seagrass beds that abut beaches have a less diverse community of organisms than deeper grass beds, and often fewer resident fish species. Mobile prey such as swimming crabs and small fish may be more important prey items for gamefish along these shallow, grassy shorelines. This is in part because the shallower areas can be harsh environments. They can become very warm and very low in oxygen during calm summer periods, and during extremely low tides they can be completely exposed to air. These phenomena are natural but create intolerable conditions for many species. Species that are best able to tolerate these conditions, or easily move in and out of these areas as conditions allow, are best suited for these habitats. Prey types that are of interest to fly anglers include swimming crabs, hermit crabs, mojarra, and mullet.

Examine the landward portion of the beach for signs of land hermit crabs: sets of parallel walking tracks on either side of a drag mark, made by the heavy shell the crab carries on its back. Other crabs—land crabs and ghost crabs—leave only the walking tracks. The land-dwelling hermit crabs sometimes forage along the water, and they search the shoreline looking for new shells to move into. They are most active at night but can be found lingering near the water's edge at dawn. A permit or bonefish foraging along a shoreline may fall for a well-placed fly imitating a hermit crab out of its shell. In addition, these same shorelines are home to marine hermit crabs, which may also be on the menu of some of your favorite gamefish.

Barjacks, bonefish, small snapper, and barracuda are the most common gamefish on these shallow shoreline grass flats, but during higher tides, especially at dawn or dusk, larger fish may venture up to the shorelines as well. Large barracuda sometimes lie in wait in depressions in the sand just off the shoreline and will make a meal out of needlefish and halfbeaks that cruise along these shallow shorelines. These large barracuda are especially wary, so it's important that you sight and cast to the fish from at least sixty feet away. Usually you get only a well-placed cast or two before the barracuda realizes something is amiss and moves off.

APPLYING WHAT YOU'VE LEARNED:

Strategy for Fishing Protected Beaches

My favorite strategy for these shallow, grass-lined beaches is to walk slowly along the beach, with the sun at my back, looking for bonefish and other gamefish cruising along the shoreline searching for food. Sometimes fish meander between the strip of sand and the seagrass; other times they remain over the sand bottom for long distances. Walking along the beach allows me to be higher up off the water, so I can see approaching fish better, and from farther away, than if I were wading. I am also able to backtrack along the beach to get a second shot at a fish that refused or didn't see my initial offering. By stooping to keep a low profile and backtracking along the beach, I once was able to try three different flies on a group of three bonefish before I finally got a take on a large crab pattern. In hindsight, a crab pattern should have been my first choice, since small swimming crabs are common in that strip of sand that parallels the beach. This brings me to an important point: Fish that are cruising along this sand strip next to the shoreline in shallow water are certainly searching for food, so a good presentation and the right fly should be the perfect combination for a hookup.

Protected shorelines provide great opportunities for using lighter-weight fly rods. My favorite rod for fishing protected beaches is a 9-foot 6-weight. It's often a long way to any substantial structure, such as reefs or rocks, along these beaches, so even if you connect with a strong fish, it is unlikely to run into structure and break off. And since you will often be casting small, lightly weighted flies, a 6-weight rod is perfectly matched to the flies and conditions and makes for an easy day of casting.

Semiprotected Beaches

Although some protected beaches are glass-calm under almost all conditions, others are exposed to waves during periods of high wind or experience a small but consistent surf. These semiprotected beaches tend to support even higher abundances of prey than fully protected beaches, in part because the occasional wave energy that washes them also mixes the water column and keeps the bottom waters from becoming depleted of oxygen. This maintains a diverse benthic community. So as long as the wave energy isn't so great that it harms the adjacent bottom habitats, semiprotected beaches can offer the most varied fly-fishing opportunities.

This does not imply that low-energy areas are not healthy ecosystems, only that a wider variety of prey species is able to take advantage of semi-protected areas.

The bottom slopes quickly off some semiprotected beaches, either to a deeper grass bed or to open sand bottom. Since sight fishing is tough in these conditions, and it is doubtful that you will sight and cast to a fish that is feeding on the deep bottom, flies that mimic moving prey, such as streamer imitations of baitfish or juvenile reef fish, are most appropriate. Species that cruise the deep grass beds along sandy beaches include bar-jacks, horse-eye jacks, permit, bonefish, barracuda, snapper, and tarpon. Barjacks and horse-eye jacks cruise the shoreline on hit-and-run attacks on baitfish schools or in search of small fish that wander too far from the safety of the seagrass. Small barracuda lie motionless in the vicinity of small patch reefs or rocks that are inhabited by small fish and take advantage of any fish that lets down its guard. Permit and bonefish cruise the shoreline in search of crabs, shrimp, or clams that lie hidden in the seagrass. Bonefish will also take advantage of a vulnerable fish, whether a baitfish, juvenile reef fish, or a small goby, as prey. In fact, bonefish will feed on rather large baitfish—sardines large enough to be caught with a size 2/0 Deceiver, for example—along these shorelines.

Along semiprotected sandy beaches with small surf and a sandy bottom, gamefish often forage just below the dropoff at the shoreline. They also ride the small surf up into the swash zone in search of prey such as small crabs, shrimp, and small fish. Standing on the beach and casting parallel to shore, you may be rewarded with hookups of palometa, jacks, and even the occasional bonefish. A cast away from shore might also result in a hookup, but usually only once the fly has been stripped almost to shore. Small shrimp or baitfish imitations, like a Gotcha, small Clouser, or Crazy Charlie, are good flies for this type of fishing.

APPLYING WHAT YOU'VE LEARNED:

Tarpon at Dusk

Another fun-filled evening of fishing for tarpon emphasizes the importance of timing. It was the first night of a full moon in July. After a twenty-minute hike to the beach, Kelly, Kurt, and I planned to spend the fading hours of sunlight casting for whatever fish we might be able to catch in the calm waters of this crescent-shaped bay. Once dusk arrived, we planned to throw out some bait for the large snapper that come into the shallow grass beds to feed on nights like this.

As we were unloading our packs, six-inch sprat erupted from the water. The small eruption suddenly turned into waves of fish. Then small tarpon, ten pounds or so, showed themselves. They rolled and splashed through the thick schools of baitfish, preceded each time by waves of flashing silver. All but the fishing gear was quickly forgotten. The air was soon filled with the sound of line being stripped from reels and whipping through the still evening air. Within the first minute of casting, someone had a fish on. A quick run, a strong jump, and the fly lay on the water surface as the small tarpon porpoised into open water.

As dusk slowly covered the cove, the action became more intense— sprat pressed ever closer to the sandy shoreline, and their attempts to escape became more and more frantic. Tarpon slashed through the bait as if this were their last meal. Then there were more tarpon, bigger, too, all within easy reach of a cast from shore. We had many fish hooked and lost, only to have the fly grabbed again as it fell from the first tarpon's mouth.

Since the fish were so close when they took the fly, many leaders were snapped. There just wasn't enough line beyond the rod tip to cushion the shock of a leaping tarpon. I thought about backing up the beach a bit to get some distance between me and the fish, but decided against it. It was better to be in the middle of the frenzy. To feel baitfish bounce against my feet as they searched for cover from slashing tarpon. To watch water boil at my feet as the tarpon chased herring from the water again and again. To see tarpon vault from the water as they chased down their prey. And to feel the power of a tarpon at point-blank range when it felt the bite of the hook. Then acrobatic leaps and rattling gill plates. Finally, the deep-water pull from far off the beach when a well-hooked fish was too tired to jump and shake the hook loose.

Dusk gave way to darkness. I could barely make out the fly as it fell to the water at the end of a cast. After action that lasted an hour and a half, the tarpon suddenly stopped feeding and disappeared. Still, I continued to cast until I could no longer see the fly before I gave up and retreated to camp. Although I knew the fishing was over long before I stopped casting, I wanted to let myself down slowly from the frantic pace of the tarpon blitz.

We set up camp, readied the small stove, and waited for the moon to rise. As we sat on the beach and gazed at the stars, we passed around the flask and talked about those fish. How this one jumped and that one headed for open water and never stopped. We wondered if the fish would return in the morning. We fell silent and listened to the surf on the reef that protected our cove, to the smaller waves that made it to shore, to the tree frogs as they stirred with the darkness, to the sounds of a tropical night.

GAMEFISH PREY

A few interesting prey species occur on semiprotected Caribbean beaches with consistent wave action. If the waves are not too rough, gamefish including palometa, bonefish, permit, and snapper will cruise along the beach, riding the wash in and out, readily slurping up mole crabs. Common species of mole crabs in the Caribbean include the Cuban mole crab, common mole crab, Puerto Rican mole crab, and purple surf crab. There are several mole crab fly patterns made of wool, chenille, spun deer hair, or a combination of these materials, weighted to ride on the bottom. Small, heavily weighted, tan Clousers are also productive. It is rare that I use a sinking line when fishing shorelines in the Caribbean, but fishing a mole crab pattern on an exposed beach is one of those rare occasions. A sinking line with a short leader will allow you to fish the fly so that it bounces along the bottom, making a good imitation of a mole crab.

Caribbean coquina clams (Donax denticulata) may be the only clam with the potential for imitation with a fly, although I am not aware of any successful attempts to date. Caribbean coquina clams are small, up to an inch long; triangular in shape; and vary in color from white to purple. They move from place to place in the intertidal zone of beaches, emerging from the sand, washing up or down the beach in the surf, and then reburrowing in the sand. They are most conducive to being imitated with a fly when they are on the move.

If you're lucky, you may come upon schools of baitfish moving back and forth along beaches in larger embayments. Often, smaller fish species such as anchovies or dwarf herring will be closer to shore, and larger species like herring will be farther off the beach. This pattern may change, however, depending on how active predators have been. I've seen schools of large sprat packed tightly against the shoreline when tarpon are present. Finding these baitfish schools is not always easy because they blend in well with their surroundings, they are often well below the surface, and the baitfish may be somewhat scattered if they are not being actively pursued by predators. Often these unmolested baitfish schools appear as shadows over the bottom. If baitfish schools are present, it's a good bet that larger fish are not far away, and it might only be a matter of time before the action begins.

I like to walk large, semiprotected bays looking for signs of baitfish. If I find baitfish, this is where I concentrate my efforts. It's always worth casting in the vicinity of schooled baitfish, even if gamefish aren't actively feeding. You never know if jacks, barracuda, snapper, bonefish, or other gamefish are merely resting and ready to pounce on a fish that gets separated from the school. If there are no obvious signs of baitfish, I stop along the beach at intervals of thirty yards or so and blind-cast for a few minutes, hoping to pick up cruising fish. The most common catch along these shorelines are jacks, although palometa (a member of the jack family and relative of the permit), small barracuda, cero mackerel, and various snappers may also grab the fly. While it is common to find jacks and barracuda eager to take a fly from midmorning to midafternoon, it is morning and evening that are generally best for tarpon.

TROPICAL BEACHROCK SHORELINES

Many Caribbean shorelines consist of hard limestone pavement called beachrock, which is the solidified remains of old sand and coral reefs. One type of beachrock shoreline is low-lying and may be intermixed with sandy beach. On the seaward side, beachrock often drops abruptly into the water. This drop may be only a foot or a few feet, and in deeper spots, an undercut has usually been eroded by wave action. At first glance, it doesn't look like great fish habitat, but if the dropoff is deep enough, this undercut can provide shelter to numerous juvenile reef fish and gamefish. With careful examination, you may find small fish in the tidepools along beachrock shorelines, which can give you an indication of appropriate sizes and colors of flies to use.

Undercut beachrock habitat seems to support more small fish when it's adjacent to seagrass because the beachrock provides shelter next to a good foraging area. But leaving the shelter of beachrock to forage in adjacent seagrass carries risks for small fish, as jacks, palometa, snapper, barracuda, and other predators are always on the prowl along these shorelines. In areas that have deeper dropoffs of a few feet or more, subadult and adult snapper and grouper may set up residence in holes or crevices and will charge from their shelters if prey swims close by. Other gamefish take advantage of invertebrate communities that can be found here. Permit and triggerfish feed on the small urchins that seem to inhabit almost every crevice of some beachrock shorelines.

Although beachrock that is bordered by a sand bottom doesn't support nearly as many small fish, it does provide a source of shelter on an otherwise open bottom, so small fish use this habitat as shelter as well.

Jacks and palometa are among the most common gamefish found here, but you will also find snook, bonefish, and small tarpon. Beachrock that is bordered by rubble is a popular spot for barjacks and blue runners, since the rubble also provides habitat for small fish. You might also find permit rummaging along beachrock edges or in nearby rubble in search of reef crabs, shrimp, and urchins.

In some locations, you might find that a low shelf of beachrock drops dramatically into the ocean, but more often the shoreline slope continues underwater. Steep shorelines often occur as points at either end of a sandy beach or may extend for a considerable distance along a coast. The deeper dropoffs usually support fringing coral reefs, so they are home to reef fish of all shapes and sizes and provide shoreline anglers access to larger fish that inhabit deeper water. In fact, these steep-sloped beachrock shorelines may provide shorebound anglers their best chance of access to large coral reef fish. Barjacks, blue runners, horse-eye jacks, and crevalle jacks can be found cruising the edges of these steep dropoffs, and these jacks are often large, as are the barracuda. Snapper and grouper are usually resident on the reefs below these shorelines but are often well hidden within the reef's many crevices. They must be coaxed out of hiding by fishing your fly dangerously close to the sharp corals. Once hooked, these fish will try their best to quickly get back into the safety of their crevices in the reef.

Fishing along steep-sloping beachrock calls for larger flies than you use along shallow beaches and on grass flats. All white Deceivers, white with blue or yellow backs and chartreuse over white (size 2/0), will do well along these steep, rocky shorelines. Although the deep water may have you thinking of sinking fly lines, the shoreline and adjacent reef are full of snags that seem to reach out and grab sinking lines, so when fishing these areas from shore, use a floating line. If gamefish are there and are hungry, they'll come up for the fly. Save the sinking line for fishing these locations from a boat. A 10-weight fly line is often necessary along these steep shorelines.

These rocky coastlines are often in high-energy areas that can be pounded by heavy seas, so fish them with caution and only in calm conditions. In addition, the limestone that makes up these rocky shores and the sedimentary rock that is sometimes mixed in are constantly being eroded, and loose rocks make for difficult footing. Erosion of limestone often creates sharp, craggy edges and crevices, which make for tough walking—and painful scrapes and bruises should you fall—so wear strong-soled shoes and choose your steps carefully. If you fish these locations from a boat, have only one person fish while the other stays at the helm. The swells and surf can be tricky along these rocky shorelines, so it's important to be in full control of the boat at all times.

STEWARDSHIP

Beaches are the launching point from which we begin many of our journeys into the saltwater world. By absorbing the force of the oceans, beaches protect barrier islands and the estuaries that lie behind them, and buffer the land from the erosive forces of the sea. And despite the dynamic nature of beach habitats, a suite of animals has evolved into beach specialists and has come to depend on the ecological integrity of these environments. Alterations that affect beaches also affect these animals.

Beaches also protect marine habitats from land-based human activities, and breaching the protective bulwark between land and sea has negative impacts on both the land and sea habitats that depend on the nature of the beaches. Hotels often import sand to create beaches for tourism. In the tropics, imported sand covers and smothers seagrass and corals, and as the sand erodes, it is carried by currents to adjacent areas, where it further damages habitats. Given a choice, consider staying at hotels that incorporate the natural environment into their marketing and development plans, such as restricting all buildings to behind the beach zone. These hotels are less likely to compromise the integrity of coastal ecosystems and more likely to provide better access to good fishing and ecotourism. Beach nourishment activities in subtropical and warm-temperate regions may have less obvious but equally damaging effects on beach-dependent organisms. A negative impact on the habitat and associated organisms will have a negative impact on gamefish. For example, mole crabs can be absent or in low abundance for years following beach renourishment, which has direct implications for gamefish.

Alterations of the longshore flow of sand can have dramatic effects on coastal habitats as well. Jetties interrupt the transport of sand via the longshore current. The beach may build up nicely around a new jetty, but beaches downstream starve for new sand and slowly lose ground. Longshore bars are similarly affected.

These are just some of the ecological considerations weighing the benefits and disadvantages of making alterations to our beaches.

Chapter 7

Rubble Flats and Sand Flats of the Tropics

Rubble flats and sand flats provide great opportunities for sight-fishing in the tropics. Neither habitat has a lot of structure, but both support sufficient numbers of prey to provide good feeding areas for bonefish, permit, snapper, and a host of other gamefish that venture into these shallow habitats to feed at high tide. Sand flats have been well covered in numerous books on flats fishing, so most of the discussion here is limited to prey of this habitat. Rubble flats, on the other hand, have been shortchanged in the fishing literature, so this section delves a bit deeper.

RUBBLE FLATS OF THE BACKREEF
Rubble flats are my favorite shallow-water habitats of Caribbean islands because they are home to permit. Even if you don't find permit, you may still find bonefish, jacks, barracuda, triggerfish, snapper, small sharks, and other gamefish on backreef rubble flats. The typical rubble flat lies behind a coral reef, offshore of which is deeper water. Seagrass and algae eventually take hold in the backreef and spread into the lagoon, which results in a further slowing of currents and more deposition of debris and sand. In some spots, small colonies of finger coral grow among the seagrass. When everything works out just right, a shallow rubble flat results.

Water depth is the primary factor affecting whether you will find gamefish on a backreef rubble flat. The two factors most influencing the water depth are tides and waves.

Tides
Tidal range in the Caribbean is generally small, the water level changing a foot or less through a normal tidal cycle. Still, gamefish respond to even minor tidal fluctuations. On shallow flats, gamefish may be completely absent during low tide but may venture far onto the flat in search of food at high tide. Many times I've seen this occur even though I've been unable to detect a difference in water depth between tides.

In general, fishing the backreef flats is best from the latter half of the incoming tide through the first hour or so of the outgoing tide. In addition, backreef flats that hold good water throughout the tidal cycle are great places to search for fish at dawn and dusk, regardless of tides. I am not a big fan of early mornings, but when living in the Caribbean, I frequently dragged myself out of bed before dawn to walk my favorite backreef flat at first light.

Waves

Waves are almost constantly assaulting the outer edge of the reef that protects backreef rubble flats. And as on sandy beaches, the surf pushes water onto the reef. Some of this water is deflected seaward by the coral reef, but some of the water passes over or around the reef and onto the flat. If the reef is relatively deep or the tide is particularly high, a considerable amount of water can push over the reef and create an appreciable current on the flat. In addition, the remnants of larger waves that crashed onto the reef can maintain some of their form and roll across the flat. Both the wave-induced current and the small waves continuing across the flat can dislodge prey hiding among the rubble.

In contrast, other reefs and flats are shallow, so under normal conditions, there is little wave energy that continues over the reef onto the flat. These shallow, more protected rubble flats offer a different challenge in presenting a fly to a feeding permit or bonefish. The shallow water means the fish may be more wary of a fly hitting the water, and since the fly can quickly become lost in the crevices among the rubble, you must cast it closer to the fish to make sure it gets noticed.

Whether or not the reef and flat are shallow, extended periods with strong surf can increase the water depth more than tides. The constant surf will actually push more water onto the flat than can escape back to sea through cuts and channels in the reef, which can result in higher-than-normal water depths for the duration of the strong surf. Gamefish will take advantage of these high-water periods just as if the high water were due to an extended high tide. An added bonus to the near constant flushing of new water from the incoming waves is that backreef rubble flats rarely get as warm as nearby shallows with less water flow, so they can be good places to fish when other flats are too warm for permit and bonefish.

Fishing for Permit on Rubble Flats

I began working my way across the flat as the light of the dawn sky slowly overtook the glow of the full moon. There was just enough wind to ripple the surface of the small surf rolling gently across the reef and spreading onto the flat. As I stripped out the usual fifty feet of fly line, I saw movement out of the corner of my eye. Glancing to my left, I saw the wake of a permit slowly cruising across the flat. I checked the knot connecting my urchin fly pattern to my tippet and false-cast to get fly line out of the rod tip. The permit tailed 40 feet away.

I made a false cast, and then dropped the fly four feet in front of the fish. The unweighted fly dropped slowly to the bottom, but the fish moved off to the left without seeing it. I made another cast, placing the fly a little closer in front of the slowly moving fish. As the fly dropped, the fish surged quickly forward. I saw the end of the fly line jump and set the hook with a strip strike.

The fish gave a small head shake, rubbed its nose in the bottom, then bulled fifty feet, rubbed its nose again, and surged another fifty feet. I followed after it as best I could, getting closer to the reef and all of its sharp coral with each step. Then, suddenly, the fish had had enough of the shallow water and bolted through the reef. The rod captured the vibration of the fly line scraping across the coral as it passed through the reef—fraying leader, shredding fly line, and testing the durability of the backing. I lightened the reel's drag and followed the path of the line as quickly as I could, carefully picking my way through the maze of mostly dead coral, freeing the line from the labyrinth of the fish's pass through the reef. All the time, the fish was still heading seaward, by now into the deeper water outside the shallow reef. Then suddenly the line was free, the curve in the backing quickly straightened—the fish was still on!

I was able to apply some pressure, and the fish slowed and finally stopped taking out line. It began swimming back and forth in the deeper water. As the fish began to tire, its dorsal and tail fins broke the surface. I slowly gained the edge in the battle for backing and finally the fly line. I began to walk back to the flat and the fish followed, tired now and finning at the surface.

As I guided the permit over the reef, the sight of shallow water gave it new energy, and the fish rubbed its nose on every coral head it passed. I worked the fish onto the flat many times, only to have it regain its strength and rush back into the reef.

Suddenly the situation worsened—after bulling its way into the reef once again, the fish refused my pressure pulling it back to the flat and began to swim back and forth in the reef. I followed as best I could, rod held high as I wove my way through the coral. Then it happened. I lost track of my footing, tripped on a piece of broken coral, and went down. Full body. Flat on my face. Rod, still in hand, fully submerged, an extension of my sprawled right arm. I was completely soaked. I regained my footing and brought the rod back into the upright position. Water gushed off my wide-brimmed hat and flooded from my soaked shirt. I couldn't believe it—the fish was still on! Then I felt a stinging pain in my legs. A quick glance down revealed a little blood, but it didn't look bad. My attention returned to the fish with even greater focus than before.

The fish continued to move back and forth across the reef, but this time I stayed put. I didn't dare try navigating the reef maze again. And I was starting to feel the pain of the coral cuts on my legs. I eventually gained enough line so there was only twenty feet of fly line and leader between us. I could clearly see the irridescent glow of the permit's silvery sides and the yellow hue to its belly brightened by the battle. Even from the side, I could see its shoulders were broad. The fish was tired and had conceded, so I began walking it back onto the flat. With only another thirty feet to a safe spot to land the fish, the line went slack. The leader had finally failed, not with a snap, but with a muted parting. It took both me and the fish by surprise. I stared at the leader in disbelief as the permit continued to swim in the direction I had been leading it. Then the fish felt its freedom, veered off, and slowly swam over the reef. The remnants of the frayed leader dangling from the rod tip and spikes of plastic protruding like cactus spines from the fly line wound tightly on the reel told the story.

The pain suddenly reminded me of my fall, and I realized the water around my legs was discolored. I looked down to see that most of my left leg and my right thigh were solid brush burn—scraped, raw, and bruised, but no blood. The blood was from a cut on my right kneecap in the distinct pattern of brain coral. I checked for urchin spines, but fortunately found none. Defeated, I walked back to shore, sat on the beach, and rested, as I let the gash in my knee dry closed. After a few minutes, I made my way back to my truck and home.

Permit like to come through the reef to access backreef rubble flats, often riding the energy of the remnant waves through the reef into the shallow water. I've even seen large fish swimming sideways to get through particularly shallow areas. This is important to know for two reasons. First, you can look for cuts in the reef that provide easier access to such large fish and focus your efforts on these portions of the flat. Second, when hooked, permit will probably hightail it right back through the reef into deeper water, and you should be prepared for this. Both points can influence your fly-fishing strategy.

Once on the flat, permit will cruise the flat, often with their dorsal fins above the water, occasionally stopping to feed, digging their noses into the bottom and flipping their large, forked tails into the air. Prey items for permit in these areas include small clams and snails, sea urchins, crabs, and shrimp. After feeding along a stretch of flat, the fish usually head back through the reef to deeper water. In my experience, for any particular flat, permit feed in the same general pattern. They cross the reef in specific areas, travel along the flat in the same direction, and feed more actively on some sections of the flat than others, often at the same time in the tidal cycle. More intriguing, an individual permit's feeding pattern often persists on the flat for a few days, so as long as you don't spook a fish while trying to catch it, you can return the next day and have a decent shot at finding the fish again under the same conditions.

Once you've spotted a permit, the challenge is to present the fly close enough that the fish will see it, but not so close that you spook the fish. When feeding on the bottom, a permit's circle of vision is limited; it seems to focus on a rather small section of bottom just in front of, or directly below, its swimming path, so getting the fly close is paramount. It's like casting to teacup moving across the bottom. One option is to cast your fly directly in front of a slowly cruising fish. This is tough because a fly that splats down on the water will often spook the permit.

A second option is to anticipate the path of a cruising fish and cast the fly along this path, well ahead of the fish. As the fish approaches the fly, give it a small twitch. Though this approach works well over deeper seagrass, it can be tough to impossible on shallow rubble flats. Either the small waves rolling across the flat will move your fly out of the fish's path, or the fly will settle to the bottom and sink into one of the crevices among the rubble and never be seen by the fish. There is nothing quite as maddening as having to wait for a permit to pass by before wading over to unsnag a fly wedged in the rubble.

The third, and best, option is to cast directly in front or to the side of a feeding, tailing fish. Let the fly drop to the bottom. If the permit doesn't react, give the fly a slight twitch, and again let it rest. Most of the prey you'll be imitating with the flies you cast to permit won't move much once they think they've been spotted. Instead, they try to hide in the bottom. Too much movement to a fly will often send a permit in the other direction.

For each of these options, small waves rolling across the flat or wave-induced currents can make fly presentation difficult. But at times when the sea is calm and the water surface is like a mirror, the permit are very wary and easily spooked. It's a challenging situation under all conditions, which is part of what makes fishing for permit on backreef flats so much fun.

If you are lucky enough to hook a permit on a backreef flat, you will be faced with the challenge of keeping your leader in one piece as the fish heads to deeper water—directly through the coral reef. Of the numerous permit I've hooked on the fly on these flats, I've lost all to leaders that were cut on corals.

So you have two options. One strategy, albeit risky, is to clamp down on the drag and hope your line and rod hold as you prevent the fish from running through the reef. A second strategy is to give the fish plenty of line to run through the reef to deeper water, and let it tire itself out. Once the fish has tired, it will come to the surface, and you can work it back over the reef onto the flat. This is the stage of the fight where I have lost many fish, due to either bad luck or impatience on my part. So take your time, even though all of your senses tell you to hurry.

SHORELINE RUBBLE FLATS
Other rubble flats lie close to or along the shoreline. It is common to come across small flats of coral rubble mixed with sand and seagrass as you drive around a Caribbean island. The land topography often continues into the water, so pay particular attention to flat stretches of land where the road passes close to the water. The road may provide shoreline access to a wadable shallow-water rubble flat.

Flats that are adjacent to busy roads or walkways are most productive at dawn and dusk, when traffic is low. However, fish that are resident in busy areas sometimes adjust to the activity and are not so easily spooked. That doesn't mean these fish will be easy to catch. They might not be easily spooked, but they might still be picky eaters or wary of poorly presented flies, or because the flats are so accessible, they might be heavily fished.

Other rubble flats are harder to find but can be worth the effort. Small flats off the beaten track will likely have less fishing pressure, so they may hold more fish. These isolated flats have provided me with great fishing over the years. If you have time before your trip, do your best to find a boater's map, or at least a topographical map. For U.S. waters, the United States Geological Survey (USGS) is a good place to start, as is the National Oceanographic and Atmospheric Administration (NOAA). The Internet is a valuable resource for both traditional maps and aerial photos that can reveal the locations of likely flats. Most islands have a government fisheries bureau, which is worth a phone call, though results are not guaranteed. I've found some very good maps in old fishing and sailing books. You don't need a map detailed enough for navigation, just one that shows you general patterns of inshore water depths and locations of reefs and shoals.

Fly-fishing strategies for fishing these flats will vary. On the narrow flats that parallel the shoreline, I prefer to slowly walk the shoreline searching for signs of fish. Walking on the shore provides a higher vantage point so I can see fish at a greater distance. I am also able to quickly move to a location down the shoreline should I see activity such as a tailing fish. Don't be surprised to see fish right up against the shoreline, especially at high tide or at dawn or dusk. If you don't see fish after a pass along the shoreline, you may want to wade the middle of the flat. If this strategy doesn't work, wade to the outer edge of the flat and try casting into deeper water. Such blind-casting might result in a nice jack, snapper, barracuda, or even the occasional small tarpon. If you don't see fish on your first visit to a flat, try again at a different time of day or a different point in the tidal cycle. I know of a few flats where large schools of bonefish cruise the rubble zone in the last hour and a half of the incoming tide but are completely absent at other points in the tidal cycle. Still other flats have feeding fish at dawn and dusk, seemingly regardless of the tide.

Gamefish Prey of Rubble Flats
The blend of rubble, seagrass, and scattered corals supports a diverse assortment of prey species. Rubble flats with seagrass mixed in have the same suite of prey as seagrass habitats, while rubble flats without seagrass harbor a subset of seagrass prey species. In addition, the many crevices among the rubble are good hiding places for an assortment of other prey species.

Chief among them are small members of the spider crab family (Majidae). These crabs feed along the bottom and scurry for the undersides of shells and rubble when chased. Green reef crab *(Mithrax sculptus)* and tan reef crab *(Mithrax coryphe),* and to a lesser extent gray pitho crab *(Pitho aculeata)* and pitho crab *(Pitho mirabilis),* top the list and are eaten by bonefish and permit.

The carapaces of reef crabs are triangular with rounded edges. The pitho crabs are teardrop-shaped, with their eyes at the narrow end of the teardrop. All four species listed here grow to one inch but are often smaller. The abundance of each species varies among locations, but the green reef crab is usually the most common in shallow rubble flats mixed with seagrass.

When choosing a fly to imitate spider crabs, your choice of color can be simplified to the basics: dark green, brown, or tan, depending on the species. The pitho and gray pitho crabs are tan to gray in color, the green reef crab is dark green, and the tan reef crab is tan.

Porcelain crabs (family Porcellanidae) also inhabit shallow rubble flats. The lined porcelain crab *(Petrolisthes galathinus)* is especially abundant on

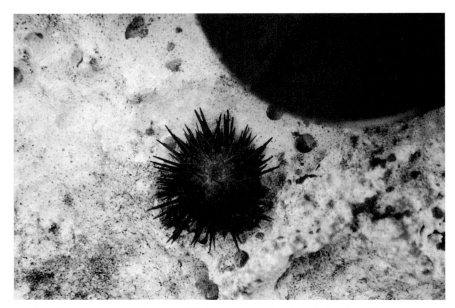

Small urchins are often abundant on rubble flats and along beach-rock shorelines. They are eaten by permit and bonefish.

finger corals growing on mixed rubble and seagrass flats. The lined por-celain crab is small, at two-thirds of an inch, and medium green. It has an oval carapace and oversize, flattened claws.

When fishing flies that imitate these small crabs, the action you give the fly should be minimal. All species of walking crabs remain close to shelter, whether under a rock, among seagrass blades or algae, or burrow-ing into the bottom, and they don't scurry over long stretches of open bot-tom when chased. You may want to give your fly a couple twitches to get the attention of the bonefish or permit, and then let it sit still.

Mantis shrimp live in holes among the rubble or shells and are simi-lar in appearance to the praying mantis land insect, thus the name. When living among sparse seagrass with coral rubble or open sand bottom, the golden mantis (*Pseudosquilla ciliata*) is tan in coloration. The rock mantis (*Gonodactylus oerstedii*) is typically dark green or black but also varies to match its habitat. It is mostly found among rock and coral crevices. Man-tis shrimp usually don't venture far from their burrows and are most active at night. When chased, their defense posture is to turn and face their adversaries while retreating backward toward their burrows. While these species of mantis shrimp can reach four inches, usually only the smaller ones are eaten by bonefish and permit.

SAND FLATS

Sand flats are pretty simple habitats. There's not much structure to shelter prey or to hold gamefish, yet sand flats can be great places to fish for bonefish, permit, snapper, and a host of other species because they present an easy habitat for gamefish to feed. The more complex the shelter of the habitat, the harder it is for predators to find and catch prey. So although open sand bottoms don't host as many prey as seagrass, a gamefish's chance of finding and catching prey are much higher.

Spend some time wading sand flats, and you'll soon conclude that not all sand flats are created equal. The type of open bottom reveals the typical wave and current conditions an area experiences and can give you a good idea of whether it is a good feeding area for bonefish. Sandy areas with waves or ridges are frequently exposed to waves or currents that cause shifting sands, which tend to have fewer prey organisms than more stable sediments. Stable sediments also tend to be softer because of mixed mud and detritus due in part to the activities of the resident animals, which makes these bottoms more hospitable to more organisms. Sand bottoms occur in areas with more wave or current energy than mud bottoms, or in locations far removed from a source of soft, fine sediments that make muddy bottoms. Rivers, streams, estuaries, or lagoons with currents that might carry sediments are potential sources of soft-bottom sediments.

The survival strategies of species that live in areas with stable sand bottoms provide clues to their presence. Many of the species that live on sand flats dig burrows, and they show themselves by the presence of these burrows. These species may filter feed, eat detritus that is delivered by tides, or emerge from their burrows to feed on the surrounding bottom. Clams bury themselves in the sand and extend tubular siphons to the surface in order to filter plankton and other food from the water. Some worm burrows are as big around as a penny, and some species of worms and shrimp discharge large amounts of sand out of their burrows. Such clues indicate that you are on a "live" sand flat that supports gamefish prey.

Finding a live flat is an essential first step to finding gamefish. Most gamefish try to get away with as little travel as possible in their search for a meal, so once they've found a good place to feed, they'll use the area repeatedly. After you've found a live flat, you can set about figuring out when and how gamefish take advantage of the food source.

Gamefish Prey on Sand Flats

Polychaetes are segmented worms that come in many body shapes. The many species can be divided into two general categories: tube dwellers and free-moving. Among the most recognizable tube dwellers are numerous filter-feeding species with large, bushy crowns that extend from the worm's tube or burrow. Christmas tree worms are typical of this group. The colorful crowns quickly retract into the tube if the worm senses danger. Weighted flies with marabou plumes are good imitations of these polychaetes. Free-moving polychaetes search for food along the bottom and may live in a tube, burrow into the sediment when seeking shelter, or simply live on the bottom. They are shaped as variations on the earthworm theme. Bonefish are the most notable gamefish that eat polychaetes with regularity.

A good number of crustacean species that occur in other habitats also live on sand flats. Those flats that border grass beds or mangroves receive an overflow of prey from these habitats; sand flats far removed from other habitats harbor a smaller list of prey species. Golden mantis shrimp dig burrows in the sand and emerge at night to feed. Mantis shrimp on sand flats are tan to closely match the color of the bottom. Snapping shrimp also inhabit sand flats. On hard sand bottoms, snapping shrimp shelter in pieces of shell or rubble, as will reef and pitho crabs. In softer-bottomed sand flats, snapping shrimp dig burrows. Juvenile common shrimp, up to three inches long, also burrow into soft sand, leaving a small hole for water exchange, and emerge at night to feed. Many species of swimming crabs also inhabit shallow sand flats and usually have excellent camouflage coloration.

Finally, numerous species of small fish are specially adapted to the sand flats, including a few species of small gobies that are either clear or blandly colored to match the sand bottom. The goldspot goby *(Gnatholepis thompsoni)*, dash goby *(Gobionellus saepepallens)*, and orangespotted goby *(Nes longus)*, which makes itself comfortable in the burrows of snapping shrimp, are examples of gobies that live in burrows on sand flats. Pearly razorfish *(Hemipteronotus novacula)* and rosy razorfish *(Hempiteronotus martinicensis)* are members of the wrasse family (Labridae) and live on sand flats four feet deep or more. Razorfish hover above the bottom and dive into the sand when threatened. When living over sand, both species are pale in coloration.

Since so many of the prey that inhabit sand flats either live permanently underground or emerge at night to feed, it makes sense that gamefish that feed on sand flats have a good sense of smell. They use this sense of smell to find prey. Filter-feeding prey, like clams and some species of worms, draw water in one burrow opening, filter plankton and other food from the water, and then expel the water out another burrow opening. Gamefish that feed on these species can detect the outflow. Even organisms that don't filter feed aren't safe. Crabs, shrimp, and other gamefish prey have to pass water over their gills to obtain oxygen from the water, and this leaves a scent on the water that exits their gills. Gamefish are sometimes able to detect this water and track down unseen prey. Bonefish and permit are especially noted for this ability to smell their prey.

Strategies for Sand Flats

Since sand flats don't offer much in the way of shelter, their primary use by gamefish is as a feeding area. Granted, bonefish can get into such shallow water that they can escape sharks, dolphins, large barracuda, and other larger predators, but when they are that shallow, they can be targeted by ospreys and thus remain wary.

Because sand flats are so shallow, they can quickly become very warm in the heat of the summer sun and very cold after the passing of a cold front, in both cases making the flats inhospitable to gamefish. Given the wide open character of sand flats, gamefish are usually on the move, and the challenge for fly anglers is to interpret the flats to figure out the best places to intercept these traveling gamefish.

The biggest factor influencing the use of sand flats by gamefish is tides. It doesn't take much of a tidal change to influence the coming and going of gamefish. The well-known standard behavior for gamefish on sand flats is to follow the rising tide onto a flat and to reverse course and leave the flat with the dropping tide. Early in the incoming tide, the edges are the first places to look for fish coming onto the flat. As the tide rises, fish come over the edge and onto the flat, often using traditional routes to access the flat. At the very least, this behavior pattern means that even exploring a flat at low tide can bring rewards. If you happen upon fish concentrated along an edge, you're probably close to one of these traditional avenues of access. With a little searching, you'll probably find a small channel nearby that, even if very shallow, serves as the first access point to the flat on the rising tide. But before you get too excited, there's a catch—the locations of these avenues may change depending on the magnitude of the tide.

Spring tides occur with every new and full moon and cause higher-than-normal high tides and lower-than-normal low tides. The high spring tides flood more of the sand flats than at any other time in the tidal cycle, so gamefish tend to venture farther onto the flats in search of prey. And since more water moves onto and off the flats during spring tides, the currents are stronger. The combined higher water and stronger currents can cause a shift toward shallower locations as avenues of access for gamefish waiting to get onto the flats and exit avenues on the dropping tide. In contrast, neap tides occur at the first and last quarters of the moon and cause lower-than-normal high tides and higher-than-normal low tides. These tend to limit gamefish to smaller portions of the flat and to deeper access points.

Each type of tide has its advantages. During spring tides, gamefish know they can access parts of the flat that are normally unreachable, so they are eager to move onto the flat once the tide begins to flood. But because the amount of time between high and low tides stays the same regardless of tide height, the permit, bonefish, snapper, or crevalle jack must cover a lot more ground in a limited amount of time. In the worst case, although the shallow sand flat is "live," it is too far from the safety of deep water to attract gamefish in all but the most extreme tides. In the best case, gamefish will flood the flat with the tide and feed aggressively as they move through. In general, because of the risk associated with traveling too far on a high spring tide, gamefish start to leave the shallows in the early part of the falling tide.

Gamefish are still keyed to the tides during the neap tides but tend not to venture as far onto the flat or to feed as aggressively on the rising tide. While this might seem like a negative, it's not, because gamefish are more likely to feed throughout the tidal cycle than to focus on the rising and early falling tides. This is especially true of bonefish and permit.

The one caveat to following the tides in your fishing is the weather. Specifically, atmospheric pressure and wind can affect water level more than the tides in much of the tropics, where the normal tidal range is minor. High pressure and strong offshore winds cause lower-than-expected high and low tides, whereas low pressure and onshore winds cause higher-than-expected water levels for both tides. Given the tuned-in nature of shallow-water gamefish, these weather changes can influence gamefish behavior much the same as spring and neap tides.

Tides and wind move water, which creates currents. Most of the time, it's true that you'll find gamefish on sand flats moving into the current, but take an occasional peek behind you as you wade a sand flat for that occasional fish that rides with the current.

A less obvious aspect of currents is that they affect water temperature. During warm times of year, the water on sand flats can become too warm for comfort for gamefish. Rather than abandon the food-rich flats for the season, gamefish use the currents to their advantage. Tidal currents carry cooler water from adjacent deeper areas onto the flats with the rising tide, and if the incoming tide is strong enough, gamefish will ride the cooler water onto the flat to feed. During colder seasons, the midday sun will heat the shallow water over the sand flats. As the tide rises and is warmed by the sun and by the sun-baked sand, gamefish move onto the flat to feed. When the sun-warmed water begins to depart the flat on a dropping tide, it's worth searching out channels that drain the flat. Game-fish holding at the ends of these channels get the benefit of intercepting prey that is washed off the flat, as well as the extra warmth of the solar-heated water.

So when coming up with a strategy for fly-fishing a sand flat, you need to consider tides, wind, atmospheric pressure, currents, and tempera-ture. Whether you find fish or not, it is worth making notes of the condi-tions on the flat, and fishing the flat under different conditions. It won't take long for you to figure out the patterns of the fish. If you are traveling to an unknown area for just a couple days, take the time to figure out the local tides and weather conditions, and make your best guess on where the fishing conditions will be optimum.

Appendix A

Table of Common Gamefish

This table shows the most common coastal gamefish caught by fly anglers, the regions where they typically occur, the habitats they most often use, and the prey groups they eat most.

Common Name	Scientific Name	Regions	Major Habitats	Major Prey Groups*
Bonefish	*Albula vulpes*	T (S)	S, M, O, B, R	crustaceans, fish, echinoderms, polychaetes
Tarpon	*Megalops atlanticus*	T, S, W	VO, VC	fish, crustaceans
Permit	*Trachinotus falcatus*	T, S	S, M, O, R, B	crustaceans, echinoderms, fish
Florida pompano	*Trachinotus carolinus*	S, W	B, VO	crustaceans
Crevalle jack	*Caranx hippos*	T, S	VO	fish
Blue runner	*Caranx crysos*	T, S	VO	fish
Bar jack	*Caranx ruber*	T	VO	fish
Horse-eye jack	*Caranx latus*	T	VO, C	fish
Common snook	*Centropomus undecimalis*	T, S	S, M, B, OB	fish, crustaceans
Red drum	*Sciaenops ocellatus*	S, W	S, M, SM, OB, O, B	crustaceans, fish, polychaetes, echinoderms
Ladyfish	*Elops saurus*	T, S	VO, VC	fish
Spotted seatrout	*Cynoscion nebulosus*	S, W	S, M, B	crustaceans, fish
Weakfish	*Cynoscion regalis*	W, S	SM, S, B	fish, crustaceans
Cobia	*Rachycentron canadum*	S, W	VO	fish, squid, crabs
Great barracuda	*Sphyraena barracuda*	T (S)	VO	fish
Gray snapper	*Lutjanus griseus*	T, S	M, S	crustaceans, fish
Mutton snapper	*Lutjanus analis*	T	S, M, C	crustaceans, fish

Common Name	Scientific Name	Regions	Major Habitats	Major Prey Groups*
Yellowtail snapper	*Ocyurus chrysurus*	T	S, C	fish
Bluefish	*Pomatomus saltatrix*	W, S	VO	fish
Striped bass	*Morone saxatilis*	W	VO, VC	fish, crustaceans
Spanish mackerel	*Scomberomorus maculatus*	W, S	B	fish
Cero	*Scomberomorus regalis*	T	B	fish
Gulf flounder	*Paralichthys albigutta*	S, T	O, S, OB	fish
Southern flounder	*Paralichthys lethostigma*	T	O, S, OB	fish

Region: T = tropics; S = subtropics; W = warm-temperate.

Habitat: S = seagrass; M = mangrove; OB = oyster bar; SM = salt marsh; O = open bottom; B = beach; C = coral reef; R = rubble flat; VO = various habitats—mobile species that can be associated with numerous habitats in open areas (e.g., seagrass bed = open area); VC = various habitats—mobile species associated with habitats in open and enclosed areas (e.g., marsh creeks = enclosed area).

* Most dominant prey in the diet. Only the major prey groups that are amenable to imitation with a fly are listed.

Appendix B

Table of Major Prey Groups

This table shows the major groups of prey most eaten by common coastal gamefish, by region and by habitat where they occur most often.

Group	Family	Family Name	Region	Major Habitats	Status
Crustaceans	Mud crabs	Xanthidae	T, S, W	S, M, OB, SM	R
	Swimming crabs	Portunidae	T, S, W	S, M, SM, B	R/S
	Spider crabs	Majidae	T, S, W	S, OB, R	R
	Common shrimp	Penaeidae	T, S, W	S, M, SM, OB	R/S
	Snapping shrimp	Alpheidae	T, S	S, M, OB, R, C	R
	Mantis shrimp	Squillidae	T	S, R, C	R
Fish	Killifish	Cyprinodontidae	T, S, W		R
	Mollies	Poeciliidae	T, S		R
	Gobies	Gobiidae	T, S, W	S, OB, M, R, C	R
	Blennies	Blenniidae	T, S, W	S, OB, M, C	R
	Mojarra	Gerreidae	T, S	S, M, OB, O, B	R/S
	Herrings	Clupeidae	T, S, W	S, OB, O, B	S
	Anchovies	Engraulidae	T, S, W	S, M, SM, O, B	R/S
	Silversides	Atherinidae	T, S, W	M, SM, OB, B	R
	Mullets	Mugilidae	T, S, W	S, M, O, B	R/S
Worms	Polychaetes	Various	T, S, W	S, M, R, C, SM	R
Echinoderms	Brittle stars	Various	T, S, W	S, OB, C, R	R
	Sea Urchins	Various	T, S	S, C, R	R

Region: T = tropics; S = subtropics; W = warm-temperate.
Habitat: S = seagrass; M = mangrove; OB = oyster bar; SM = salt marsh; O = open bottom;
  B = beach; C = coral reef; R = rubble flat; VO = various habitats—mobile species that can
  be associated with numerous habitats in open areas (e.g., seagrass bed = open area);
  VC = various habitats—mobile species associated with habitats in open and enclosed
  areas (e.g., marsh creeks = enclosed area).
Status: R = resident; S = seasonal.

References and Further Reading

Adams, A. J., and J. P. Ebersole. "Use of back-reef and lagoon habitats by coral reef fishes." *Marine Ecology Progress Series* 228: 213–226. 2002.

Adams, D. H., and D. M. Tremain. "Association of large juvenile red drum, *Sciaenops ocellatus*, with an estuarine creek on the Atlantic coast of Florida." *Environmental Biology of Fishes* 58: 183–194. 2000.

Anonymous. *Red drum*. North Carolina Division of Marine Fisheries Publication.

Anonymous. *Spotted seatrout*. North Carolina Division of Marine Fisheries Publication.

Arrivillaga, A., and D. Baltz. "Comparison of fishes and macroinvertebrates of seagrass and bare-sand sites on Guatemala's Atlantic coast." *Bulletin of Marine Science* 65(2): 301–319. 1999.

Austin, H. M. "A survey of the ichthyofauna of the mangroves of western Puerto Rico during December, 1967–August, 1968." *Caribbean Journal of Science* 111-2: 27–39. 1971.

Austin, H., and S. Austin. "The feeding habits of some juvenile marine fishes from the mangroves in western Puerto Rico." *Caribbean Journal of Science* 113-4: 171–178. 1971.

Austin, H. M. and S. E. Austin. "Juvenile fish in two Puerto Rican mangroves." *Caribbean Journal of Science* 111-12: 26–31. 1971.

Baelde, P. "Differences in the structures of fish assemblages in *Thalassia testudinum* beds in Guadeloupe, French West Indies, and their ecological significance." *Marine Biology* 105: 163–173. 1990.

Baltz, D. M., J. W. Fleeger, C. F. Rakocinski, J. N. McCall. "Food, density, and microhabitat: factors affecting growth and recruitment potential of juvenile saltmarsh fishes." *Environmental Biology of Fishes* 53: 89–103. 1998.

Bass, R. J., and J. W. J. Avault. "Food habits, length-weight relationship, condition factor, and growth of juvenile red drum, *Sciaenops ocellatus*, in Louisiana." *Transactions of the American Fisheries Society* 104(1): 35–45. 1975.

Beach, D. "Coastal sprawl: the effects of urban design on aquatic ecosystems in the United States." Arlington, VA: Pew Oceans Commission. 2002.

Bell, S. S., R. A. Brooks, B. D. Robbins, M. S. Fonseca, M. O. Hall. "Faunal response to fragmentation in seagrass habitats: implications for seagrass conservation." *Biological Conservation* 100: 115–123. 2001.

Bohlke, J. E., and C. C. G. Chaplin. "Family Centropomidae: snooks or robalos." *Fishes of the Bahamas and adjacent tropical waters.* Wynnewood, PA: Livingston Publishing Company, 253–254. 1968.

Bologna, P. A. X. and K. L. Heck, Jr. "Macrofaunal associations with seagrass epiphytes: relative importance of trophic and structural characteristics." *Journal of Experimental Marine Biology and Ecology* 242: 21–39. 1999.

Bortone, S. A., ed. *Biology of the Spotted Seatrout.* S. A. Bortone, CRC Press: 1–3. 2003.

Boulon, R. H. J. "Use of mangrove prop root habitats by fish in the northern U.S. Virgin Islands." *Proceedings of the Gulf and Caribbean Fisheries Institute* 41: 189–204. 1987.

Brook, I. M. "Trophic relationships in a seagrass community *Thalassia testudinum,* in Card Sound, Florida: fish diets in relation to macrobenthic and cryptic faunal abundance." *Transactions of the American Fisheries Society* 1063: 219–229. 1977.

Brown, D. *Fly fishing for bonefish.* New York: Lyons & Burford, Publishers, 1993.

Brown-Peterson, N. J., M. S. Peterson, D. L. Nieland, M. D. Murphy, R. G. Taylor, and J. R. Warren. "Reproductive biology of female spotted seatrout, *Cynoscion nenbulosus,* in the Gulf of Mexico: differences among esturies?" *Environmental Biology of Fishes* 63: 405–415. 2001.

Bruger, G. E. "Age, growth, food habits, and reproduction of bonefish, *Albula vulpes,* in south Florida waters." Florida Department of Natural Resources Marine Research Laboratory. Research Publication no. 3. 20 p. 1974.

Carmona-Suarez, C. A., and J. E. Conde. "Local distribution and abundance of swimming crabs *Callinectes* spp. and *Arenaeus cribrarius* on a tropical sand beach." *Fisheries Bulletin* 100: 11–25. 2002.

Carr, W. E. S., and C. A. Adams. "Food habitat of juvenile marine fishes occupying seagrass beds in the estuarine zone near Crystal River, Florida." *Transactions of the American Fisheries Society* 1023: 511–540. 1973.

Catano, S., and J. Garzon-Ferreira. "Ecologia trofica del sabalo *Megalops atlanticus* (Pisces: Megalopidae) en el area de Cienega Grande de Santa Marta, Caribe colombiano." *Revista de Biologia Tropical* 42(3): 673–684. 1994.

Cocheret de la Moriniere, E. "Post-settlement life cycle migrations of reef fish in the mangrove-seagrass-coral reef continuum" Dissertation. University of Nijmegen, the Netherlands. 165 p. 2002.

Coen, L. D., K. L. Heck, Jr., and L. G. Abele. "Experiments on competition and predation among shrimps of seagrass meadows." *Ecology* 626: 1484–1493. 1981.

Colton, D. E., and W. S. Alevizon. "Feeding ecology of bonefish in Bahamian waters." *Transactions of the American Fisheries Society* 12: 178–184. 1983.

Connolly, R. M. "Differences in composition of small, motile invertebrate assemblages from seagrass and unvegetated habitats in a southern Australian estuary." *Hydrobiologia* 346: 137–148. 1997.

Cowper, S. W. "The drift algae community of seagrass beds in Redfish Bay, Texas." *Contributions in Marine Science* 21: 125–132. 1978.

Crabtree, R. E. "Relationship between lunar phase and spawning activity of tarpon, *Megalops atlanticus,* with notes on the distribution of larvae." *Bulletin of Marine Science* 56(3): 895–899. 1995.

Crabtree, R. E., P. B. Hood, and D. Snodgrass. "Age, growth, and reproduction of permit *Trachinotus falcatus* in Florida waters." *Fisheries Bulletin* 100: 26–34. 2002.

Crabtree, R. E., E. C. Cyr, R. E. Bishop, L. M. Falkenstein, and J. M. Dean. "Age and growth of tarpon, *Megalops atlanticus,* larvae in the eastern Gulf of Mexico, with notes on relative abundance and probable spawning areas." *Environmental Biology of Fishes* 35: 361–370. 1992.

Crabtree, R. E., E. C. Cyr, and J. M. Dean. "Age and growth of tarpon, *Megalops atlanticus,* from South Florida waters." *Fishery Bulletin* 93: 619–628. 1995.

Crabtree, R. E., C. W. Harnded, D. Snodgrass, and C. Stevens. "Age, growth, and mortality of bonefish, *Albula vulpes,* from the waters of the Florida Keys." *Fishery Bulletin* 94: 442–451. 1996.

Crabtree, R. E., D. Snodgrass, and C. W. Harnden. "Maturation and reproductive seasonality in bonefish, *Albula vulpes,* from the waters of the Florida Keys." *Fishery Bulletin* 95: 456–465. 1997.

Crabtree, R. E., C. Stevens, D. Snodgrass, and F. J. Stengard. "Feeding habitats of bonefish, *Albula vulpes,* from the waters of the Florida Keys." *Fishery Bulletin* 96: 754–766. 1998.

Dennis, G. D. "Island mangrove habitats as spawning and nursery areas for commercially important fishes in the Caribbean." *Proceedings of the Gulf and Caribbean Fisheries Institute* 41: 205–225. 1998.

Denson, M. R., W. E. Jenkins, A. J. Woodward, and T. I. J. Smith. "Tag-reporting levels for red drum *(Sciaenops ocellatus)* caught by anglers in

South Carolina and Georgia estuaries." *Fisheries Bulletin* 100: 35–41. 2002.

Doering, P. H., and R. H. Chamberlain. "Experimental studies on the salinity tolerance of turtle grass, *Thalassia testudinum.*" In M. J. Kennish, ed. *Seagrasses: Monitoring, ecology, physiology, and management* CRC Press: 81–98. 2000.

Duarte, L. O., and C. B. Garcia. "Diet of the mutton snapper *Lutjanus analis* (Cuvier) from the Gulf of Salamanca, Colombia, Caribbean Sea." *Bulletin of Marine Science* 65(2): 453–465. 1999.

Durako, M. J., R. C. Phillips, and R. R. Lewis III. "Proceedings of the symposium on subtropical-tropical seagrasses of the southeastern United States." *Florida Marine Research Institute Research Publication* 42: 209 p. 1987.

Durako, M. J., M. D. Murphy, and K. D. Haddad. "Assessment of fisheries habitat: northeast Florida." *Florida Marine Research Institute Research Publication* 45: 51 p. 1988.

Durako, M. J., M. O. Hall, F. Sargent, and S. Peck. "Propeller scars in seagrass beds: an assessment and experimental study of recolonization in Weedon Island State Preserve, Florida." *Proceedings of the Nineteenth Annual Conference on Wetlands Restoration and Creation.* F. J. J. Webb. Hillsborough Community College Institute of Florida Studies, 42–53. 1992.

Faunce, C. H., J. J. Lorenz, J. A. Ley, and J. E. Serafy. "Size structure of gray snapper *Lutjanus griseus* within a mangrove 'no-take' sanctuary." *Bulletin of Marine Science* 701: 211–216. 2002.

Fay, C. W., R. J. Neves, and G. B. Pardue. "Species profiles: life histories and environmental requirements of coastal fishes and invertebrates (mid-Atlantic)—striped bass." *U.S. Fish and Wildlife Service Biological Report* 82(11.8). U.S. Army Corps of Engineers, TR EL-82-4. 1983.

Finucane, J. H. "Ecology of the pompano *Trachinotus carolinus* and the permit *T. falcatus* in Florida." *Transactions of the American Fisheries Society* 3: 478–486. 1969.

Fonseca, M. S. and S. S. Bell. "Influence of physical setting on seagrass landscapes near Beaufort, North Carolina, USA." *Marine Ecology Progress Series* 171: 109–121. 1998.

Fonseca, M., P. E. Whitfield, N. M. Kelly, and S. S. Bell. "Modeling seagrass landscape pattern and associated ecological attributes." *Ecological Applications* 121: 218–237. 2002.

Fourqurean, J. W., A. Willsie, C. D. Rose and L. M. Rutten. "Spatial and temporal pattern in seagrass community composition and productivity in south Florida." *Marine Biology* 138: 341–354. 2001.

Franks, J. S., J. R. Warren, and M. V. Buchanan. "Age and growth of cobia, *Rachycentron canadum*, from the northeastern Gulf of Mexico." *Fisheries Bulletin* 97: 459–471. 1998.

Geary, B. W., J. R. Rooker, and J. W. Webb. "Utilization of saltmarsh shorelines by newly settled Sciaenids in a Texas Estuary." *Gulf and Caribbean Research* 13: 37–49. 2001.

Gilmore, R. G., C. J. Donohoe, and D. W. Cooke. "Observations on the distribution and biology of east-central Florida populations of the Common Snook." *Florida Science* 46(3/4): 306–313. 1983.

Gotceitas, V., Colgan, P. "Predator foraging success and habitat complexity: quantitative test of the threshold hypothesis." *Oecologia* 80: 158–166. 1989.

Grabowski, J. H., M. A. Dolan, A. R. Hughes, and D. L. Kimbo. "The biological and economic value of restored intertidal oyster reef habitat to the nursery function of the estuary." *North Carolina Marine Fisheries Commission*, Fishery Resource Grant Program, Fishery Grant #EP-6. 2001.

Greening, H. S., and R. J. Livingston. "Diel variation in the structure of seagrass associated epibenthic macroinvertebrate communities." *Marine Ecology Progress Series* 7: 147–156. 1982.

Heck, K. L., Jr. "Comparative species richness, composition, and abundance of invertebrates in Caribbean seagrass *Thalassia testudinum*." *Marine Biology* 41: 335–348. 1977.

Heck, K. L., Jr., and G. S. Wetstone. "Habitat complexity and invertebrate species richness and abundance in tropical seagrass meadows." *Journal of Biography* 4: 135–142. 1977.

Heck, K. L., Jr., and T. A. Thoman. "Experiments on predator-prey interactions in vegetated aquatic habitats." *Journal of Experimental Marine Biology and Ecology* 53: 125–134. 1981.

Heck, K. L., Jr., and M. P. Weinstein. "Feeding habits of juvenile reef fishes associated with Panamanian seagrass meadows." *Bulletin of Marine Science* 453: 629–636. 1989.

Hildebrand, S. F. "Family Albulidae. In H. B. Bigelow, ed., *Fishes of the western North Atlantic*." pp. 111–131. Memoir Sears Foundation for Marine Research. 1: 3. 1963.

Hildebrand, S. F. "Family Elopidae. In H. B. Bigelow, ed., *Fishes of the western North Atlantic*." pp. 132–147. Memoir Sears Foundation for Marine Research. 1: 3. 1963.

Hill, J., J. W. Evans, and M. J. Van Den Avyle. "Species profiles: life histories and environmental requirements of coastal fishes and invertebrates (south Atlantic)—striped bass." *U.S. Fish and Wildlife Service*

Biological Report 82(11.118). U.S. Army Corps of Engineers, TR EL-82-4. 1989.

Hindell, J. S., G. P. Jenkins, and M. J. Keough. "Variability in abundances of fishes associated with seagrass habitats in relation to diets of predatory fishes." *Marine Biology* 136: 725–737. 2000.

Hindell, J. S., G. P. Jenkins, and M. J. Keough. "Evaluating the impact of predation by fish on the assemblage structure of fishes associated with seagrass *Heterozostera tasmanica* (Martens ex Ascherson den Hartog) and unvegetated sand habitats." *Journal of Experimental Marine Biology and Ecology* 255: 153–174. 2000.

Hixon, M. A., and J. P. Beets. "Predation, prey-refuges, and the structure of coral-reef fish assemblages." *Ecological Monographs* 63(1): 77–101. 1993.

Hoese, H. D., and R. H. Moore. *Fishes of the Gulf of Mexico: Texas, Louisiana, and adjacent waters.* 2nd ed. College Station, TX: Texas A&M University Press, 1998.

Holt, S. A., C. L. Kitting, and C. R. Arnold. "Distribution of young red drums among different seagrass meadows." *Transactions of the American Fisheries Society* 112: 267–271. 1983.

Howard, R. K. "Diel variation in the abundance of epifauna associated with seagrasses of the Indian River, Florida USA." *Marine Biology* 96: 137–142. 1987.

Johannes, R. E. "Reproductive strategies of coastal marine fishes in the tropics." *Environmental Biology of Fishes* 31: 65–84. 1978.

Jordan, F., M. Bartolini, C. Nelson, P. E. Patterson, and H. L. Soulenet. "Risk of predation affects habitat selection by the pinfish *Lagodon rhomboides* Linnaeus." *Journal of Experimental Marine Biology and Ecology* 208: 45–56. 1996.

Kalbfleisch, W. B. C., and B. Jones. "Sedimentology of shallow, hurricane-affected lagoons: Grand Cayman, British West Indies." *Journal of Coastal Research* 141: 140–160. 1998.

Kaplan, E. H. *A field guide to coral reefs: Caribbean and Florida.* Boston: Houghton Mifflin Company, 1982.

Kaplan, E. H. *A field guide to southeastern and Caribbean seashores: Cape Hatteras to the Gulf Coast, Florida, and the Caribbean.* Boston: Houghton Mifflin Company, 1988.

Kathiresan, K., and B. L. Bingham. "Biology of mangroves and mangrove ecosystems." *Advances in Marine Biology* 40: 81–251. 2001.

Kilby, J. D. "The fishes of two Gulf coastal marsh areas of Florida." *Tulane Studies in Zoology* 2(8): 175–247. 1955.

Knowles, L. L., and S. S. Bell. "The influence of habitat structure in faunal-habitat associations in a Tampa Bay seagrass system, Florida." *Bulletin of Marine Science* 62(3): 781–794. 1998.

Kulczycki, G. R., R. W. Virnstein, and W. G. Neslon. "The relationship between fish abundance and algal biomass in a seagrass–drift algae community." *Estuarine and Coastal Shelf Science* 12: 341–347. 1981.

Laegdsgaard, P., and C. Johnson. "Why do juvenile fish utilise mangrove habitats?" *Journal of Experimental Marine Biology and Ecology* 257: 229–253. 2001.

Larmouth, D., and R. Fordyce. *Tarpon on Fly.* Portland, OR: Frank Amato Publications, 2002.

Leber, K. M. "The influence of predatory decapods, refuge, and micro-habitat selection on seagrass communities." *Ecology* 666: 1951–1964. 1985.

Leber, K. M., and H. S. Greening. "Community studies in seagrass meadows: a comparison of two methods for sampling macroinvertebrates and fishes. *Fishery Bulletin* 842: 443–450. 1985.

Ley, J., C. L. Montague, and C. C. McIvor. "Food habits of mangrove fishes: a comparison along estuarine gradients in northeastern Florida Bay." *Bulletin of Marine Science* 54(30), 881–899. 1994.

Lin, J., and J. L. Beal. "Effects of mangrove marsh management on fish and decapod communities." *Bulletin of Marine Science* 571: 193–201. 1995.

Linke, T. E., M. E. Platell, and I. C. Potter. "Factors influencing the partitioning of food resources among six fish species in a large embayment with juxtaposing bare sand and seagrass habitats." *Journal of Experimental Marine Biology and Ecology* 266: 193–217. 2001.

Livingston, R. J. "Organization of fish in a coastal seagrass system: the response to stress." *Fish Community Ecology in Estuaries and Coastal Lagoons* 20 (16): 367–382. 1985.

Louis, M., C. Bouchon, and Y. Bouchon-Navaro. "Spatial and temporal variations of mangrove fish assemblages in Martinique French West Indies." *Hydrobiologia* 295: 275–284. 1995.

Luczkovich, J. J., H. J. Daniel III, M. W. Sprague, S. E. Johnson, R. C. Pullinger, T. Jenkins, and M. Hutchinson. "Characterization of critical spawning habitats of weakfish, spotted seatrout, and red drum in Pamlico Sound using hydrophone surveys." North Carolina Division of Marine Fisheries Final Report and Annual Performance Report Grants F-62-1 and F-62-2.

Mackey, G. "Juvenile nursery grounds in the British Virgin Islands, Eastern Caribbean: two sampling strategies reveal complex interactions between mangroves, seagrass beads and backreef habitats of juvenile coral reef fishes." Master's thesis. University of York, United Kingdom. 41 p. 1999.

Main, K. L. "Predator avoidance in seagrass meadows: prey behavior, microhabitat selection, and cryptic coloration." *Ecology* 68: 170–180. 1986.

Manooch, C. S., III, and D. Raver, Jr. *Fisherman's guide: fishes of the southeastern United States.* Raleigh, NC: North Carolina State University Museum of Natural History, 1991.

Marshall, A. R. *A survey of the snook fishery of Florida, with studies of the biology of the principal species,* Centropomus undecimalis *Bloch.* Miami, FL: State Board of Conservation, Marine Laboratory, 1958.

McCoy, E. D., H. R. Mushinsky, D. Johnson, and W. E. Meshaka, Jr. "Mangrove damage caused by hurricane Andrew on the southwestern coast of Florida." *Bulletin of Marine Science* 59(1): 1–8. 1996.

McMichael, R. H., Jr., K. M. Peters, and G. R. Parsons. "Early life history of the snook, *Centropomus undecimalis,* in Tampa Bay, Florida." *Northeast Gulf Science* 102: 113–125. 1989.

Mense, D. J., and E. L. Wenner. "Distribution and abundance of early life history stages of the blue crab, *Callinectes sapidus,* in tidal marsh creeks near Charleston, South Carolina." *Estuaries* 12(3): 157–168. 1989.

Mercer, L. P. "Species profiles: life histories and environmental requirements of coastal fishes and invertebrates (Mid-Atlantic)—weakfish." *U.S. Fish and Wildlife Service Biological Report* 82(11.109): 17. 1989.

Mojica, R., Jr., J. M. Shenker, C. W. Harnden, and D. E. Wagner. "Recruitment of bonefish, *Albula vulpes,* around Lee Stocking Island, Bahamas." *Fisheries Bulletin* 93: 666–674. 1995.

Montague, C. L., and J. A. Ley. "A possible effect of salinity fluctuation on abundance of benthic vegetation and associated fauna in northeastern Florida Bay." *Estuaries* 16(4): 703–717. 1993.

Moody, K. M. "The role of drift macroalgae as a predation refuge or foraging ground for the seagrass fish, *Gobiosoma robustum.*" Master's thesis. University of South Florida. 53 p. 1996.

Mueller, K. W., G. D. Dennis, D. B. Eggleston, and R. I. Wicklund. "Size-specific social interactions and foraging styles in a shallow water population of mutton snapper, *Lutjanus analis* (Pisces: Lutjanidae), in the central Bahamas." *Environmental Biology of Fishes* 40: 175–188. 1994.

Muller, R. G. *The 2000 stock assessment update of common snook,* Centropomus undecimalis. Fish and Wildlife Conservation Commission, Florida Marine Research Institute, St. Petersburg. 2000.

Mullin, S. J. "Estuarine fish populations among red mangrove prop roots of small overwash islands." *Wetlands* 154: 324–329. 1995.

Murphey, P. L., and M. S. Fonseca. "Role of high and low energy seagrass beds as nursery areas for *Penaeus duorarum* in North Carolina." *Marine Ecology Progress Series* 121: 91–98. 1995.

Murphy, M. D., and R. G. Taylor. "Reproduction, growth, and mortality of red drum, *Sciaenops ocellatus*, in Florida waters." *Fisheries Bulletin* 88: 531–542. 1990.

Nagelkerken, I., G. van der Velde, M. W. Gorissen, G. J. Meijer, T. van't Hof, and C. den Hartog. "Importance of mangroves, seagrass beds and the shallow coral reef as a nursery for important coral reef fishes, using visual census technique." *Estuarine and Coastal Shelf Science* 51: 31–44. 2000.

Nagelkerken, I., M. Dorenbosch, W. C. E. P. Verberk, E. Cocheret de la Moriniere, and G. van der Velde. "Day-night shifts of fishes between shallow-water biotopes of a Caribbean bay, with emphasis on the nocturnal feeding of Haemulidae and Lutjanidae." *Marine Ecology Progress Series* 194: 55–64. 2000.

Naughton, S. P., and C. H. Saloman. "Fishes of the nearshore zone of St. Andrew Bay, Florida, and adjacent coast." *Northeast Gulf Science* 21: 43–55. 1978.

Nieland, D. L., R. G. Thomas, and C. A. Wilson. "Age, growth, and reproduction of spotted seatrout in Barataria Bay, Louisiana." *Transactions of the American Fisheries Society* 131: 245–259. 2002.

Ong, J. E. "The ecology of mangrove conservation and management." *Hydrobiologia* 295: 343–351. 1995.

Orth, R. J., K. L. Heck, Jr., and J. van Montfrans. "Faunal communities in seagrass beds: a review of the influence of plant structure and prey characteristics on predator-prey relationships." *Estuaries* 7(4A), 339–350. 1984.

Peters, D. J., and W. G. Nelson. "The seasonality and spatial patterns of juvenile surf zone fishes of the Florida east coast." *Florida Scientist* 50: 85–99. 1987.

Peters, K. M., and R. H. J. McMichael. "Early life history of the red drum, *Sciaenops ocellatus* (Pisces: Sciaenidae), in Tampa Bay, Florida." *Estuarine Research Federation:* 92–107. 1987.

Peters, K. M., J. R. E. Matheson, and R. G. Taylor. "Reproduction and early life history of common snook, *Centropomus undecimalils* (Bloch), in Florida." *Bulletin of Marine Science* 62(2): 509–529. 1998.

Peterson, B. J., K. R. Thompson, J. H. Cowan, Jr., and K. L. Heck, Jr. "Comparison of predation pressure in temperate and subtropical seagrass habitats based on chronographic tethering." *Marine Ecology Progress Series* 224: 77–85. 2001.

Porch, C. E., C. A. Wilson, and D. L. Nieland. "A new growth model for red drum *(Sciaenops ocellatus)* that accommodates seasonal and ontogenic changes in growth rates." *Fisheries Bulletin* 100: 149–152. 2002.

Pottern, G. B., M. T. Huish, and J. H. Kerby. "Species profiles: life histories and environmental requirements of coastal fishes and invertebrates (Mid-Atlantic)—bluefish." *U.S. Fish and Wildlife Service Biological Report* 82(11.94). U.S. Army Corps of Engineers, TR EL-82-4. 20 p. 1989.

Poulakis, G. R., J. M. Shenker, and D. S. Taylor. "Habitat use by fishes after tidal reconnection of an impounded estuarine wetland in the Indian River Lagoon, Florida, USA." *Wetlands Ecology and Management* 10: 51–69. 2002.

Primavera, J. H. "Fish predation on mangrove-associated penaeids. The role of structure and substrate." *Journal of Experimental Marine Biology and Ecology* 215: 205–216. 1997.

Rakocinski, C. F., S. S. Brown, G. R. Gaston, R. W. Heard, W. W. Walker, and J. K. Summers. "Macrobenthic responses to natural and contaminant-related gradients in northern Gulf of Mexico estuaries." *Ecological Applications* 74: 1278–1298. 1997.

Reagan, R. E. "Species profiles: life histories and environmental requirements of coastal fishes and invertebrates (Gulf of Mexico)—red drum." *U.S. Fish and Wildlife Service Biological Report* 82(11.36) (U.S. Army Corps of Engineers, TR EL-82-4): 16. 1985.

Robbins, B. D., and S. S. Bell. "Dynamics of a subtidal seagrass landscape: seasonal and annual change in relation to water depth." *Ecology* 81(5): 1193–1205. 2000.

Robblee, M. B. "The spatial organization of the nocturnal fish fauna of a tropical seagrass feeding round." *Dissertation.* University of Virginia. 144 p. 1987.

Robertson, A. I. "The structure and organization of an eelgrass fish fauna." *Oecologia* 47: 76–82. 1980.

Robertson, A. I., and N. C. Duke. "Mangrove fish-communities in tropical Queensland, Australia: spatial and temporal patterns in densities, biomass and community structure." *Marine Biology* 104: 369–379. 1990.

Robins, C. R., G. C. Ray, J. Douglas, and R. Freund. *A field guide to Atlantic coast fishes of North America.* Boston: Houghton Mifflin, Co., 1986.

Rooker, J. R., and G. D. Dennis. "Diel, lunar and seasonal changes in a mangrove fish assemblage off southwestern Puerto Rico." *Bulletin of Marine Science* 493: 684–698. 1991.

Rooker, J. R., G. J. Holt, and S. A. Holt. "Vulnerability of newly settled red drum *Sciaenops ocellatus* to predatory fish: is early-life survival enhanced by seagrass meadows?" *Marine Biology* 131: 145–151. 1998.

Rooker, J. R., S. A. Holt, M. A. Soto, and G. J. Holt. "Postsettlement patterns of habitat use by Sciaenid fishes in subtropical seagrass meadows." *Estuaries* 212: 318–327. 1998.

Ross, D. A. *The fisherman's ocean*. Mechanicsburg, PA: Stackpole Books, 2000.

Ross, J. L., and T. M. Stevens. *Life history and population dynamics of red drum* (Sciaenops ocellatus) *in North Carolina waters*. Morehead City, NC: Division of Marine Fisheries, 1992.

Ross, J. L., T. M. Stevens, and D. S. Vaughan. "Age, growth, mortality, and reproductive biology of red drums in North Carolina waters." *Transactions of the American Fisheries Society* 124: 37–54. 1995.

Ross, M. S., P. L. Ruiz, G. J. Telesnicki, and J. F. Meeder. "Estimating aboveground biomass and production in mangrove communities of Biscayne National Park, Florida, USA." *Wetlands Ecology and Management* 9: 27–37. 2001.

Saloman, C. H., and S. P. Naughton. "Fishes of the littoral zone, Pinellas County, Florida." *Florida Scientist* 42: 85–93. 1979.

Sargent, F. J., T. J. Leary, D. W. Crewz, and C. R. Kruer. "Scarring of Florida's seagrasses: assessment and management options." *Florida Marine Research Institute Technical Report*. TR-1: 37. 1995.

Savino, J. F., and R. A. Stein. "Behavior of fish predators and their prey: habitat choice between open water and dense vegetation." *Environmental Biology of Fishes* 24(4): 287–293. 1989.

Schneider, F. I., and K. H. Mann. "Species specific relationships of invertebrates to vegetation in a seagrass bed." *Journal of Marine Biology and Ecology* 145: 101–117. 1991.

Seaman, W., Jr., and M. Collins. "Species profiles: life histories and environmental requirements of coastal fishes and invertebrates (South Florida)—snook." U.S. Fish and Wildlife Service FWS/OBS-82/11.16: 16. 1983.

Sedberry, G. R., and J. Carter. "The fish community of a shallow tropical lagoon in Belize, Central America." *Estuaries* 162: 198–215. 1993.

Sexton, W .J. "The post-storm hurricane Hugo recovery of the undeveloped beaches along the South Carolina coast, Capers Islands to the Santee Delta." *Journal of Coastal Research* 114: 1020–1025. 1995.

Sheaves, M. J. "Patterns of distribution and abundance of fishes in different habitats of a mangrove-lined tropical estuary, as determined by fish trapping. *Australian Journal of Marine and Freshwater Research* 43: 1461–1479. 1992.

Shenker, J. M., and J. M. Dean. "The utilization of an intertidal salt marsh creek by larval and juvenile fishes: abundance, diversity, and temporal variation." *Estuaries* 23: 154–163. 1979.

Sheridan, P. "Comparative habitat utilization by estuarine macrofauna within the mangrove ecosystem of Rookery Bay, Florida." *Bulletin of Marine Science* 501: 21–39. 1992.

Sklar, F. H., and J. A. Browder. "Coastal environmental impacts brought about by alterations in freshwater flow in the Gulf of Mexico." *Environmental Management* 22(4): 547–562. 1998

Smithsonian Marine Station at Fort Pierce, Florida. Web resources. http://www.sms.si.edu. 2002.

Sogard, S. M. "Size-selective mortality in the juvenile stage of teleost fishes: a review." *Bulletin of Marine Science* 60(3): 1129–1157. 1997.

Sogard, S. M., G. V. N. Powell, and J. G. Holmquist. "Epibenic fish communities on Florida Bay banks: relations with physical parameters and seagrass cover." *Marine Ecology Progress Series* 40: 25–39. 1987.

Sogard, S. M., and K. W. Able. "A comparison of eelgrass, sea lettuce macroalgae, and marsh creeks as habitats for epibenthic fishes and decapods." *Estuarine and Coastal Shelf Science* 33: 501–519. 1991.

Sogard, S. M., and. B. L. Olla. "The influence of predator presence on utilization of artificial seagrass habitats by juvenile walleye pollack, *Theragra chalcogramma.*" *Environmental Biology of Fishes* 37: 57–65. 1993.

Stoner, A. W., and I. F. G. Lewis. "The influence of quantitative and qualitative aspects of habitat complexity in tropical seagrass meadows." *Journal of Experimental Marine Biology and Ecology* 94: 19–40. 1985.

Taylor, R. G., J. A. Whittington, H. J. Grier, and R. E. Crabtree. "Age, growth, maturation, and protandric sex reversal in common snook, *Centropomus undecimalis,* from the east and west coasts of Florida." *Fisheries Bulletin* 98: 612–624. 2000.

Taylor, R. G., J. A. Whittington, and D. E. Haymans. "Catch-and-release mortality rates of common snook in Florida." *North American Journal of Fisheries Management* 21: 70–75. 2001.

Thayer, G. W., D. R. Colby, and W. F. Hettler, Jr. "Utilization of the red mangrove prop root habitat by fishes in south Florida." *Marine Ecology Progress Series* 35: 25–38. 1987.

Tremain, D. M., and D. H. Adams. "Seasonal variations in species diversity, abundance, and composition of fish communities in the northern Indian River Lagoon Florida." *Bulletin of Marine Science* 57(1): 171–192. 1995.

Tucker, J. W. J., and S. W. Campbell. "Spawning season of common snook along the east central Florida coast." *Biological Sciences* 51(1): 1–6. 1988.

Valiela, I. *Marine ecological processes.* 2nd ed. New York: Springer-Verlag, 1995.

Valiela, I., J. L. Bowen, and J. K. York. "Mangrove forests: one of the world's most threatened major tropical environments. *Bioscience* 5110: 807–815. 2001.

Virnstein, R. W., P. S. Mikkelsen, K. D. Carns, and M. A. Capone. "Seagrass beds versus sand bottoms: the trophic importance of their associated benthic invertebrates." *Florida Scientist* 46(3/4): 363–381. 1983.

Virnstein, R. W., and P. A. Carbonara. "Seasonal abundance and distribution of drift algae and seagrasses in the mid-Indian River Lagoon, Florida." *Aquatic Botany* 23: 67–82. 1985.

Volpe, A. V. *Aspects of the biology of the common snook,* Centropomus undecimalis *(Bloch), of southwest Florida.* University of Miami, State of Florida Board of Conservation. Technical Series no. 31. 1959.

Walsh, C. J., and B. D. Mitchell. "Factors associated with variations in abundance of epifaunal caridean shrimps between and within estuarine seagrass meadows." *Marine and Freshwater Research* 49: 769–777. 1998.

Wenner, C. *Red drum: natural history and fishing techniques in South Carolina.* South Carolina Department of Natural Resources. Educational Report no. 17. 1992.

Wenner, C., and J. Archambault. *Spotted seatrout: natural history and fishing techniques in South Carolina.* South Carolina Department of Natural Resources. Educational Report no. 18. 1995.

USEFUL FISHING PERIODICALS WITH INFORMATION FOR FLY ANGLERS

Saltwater Fly Fishing
Fly Fishing in Salt Water
Game and Fish Magazine
Florida Sportsman

Index

adult stage, 11–12
algae, drift, 22–23, 32–33
amberjack, juveniles, 7
anchovies, 47, 48–49, 65, 69, 70, 109, 157
   regions and habitats of, 191

baitfish species
   along beaches, 155–158, 170–171
   in mangroves, 69–72
   in oyster bars, 109
   in seagrass, 47–49
barjacks, 11
barracuda
   ambush strategy used by, 31
   nursery habitat, 10
   regions, habitats, and prey of, 189
bass, 190
beaches
   beachrock shorelines, 171–172
   exposed, fishing tips, 161–162
   fall feeding frenzy, 158–169
   fishing tips, 146–149
   protects, fishing tips, 165–167
   sands, shifting, 149–152
   sediment content of, 143–144
   semiprotected, fishing tips, 167–168
   snook, summertime, 152–153
   threats to, 173
   tidal ranges, 144
   waves, role of, 144–146
beaches, gamefish prey in, 153
   baitfish species, 155–158, 170–171
   clams, 170
   crabs, 154, 170
   shrimp, 154–155
black drum, 35
blennies, 33, 42, 43, 65–66, 104, 105, 106
   regions and habitats of, 191
bluefish, 190
blue runner, 11
   regions, habitats, and prey of, 189
bonefish, 1
   fishing tips, 50–51, 79
   in mangroves, 56–57
   nursery habitat, 10

regions, habitats, and prey of, 189
seasonal diet changes, 14
spawning of, 15
broadcast spawning, 6
brittle stars, 102
   regions and habitats of, 191

clams, 170
clingfish, 104
cobia, 38
   regions, habitats, and prey of, 189
crabs
   blue, 38, 62, 68, 101, 136
   fiddler, 62–64, 132–133
   hermit, 101, 134–135
   mangrove, 62
   marsh, 62, 133
   mole/sand, 154, 170
   mud, 33, 38–39, 64, 99–101, 133, 191
   porcelain, 182
   reef, 38, 39, 181
   regions and habitats of, 191
   speckled, 154
   spider, 101, 181, 191
   swimming, 36–38, 62, 154, 184, 191
   walking, 37, 38–39
croaker, 43, 45
crustaceans, 41–42

eelgrass, 18, 23
epibionts, 26
epifauna, 26
epiphytes, 26

flounder, 190
fly patterns
   for baitfish, 109
   for beaches, 155
   for beachrock shorelines, 172
   for blennies, 43, 106
   for crabs, 64, 133–134, 181
   for crustaceans, 42
   for gobies, 43, 105
   for grass shrimp, 39, 41
   for grunts, 44, 67
   for herrings, 48, 69

fly patterns *continued*
   for jacks, 68
   for killifish, 107
   for lobsters, 68
   for mojarras, 107
   for mole/sand crabs, 170
   for mollies, 107
   for parrotfish, 44
   for pinfish, 46–47
   selecting, 109–110
   for shrimp, 64–65
   for silversides, 49
   for spotted seatrout, 45
   for swimming crabs, 37–38, 62
   for toadfish and skilletfish, 105–106
   for walking crabs, 39
   for wrasses, 44
fry, 14

gobies, 33, 42, 43, 65–66, 104, 105, 184
   regions and habitats of, 191
grouper, 10
grunts, 13, 44, 67

herrings, 47, 48, 65, 69, 109, 155
   regions and habitats of, 191
horse-eye jacks, 10–11

jack family
   fishing tips, 79
   juveniles as prey, 67–68, 69
   nursery habitat, 10–11
   regions, habitats, and prey of, 189
juvenile stage, 7–11
juveniles, as prey
   in mangroves, 66–68
   in oyster bars, 107–108
   in seagrass, 44–47

killifish, 43, 65, 66, 106–107, 135, 136,
   158
   regions and habitats of, 191
kingfish, 158

ladyfish, 154
   regions, habitats, and prey of, 189
larval stage, 6–7
lobsters, juvenile, 68
local nuances, 16

mackerel, 190
manatee grass, 18, 23–24

mangroves
   black, 54, 59–61
   fishing tips, 77–80
   location of, 72–74
   pneumatophores, 59
   prop foot communities in the sub-
      tropics, 57–58
   prop foot communities in the trop-
      ics, 55–56
   red, 54, 55–58
   role of, 53–54
   salinity and, 53
   seasonal changes, 74–77
   threats to, 80–81
mangroves, gamefish prey in
   baitfish species, 69–72
   crabs, 61–64, 68
   feeding times, 74
   insects, 64–65
   juveniles, 66–68
   resident, 65–66
   seasonal, 66–68
   shrimp, 64–65, 68
minnows, 66, 79–80, 107, 136
mojarra, 43, 45, 65, 66, 107, 157
   regions and habitats of, 191
mollies, 66, 106, 107, 135
   regions and habitats of, 191
mosquitofish, 66, 135
mullets, 49, 65, 70–72, 109, 136–137,
   157, 158–159
   regions and habitats of, 191

nursery habitats
   without plants, 10–11
   with plants, 9–10

oyster bars
   currents and, 88–89
   difference between oyster reefs and,
      84, 85
   fishing tips, 92–95, 103–104, 110–111
   formation of, 85
   habitats, 96–98
   locating and exploring, 91–92
   role of, 83
   salinity and, 90
   seasonal changes, 98
   threats to, 112
   tidal range, 89–90
   types of, 86–87

oyster bars, gamefish prey in, 98
  baitfish species, 109
  brittle stars, 102
  crabs, 99–101
  feeding times, 103–104
  juveniles, 107–108
  resident, 104–107
  seasonal, 107–108
  shrimp, 101–102
oyster drill, 90
oysters, 57–58
  ecological requirements, 85–86
  species of, 84

parrotfish, 43–44, 67
permit, 176–180
  regions, habitats, and prey of, 189
pigfish, 108
pinfish, 8, 43, 45–47, 108
pompano, 189
potholes, 31
prey, use of seasonal, 12–14
prop-scarring, 52

razorfish, 184
red drum, 1
  along beaches, 158
  diet and age of, 12
  fishing tips, 51
  nursery habitat, 10
  regions, habitats, and prey of, 189
  in salt marshes, 121–123
  seasonal diet changes, 13
  tailing, 34–35
  typical stomach contents of, 33
rubble flats
  gamefish prey in, 181–183
  permit in, 176–180
  shoreline, 180–181
  tides and, 175–176
  waves and, 176

salt marshes
  fishing tips, 125–127, 137–140
  formation of, 113–115
  Gulf of Mexico versus Atlantic
    coastal, 127–130
  high and low zones, 115–119
  locating gamefish in, 119–120
  red drum in, 121–123
  role of, 113, 114–115
  species in, 130–131

threats to, 140–141
tides and, 123–127
salt marshes, gamefish prey in, 131
  crabs, 132–135
  resident, 135–136
  seasonal, 136–137
  shrimp, 134
  worms, 135
sand flats
  fishing tips, 185–187
  gamefish prey in, 184–185
  habitat, 183
sardines, 69, 155
scad, 155
seagrass
  fishing in patchy, 30–35
  fishing tips, 50–52
  forms of, 17
  as habitat, 26–30
  location of beds, 18
  reading, 24–25
  role of, 18–19
  salinity and, 19–20
  species and requirements, 18, 20–24
  time of day/night feeding, 50–52
seagrass, gamefish prey in, 35
  baitfish species, 47–49
  crabs, 36–39
  crustaceans, 41–42
  feeding times, 50
  imitating behavior of, 47
  juveniles, 44–47
  resident, 42–44
  seasonal, 44–47
  shrimp, 39–41
  threats to, 52
seasonality of prey, 12–14
sheepshead, 96
shoal grass, 18, 21–22
shrimp
  common, 39–40, 64, 68, 101, 136, 184,
    191
  ghost, 134, 154–155
  grass, 28, 39, 41, 101, 134
  mantis, 40–41, 182–183, 184, 191
  mud, 134
  regions and habitats of, 191
  snapping, 41, 64, 101, 184, 191
silver jenny, 157
silversides, 48–49, 65, 69, 109, 136, 157
  regions and habitats of, 191
skilletfish, 104, 105–106

snapper
 ambush strategy used by, 31
 fishing tips, 80
 juveniles as prey, 44–45, 67
 nursery habitat, 10
 regions, habitats, and prey of,
 189–190
snook
 ambush strategy used by, 31
 at beaches, 152–153
 fishing tips, 51, 77, 152–153
 nursery habitat, 10
 regions, habitats, and prey of, 189
 spawning of, 6, 14–15
spawning behavior, 14–15
spotted seatrout
 along beaches, 158
 ambush strategy used by, 31
 fishing tips, 51
 juveniles as prey, 45
 locating, 26

regions, habitats, and prey of, 189
seasonal diet changes, 11–12, 13

tarpon
 adult habitat, 11
 ambush strategy used by, 31
 feeding frenzy, 159
 fishing tips, 50, 162–165, 168–170
 juveniles, 7
 nursery habitat, 10
 regions, habitats, and prey of, 189
temperatures, effects of, 15–16
toadfish, 104–106
tonguefish, 107
turtle grass, 18, 20–21

weakfish, 189
widgeon grass, 18, 23
worms, 135, 184
 regions and habitats of, 191
wrasses, 42, 43–44, 184